World Series '64

Also by John G. Robertson and Carl T. Madden

*Five Overtimes: The Habs and the Leafs
in the 1951 Stanley Cup Finals* (2024)

*World Series '48: The Cleveland Indians
and Boston Braves in Six Games* (2023)

*The Bruins in 25 Games: Boston's Most Unforgettable
Wins and Heartbreaking Losses* (2023)

*Cold War on Ice: The NHL versus the Soviet Union
in Hockey's Super Series '76* (2023)

*The Mustache Gang Battles the Big Red Machine:
The 1972 World Series* (2022)

*Amazin' Upset: The Mets, the Orioles
and the 1969 World Series* (2021)

Also by John G. Robertson

*Hockey's Wildest Season: The Changing
of the Guard in the NHL, 1969–1970* (2021)

*When the Heavyweight Title Mattered: Five Championship Fights
That Captivated the World, 1910–1971* (2019)

*Too Many Men on the Ice: The 1978–1979 Boston Bruins
and the Most Famous Penalty in Hockey History* (2018)

*The Babe Chases 60: That Fabulous 1927 Season, Home
Run by Home Run* (1999; paperback 2014)

*Baseball's Greatest Controversies: Rhubarbs, Hoaxes,
Blown Calls, Ruthian Myths, Managers' Miscues
and Front-Office Flops* (1995; paperback 2014)

Also by John G. Robertson and Andy Saunders

*The Games That Changed Baseball: Milestones
in Major League History* (2016)

*A's Bad as It Gets: Connie Mack's
Pathetic Athletics of 1916* (2014)

All From McFarland

World Series '64

The Cardinals, the Yankees and the End of a Dynasty

John G. Robertson *and*
Carl T. Madden

McFarland & Company, Inc., Publishers
Jefferson, North Carolina

LIBRARY OF CONGRESS CATALOGING-IN-PUBLICATION DATA

Names: Robertson, John G., 1964– author. | Madden, Carl T., author.
Title: World Series '64 : the Cardinals, the Yankees and the end of a dynasty / John G. Robertson and Carl T. Madden.
Description: Jefferson, North Carolina : McFarland & Company, Inc., Publishers, 2024 | Includes bibliographical references and index.
Identifiers: LCCN 2024033185 | ISBN 9781476696782 (paperback : acid free paper) ∞
 ISBN 9781476654317 (ebook)
Subjects: LCSH: World Series (Baseball) (1964) | St. Louis Cardinals (Baseball team)—History—20th century. | New York Yankees (Baseball team)—History—20th century. | Baseball—United States—History—20th century.
Classification: LCC GV878.4 .R63 2024 | DDC 796.357/646—dc23/eng/20240726
LC record available at https://lccn.loc.gov/2024033185

BRITISH LIBRARY CATALOGUING DATA ARE AVAILABLE

ISBN (print) 978-1-4766-9678-2
ISBN (ebook) 978-1-4766-5431-7

© 2024 John G. Robertson and Carl T. Madden. All rights reserved

No part of this book may be reproduced or transmitted in any form or by any means, electronic or mechanical, including photocopying or recording, or by any information storage and retrieval system, without permission in writing from the publisher.

Front cover: (top) St. Louis Cardinals pitcher Bob Gibson (Missouri Sports Hall of Fame); (bottom inset) New York Yankees center fielder Mickey Mantle (National Baseball Hall of Fame and Museum, Cooperstown, New York)

Printed in the United States of America

McFarland & Company, Inc., Publishers
 Box 611, Jefferson, North Carolina 28640
  www.mcfarlandpub.com

Dynasties are good for sports. They create the dynamic of the underdog versus the perennial champion. Their rise and fall create discernible eras. Accordingly, this book is dedicated to baseball's greatest dynasties: the Boston Beaneaters and Baltimore Orioles of the 1890s; Connie Mack's Philadelphia Athletics of the early 1910s and early 1930s; the long NL dominance of the Brooklyn/Los Angeles Dodgers from the late 1940s to the mid-1960s; the New York Yankees from 1947 to 1964; the Oakland A's of the early 1970s; the Cincinnati Reds of the mid-1970s; and onward into the 21st century. Baseball history would be poorer without such periods of a single team's championship reign. To all the MLB dynasties that came before us, to those we personally witnessed in the past, and to the ones that are yet to be, the authors of this book thank you.

Acknowledgments

The authors of this book would like to express their gratitude to the following:

- the interlibrary loan department of the Cambridge, Ontario, public library system for helping us acquire difficult-to-find source materials;
- Bob Cullum, the curator of the Leslie Jones Collection of historic photographs held by the Boston Public Library, for his generous permission and assistance in providing some of the photographs found in this book;
- the Library of Congress for its continuing commitment to allowing the public to download thousands of images for publication free of charge;
- those anonymous folks who, free of charge to the public, maintain the wonderful websites chock full of accurate historical MLB data, such as Retrosheet, Baseball-Almanac.com and Baseball-Reference.com.
- Mike Tomkins for his help in identifying Preston Ward in the photograph on page 12.

Table of Contents

Acknowledgments   vi
Introduction   1

1. The Philly Phlop   7
2. The NL Pennant Chase: The Cardinals Prevail   15
3. Another AL Pennant: The Yankees Take the Fifth   28
4. A World Series Without Mel Allen   40
5. Before the First Pitch: Anticipating the Series   48
6. Game One: October 7   56
7. Game Two: October 8   71
8. Game Three: October 10   84
9. Game Four: October 11   96
10. "Let's All Play What's My Line?"   109
11. Game Five: October 12   111
12. Game Six: October 14   125
13. Game Seven: October 15   137
14. The Yankees Get Old ... Then They Get Sold   153
15. Managerial Musical Chairs   156
16. The Short Life of Johnny Keane   160
17. The Rapid Descent of the New York Yankees   163
18. The Cardinal Juggernaut   168
19. Fiftieth Anniversary Championship Reunion   173

20. Where Have You Gone, Chet Trail?	175
21. Whatever Happened To…	177
1964 World Series Statistics	197
Chapter Notes	201
Bibliography	209
Index	211

Introduction

> "The World Series is played in my doubtless too-nostalgic imagination in some kind of autumn afternoon light.... Seeing it exclusively in the bitter chill of midnight breaks the spell of even the best of games."
> —essayist Adam Gopnik

The year 1964 saw great changes on many fronts, social, political, and otherwise. It witnessed the Beatles sensationally arrive on the North American popular music scene with a seismic impact that could scarcely have been imagined just a year earlier. At one point in July, Beatles songs remarkably occupied every top-ten spot on CHUM, a hugely popular Toronto radio station. The Fab Four also kicked opened the door to an overwhelming but peaceable British invasion of the musical kind. Within a short time, the Rolling Stones, Gerry & the Pacemakers, Herman's Hermits, Dusty Springfield, and Petula Clark would all be staples in American jukeboxes.

All things British-related seemed to be popular in 1964, as *My Fair Lady* finally made the inevitable jump from Broadway to Hollywood and won the Oscar for Best Picture. It was not without controversy, however. Julie Andrews, despite playing Eliza Doolittle superbly on stage for years, was deemed too much of an unknown to America's filmgoers to reprise the role in the cinematic version. Audrey Hepburn took her place—but she had all her songs dubbed by "ghost singer" Marni Nixon.

Two weeks after the Beatles drew 73 million viewers to *The Ed Sullivan Show*, a remarkable, vociferous, 22-year-old self-promoting boxer from Louisville, Kentucky, named Cassius Clay made headlines. On February 25 in Miami Beach, he stunned the fight game by dethroning 7:1 favorite and fearsome defending champion Sonny Liston to seize the world heavyweight crown. It was a wild, six-round fight that featured no knockdowns, but it had more plot twists than several O. Henry short stories combined.

The surprises continued the next day when Clay publicly renounced what he deemed to be his "slave name" and insisted henceforth on being called Cassius X. (Boxing's foremost chronicle, *The Ring* magazine, did not quite get it, and amusingly referred to the youthful new champ as "Cassius X. Clay" for a time.) Not long afterward Cassius Clay came to be known as Muhammad Ali, someone who would transcend his sport to become the most famous person on the planet.

The assassination of John F. Kennedy in November 1963 shocked the world, and the American public understandably sought escapism wherever it could be found. New York City hosted a successful world's fair in its Flushing Meadows-Corona Park section of Queens. It featured 140 pavilions and 110 restaurants representing 80 nations. It was the place to be as more than 51.6 million visitors paid $2 apiece—even less for children—over a pair of six-month runs before the exhibition closed in April 1965. Its hopeful and promising motto was "Peace Through Understanding."

However, nothing reflected the desire to temporarily abandon life's harsh realities more than the number-one rated TV show in America in 1964: *The Beverly Hillbillies*. The program shot to the top spot in the ratings after just three episodes in 1962 and stayed firmly there for two full seasons. Early in 1964, *The Beverly Hillbillies* was pulling in phenomenal viewership totals on CBS for its weekly 30 minutes of lowbrow laughs. Television critics generally hated the sitcom's cornball humor about an oil-rich bumpkin family from rural Missouri that relocated to California's wealthiest neighborhood, but the public adored it. Irene Ryan, who played the tiny but feisty Granny Clampett, just laughed at the elitist snobbery. She opined that 50 million Americans could not possibly be wrong.

In more serious matters, the Civil Rights Act was passed. Upon its passage, the new U.S. president, Lyndon Johnson, optimistically commented, "Let us close the springs of racial poison. Let us pray for wise and understanding hearts. Let us lay aside irrelevant differences and make our nation whole."[1] In 1964, those hopeful words were far from being universally embraced across America.

After beginning in 1946, the Baby Boom era in the United States and Canada concluded in 1964, but the impact of the arrival of millions of youngsters would be felt for generations in North American society in innumerable ways. Their vast needs, desires, and general affluence would greatly influence the economy well into the 21st century—and still does. Times were generally on an upswing. Looking back six decades, prices of everyday items in 1964 seem truly quaint to the modern eye. A gallon of gasoline was just a quarter. A first-class postage stamp cost a nickel. An adult movie ticket cost $1 while the typical price of a man's haircut, according to an alarming front-page story that ran in the *Boston Globe* in mid–October, was about to rise to $2. Bread was 22 cents per loaf. A gallon of milk was $1.08. Coffee was 79 cents per pound. An absolute necessity for teens, the American debut album of Beatles tunes (on vinyl, of course) was priced at $5.98.

There were ominous warnings, though. On January 11, Dr. Luther L. Terry, the surgeon general of the United States, officially announced what many observant people had suspected for decades: cigarette smoking was dangerous to one's health. Furthermore, it was so great a hazard that it warranted "appropriate remedial action."[2] The announcement was purposely made on a Saturday when the stock markets were closed so shares in tobacco companies would not collapse and to get maximum exposure in the nation's plentiful and popular Sunday newspapers. Despite the dire warning for puffers, cigarette consumption in the United States was barely impacted by Dr. Terry's findings. Sentiments in a front-page sidebar story in the January 12 *Boston Globe* written by Jeremiah V. Murphy were typical. It noted that "the validity of the report was unquestioned, but few of the smokers [I] interviewed planned on giving up cigarettes completely. Most said they would 'cut down.'"[3] Few even did that, apparently. By 1965 a new plateau in national tobacco sales would be reached. Moreover, it was estimated that about 40 percent of American adults had willfully adopted the smoking habit as the one-time social taboo of women lighting up had long vanished.

Geopolitical tensions were the focus of British writer John le Carré's work *The Spy Who Came in from the Cold*; it was the top selling novel in America that year. That was a fictional tale. In real life on the other side of the Iron Curtain, 1964 saw the fall from grace of 70-year-old Nikita Khrushchev as the leader of the Soviet Union after 11 years in power. (The news came as the climax to the World Series approached, driving the game reports from the front pages of many U.S. dailies—a development that likely irked baseball fanciers.) The bland Leonid Brezhnev, at age 57, became the new head of the country's Communist Party, thus replacing the diminutive firebrand who had blinked during the 1962 Cuban Missile Crisis and whose ambitious agricultural policies for his motherland had badly misfired.

It was also an Olympic year, which meant in 1964 that both the Winter and Summer Olympic Games were held. The winter version was held in Innsbruck, Austria, from January 29 to February 9 where a lack of snow nearly threatened its postponement. Hundreds of tons of it had to be trucked in from mountainous regions for the Games to take place. Few Americans paid much attention or really cared that Terry McDermott, a speed skater in the men's 500-meter event, was the only champion from the United States. In stark contrast, at the Summer Games in Tokyo,

American athletes fared far better. From October 9 to 24, they won 36 championships and 90 medals overall, three shy of what the Soviet Union's competitors took home. However, most American sports fans had their attention fixed elsewhere at that time.

Although professional football was steadily rising in popularity, baseball remained America's favorite sporting pastime in 1964. Television was slowly killing the once-vibrant professional minor leagues, though. ("Fewer and fewer fans followed the fortunes of the Kalamazoo Kazoos,"[4] noted documentarian Ken Burns in his superb *Baseball* project for PBS.) Nevertheless, the World Series was still the premier event on America's sporting calendar. Huge audiences tuned in to watch the Fall Classic in an era when Major League Baseball still quaintly played all its championship games in the October sunshine, even on weekdays. (Nighttime World Series play was still seven long years away.) World Series radio listenership was also strong, as people tuned in at work or school, even if it meant smuggling a transistor radio and an earpiece into locations where they were not particularly welcomed. In 1964, MLB was comprised of 20 teams—ten in each of the National and American leagues. Every team played 18 games against the other nine in its circuit. Pitchers, of course, still came to bat like any other player. (Why shouldn't they?) Nobody thought that splitting the AL or NL into divisions or radically adopting inter-league play was a particularly good idea. There were no tiers of playoffs, either. Only winning the pennant—and nothing less—got a club an invitation to postseason play. There was no prize for second place.

That autumn the featured clubs were the NL champions, the St. Louis Cardinals, and the AL kingpins, the New York Yankees. The maximum seven games were played from October 7 through 15 to determine a winner. No one knew it at the time, but the 1964 World Series was a contest that pitted an ascending, exciting, fast-paced club against an aging and somewhat stodgy one that was about to begin a decade-long decline in on-field success and prestige.

The New York Yankees were still the vaunted club of Mickey Mantle, Roger Maris and Whitey Ford. Yogi Berra was still in pinstripes, too—but as the team's first-year manager, not its catcher. (In a truly weird development, Berra would be fired after Game Seven and replaced by Johnny Keane, the man who had promptly resigned after defeating the Yankees!) The Yanks won 99 games, just one game more than the surprising Chicago White Sox. The hard-fought 1964 AL pennant was New York's fifth in a row and 15th in 18 years. Certainly, having any AL champion other than the glamorous Yankees participating in the Fall Classic would have been a genuine novelty. However, in an era when the participating teams' broadcasters called the World Series games on television for NBC, the familiar voice of Mel Allen was noticeably absent. He had been coldly notified by the Yankees on September 21 that the 1964 season would be his last for the club. His broadcasting partner, Phil Rizzuto, took Allen's spot at the microphone for the Fall Classic—and did quite well at the task.

In contrast, the NL was much more democratic with its constantly changing array of champions. Of the eight traditional NL franchises, only the Chicago Cubs had not been pennant winners at least once between 1946 and 1963. In 1964, the St. Louis Cardinals were making their first Fall Classic appearance since 1946—which was the last year the World Series was not televised. Under the guidance of manager Johnny Keane, the racially diverse Cards had pulled off a remarkable comeback, winning 93 games by season's end in overtaking the Philadelphia Phillies who had held a substantial lead in the pennant chase for most of 1964. Most baseball historians, however, tend to recall the final weeks of the 1964 NL campaign as more of a spectacular collapse by the Phillies (who actually dropped into a tie for second place with Cincinnati), an assessment very much unfair to the talented Cardinal club who proved they were deserving titlists. They played an exciting and aggressive brand of baseball that had become a trademark of the best NL clubs. The names of Curt Flood, Lou Brock, Ken Boyer, Tim McCarver, Mike Shannon and—most prominently—Bob Gibson were suddenly in the limelight.

This book will relive every play and every at-bat of the exciting, seesaw 1964 World Series—ranked the 21st best Fall Classic of all time by ESPN in 2020—and the events leading up to the Cards-Yankees clash. It is a retrospective look at a time when baseball was still king of American sports and its players and peripheral figures still attracted huge amounts of national attention.

Paul Simon once noted that 1964 had been both the year of the Beatles and of the Rolling Stones. Yes, that was true. It was also the year the St. Louis Cardinals ended the MLB dynasty of the New York Yankees.

— 1 —

The Philly Phlop

> "The chilling collapse of losing ten straight games at the most inopportune time had a negative effect on the city's psyche for years."[1]
> —Philadelphia Phillies historian Mel Marmer

One of the most excruciating experiences a baseball fan can endure is watching a favorite team squander a huge lead late in a pennant race. Those supporters who helplessly witnessed the '51 Dodgers, '78 Red Sox or '87 Blue Jays suddenly unravel when victory was all but assured can attest to one thing: the ordeal is a slow form of torture.

But of all the teams that fell apart at the end, perhaps the most famous "chokers" were the 1964 Philadelphia Phillies. In some respects, the Philly Phlop (as it came to be known) was the cruelest of them all. Their sudden demise haunted their players and beleaguered manager for decades.

When the 1964 National League season began, nobody gave the Phillies much of a chance to win the pennant. Three summers before, during the 1961 season, Philadelphia set an unflattering modern NL record by losing 23 consecutive games. (In the 63 years since the 1961 MLB season was played, only two teams have lost as many as 20 games in a row.) That season they won just 47 times in 154 outings and finished 17 games behind the *ninth-place* club, the Chicago Cubs. By 1962, the Phillies were a barely mediocre seventh-place outfit in a 10-team circuit. A late charge in the 1963 season, featuring a sweep of the soon-to-be World Series champion Los Angeles Dodgers, enabled the Phillies to clinch a tie for fourth place. That was considered a heady achievement for a ballclub with a substantial history of underperforming. Still, the idea that the league's longtime laughingstocks might win the pennant in 1964 was thought to be absurd. One dissenter was the Phillies upbeat manager Gene Mauch. He was quoted during spring training as saying a 92-win season for Philadelphia was absolutely doable for his club.

To the delight of their traditionally cynical fans, everything was going perfectly for the Phillies early in the 1964 season. They won 10 of their first 12 games and 27 of their first 42. Even when promising young pitcher Rick Wise was sidelined with the measles for a week, the club's frequent wins continued unabated. Optimistic Philadelphia supporters openly discussed the possibility of both outfielder Johnny Callison being named NL MVP and Dick Allen, a moody third baseman, winning Rookie of the Year honors. (Callison was also named the MVP of the 1964 All-Star Game in which he hit a walk-off homer in the NL's 7–4 win at Shea Stadium; he was the third and most recent player to achieve this feat.) Manager Mauch was seemingly making all the right moves all the time as the Phillies confidently climbed up the NL ladder.

Gene Mauch, a journeyman MLB player for more than a decade, was often regarded within the sport as the smartest manager in the majors in 1964. His one fault was, perhaps, a tendency to overthink situations. When the Phillies began to pile up the wins, the modest Mauch typically credited his team for its initial success rather than anything he had specifically done to achieve any particular victory. A quarter century later, he continued to sing the same tune. At a 1989 team reunion, Mauch generously told a group of nostalgic reporters,

> I've had more talented clubs, but I've never had a smarter, more unselfish club than this one. They prided themselves on the little things. If we were playing the Cubs, [my team] would practice bunting down the first base line to make Ernie Banks field the ball, not Ron Santo at third. They did what they had to do to win.[2]

The Phillies briefly ascended to the top of the NL standings on Thursday, June 11. Ten days later, 33-year-old Jim Bunning, who had been acquired from Detroit after the 1963 season, pitched a 6–0 perfect game on Father's Day in the brutally hot first game of a doubleheader against the New York Mets at brand new Shea Stadium. It was the first perfecto in the modern era of the NL, as the last one had occurred in 1880. (Bunning would later serve Kentucky in Congress as a Republican senator from 1999 to 2011.) Interviewed nearly three decades after the 1964 season by historian David Halberstam, Bunning possessed something akin to an encyclopedic memory regarding details about what unfolded for the Phillies in late September.

Chris Short—Philadelphia's ace lefthanded hurler—was also winning consistently. Johnny Callison and Richie Allen were both getting timely hits. On July 16 the Phillies surged into first place in the NL—seemingly to stay. "When they returned from road trips," Boston sports journalist Harold Kaese penned, "it was like Caesar's victorious legions marching into

Rome."[3] When the Phillies acquired slugging outfielder Frank Thomas from the woeful Mets on August 7, he seemed to be the last piece needed for a perfectly constructed team. Thomas thrived in the atmosphere of an apparent winner. By August, Phillies backup catcher Gus Triandos had personally dubbed the joyful and thoroughly surprising campaign "The Year of the Blue Snow." The quirky and amusing term took on an entirely different and dark meaning for the players and the team's fans by season's end, however.

Philadelphia's lead steadily grew as the tail end of July approached. The St. Louis Cardinals were 10 full games out of first place after Bob Gibson was handed a humbling 9–1 shellacking by the Phillies on July 24 at Connie Mack Stadium, Philadelphia's home ballpark. However, the Cardinals won the next three games in the series to get within seven games of the NL leaders and remain within striking distance. Had the Phillies swept St. Louis, the Cardinals would have fallen 13 games off the pace—probably an insurmountable deficit to erase considering the season was more than half over.

The Phillies seemed comfortably ahead in the NL pennant chase when autumn came. Following a tight 3–2 victory in Los Angeles on September 20, Mauch's wonder club held a daunting 6½-game lead over both St. Louis and Cincinnati with just 12 games left to play on the schedule. "The triumph reduced the Phillies' magic number to seven,"[4] reported the Associated Press. Surely the team's first NL pennant since the 1950 Whiz Kids did it was in the bag. Plans were in the works to construct more field boxes in beautiful but aging Connie Mack Stadium for the World Series. With permission granted from MLB's Commissioner's Office, tickets for the Fall Classic had already been printed by the team and were ready to be sold. There were certainly plenty of eager customers willing to buy them. Some 90,000 orders from fans poured into the club's office. (One local news photo showed a smiling group of secretaries dumping mailbags full of them onto a large table, ready for sorting and processing.) So confident were the players of receiving World Series bonuses that several Phillies bought expensive hunting rifles during a road trip to Houston. (With the aid of 20/20 hindsight, those purchases were later considered to have been an act of hubris by those who lived through the nightmare of what was about to happen.) To the everlasting horror of Philadelphia's baseball fans, what became known in the city's folklore as the Phlop—a dreadful ten-game losing streak, including seven home defeats—began on Monday, September 21.

The first game of the Phlop served as an omen: The Phillies lost 1–0 to Cincinnati when a Reds rookie, Chico Ruiz, against the orders of manager Dick Sisler, attempted to steal home in the top of the sixth inning while their best hitter, Frank Robinson, was batting. Pitcher Art Mahaffey, rattled by this daring move, uncorked a very wild pitch that sailed to the backstop, allowing Ruiz to score easily on the play. "If Chico hadn't scored," Sisler noted afterward with a straight face, "he'd still be running—all the way to San Diego."[5] (That was where the Reds' AAA affiliate was located in 1964.) In the Phillies clubhouse after the game, manager Mauch was furious that they had lost on a steal of home—but even more irked that Ruiz would even try such a thing with the dangerous Robinson batting. To the analytical Mauch, such a play defied baseball logic and therefore should not have been rewarded. Consecutive 9–2 and 6–4 victories by Cincinnati over the next two days vaulted the Reds back into the NL pennant race.

The out-of-contention Milwaukee Braves arrived in Philadelphia for a four-game set beginning on Thursday, September 24. The Braves won the opener 5–3, but the tough Philadelphia loss on September 25 best symbolized the Phlop. With the Phillies leading 1–0 in the top of the seventh, catcher Clay Dalrymple accidentally touched Dennis Menke's bat. The rare catcher's interference call set up two Milwaukee runs. Twice the feisty Phillies rallied to tie the score, but the game was lost in the top of the twelfth inning when first baseman Frank Thomas (who was playing with a broken thumb) booted what appeared to be an easy double-play grounder. The Braves won the marathon game, 7–5.

After Milwaukee again beat the Phillies, this time 6–4 on Saturday, September 26, panic truly began to set in. Manager Gene Mauch overreacted: He opted to pitch his pair of best starters on just two days' rest. "Bunning and Short ... and hold the fort!" was apparently Philadelphia's new battle cry. The strategy failed miserably. Johnny Callison hit three homers for the Phillies on Sunday, September 27, but Bunning still lost 14–8 to the Braves. That setback occurred on the same day that Cincinnati won a doubleheader versus the New York Mets to move into first place in the NL. When congratulated on his slugging feat by a reporter, Callison rightly asked him with a frown, "What good did it do?"[6]

"Maybe we're better at chasing something than holding onto it," a glum Mauch, trying to make the best of an ongoing catastrophe, told the media afterward. "We've got to do in five days what Cincinnati took 5½ months to do. And you can bet we will do it—I hope."[7] Mauch's optimism was unfortunately misguided. Chris Short was soundly beaten, 5–1, in St. Louis by the also ascending Cardinals the very next night. Two more losses to the sizzling Cards at Busch Stadium (by scores of 4–2 and 8–5) followed in rapid succession in what was now a highly compelling three-team pennant race. Years later, many Cardinals remembered how frightened the Phillies looked during that series—afraid of blowing such a big lead in such a short span of time. Before facing the Phillies, St. Louis had gotten into the NL pennant picture with a five-game sweep of the Pirates in Pittsburgh. (The Phillies were annoyed that Pittsburgh's best starter, Bob Friend, had benched himself during the series because of a sore throat.) In contrast, the Cardinals were extremely loose, had smiles on their faces, and could not wait to get to the ballpark each day. In midsummer they had not expected to be in the NL pennant chase come September. Now they were in the thick of it. It was all a huge, positive surprise for them. Unlike Philadelphia, they had not had time to fret about anything.

For Phillies fans young and old, the slide was pure agony to endure. *Sports Illustrated*'s Steve Wulf, who was a 13-year-old in 1964, wrote this melancholy recollection in an article he penned for the magazine 25 years later:

> I would listen to the Phillies' games on a wonderful old brown Zenith. Each night I'd tune into the faint and floating signal from WFIL in Philadelphia. After each loss during the skid, I'd turn off the lights and lie awake forever. I came down the steps to breakfast slower and slower each morning, and the bags under my eyes grew heavier and heavier.[8]

Philadelphia's Cookie Rojas, an often-used utility player, concocted a grim, succinct simile to describe what was happening to his team. "It was like swimming in a long, long lake," he said, "...and then you drown."[9]

After losing their tenth straight game, the desperate Phillies arrived in Cincinnati for their final two contests on their 1964 schedule. Now *trailing* St. Louis by 2½ games in the NL standings, Philadelphia's fate was no longer in their hands. The Phillies teased their fans by winning both games against the Reds, including a 10–0 rout in the finale at Crosley Field. It was the team's 92nd victory of 1964—precisely the sum that manager Mauch had optimistically predicted for his squad six months earlier, but it was not enough. After the World Series was played—without the Phillies in it—Johnny Callison would finish second in league MVP voting. The 25-year-old Callison, who had deceptive power and movie-star looks, would stay in MLB through 1973 and never have a better season. However, Dick Allen did win the NL's Rookie of the Year award (and finish seventh in MVP voting, too).

Just 36 minutes after the game in Cincinnati ended, the final result was also known from Busch Stadium. The Cardinals trailed the last-place New York Mets at home for a time on Sunday, October 4, the final day of the regular season. However, the Cards rallied to win the game handily, 11–5, to edge both Philadelphia and Cincinnati by a single game. The 30,146 fans jammed into the ballpark in St. Louis had roared when the ballpark's out-of-town scoreboard showed the Phillies-Reds game had concluded.

That result, combined with St. Louis' victory, eliminated both the Phillies and Reds from the pennant chase. "An all-time record for the cancellation of hotel accommodations must have been set," remarked Harold Kaese of the *Boston Globe* the next day. The Reds too had issued World Series tickets. The NL reimbursed the club's printing expenses, but an estimated $1.4 million in revenue had to be refunded to disappointed Cincinnati fans.

Mauch later said, "I knew we'd beat Cincinnati [on the last day], but asking the Mets to take three from St. Louis was too much. If we'd done as good a job in St. Louis as the Mets did, this would have been a cakewalk." He continued, "I can't let this affect me forever. It's just a lot of long, hard work … gone down the drain. This is the first thing in my life I wanted, and I came so close to getting it, and I missed."[10]

Mauch, who managed in the majors for 26 seasons—and won 1,902 MLB games without ever capturing a pennant—always blamed himself for

Gene Mauch, third from the left, as a player with the Brooklyn Dodgers in 1948. The well-traveled Mauch played 304 MLB games from 1944 through 1957. He became much more famous as a manager who never won a pennant despite coming close several times. He is pictured here with teammates Billy Cox (left) and Pee Wee Reese (second from left); the player at right is Preston Ward (courtesy Boston Public Library, Leslie Jones Collection).

the Phlop. "He was wrong," said a sympathetic Rojas in defense of Mauch's handling of the team. "We couldn't have gotten as far as we did without him."[11]

In an interview with *The Sporting News* after the 1964 season had concluded, Mauch said of his club's stunning collapse, "We had a complete reversal of form. Maybe if we had one more Short or Bunning, it's no contest. And maybe I failed to make a move that would have won it. But I tell you truthfully, I don't know what it could have been."[12]

The team's upper management seemed to agree. While the San Francisco Giants fired their manager Alvin Dark at season's end and the Houston Colts dumped their pilot, Harry Craft, with 13 games remaining on the schedule, the day after the regular season concluded, the 38-year-old Mauch was spared from the same harsh fate. In fact, he was rewarded with a two-year contract extension to remain as the Phillies' skipper by club owner Bob Carpenter. Mauch had been with Philadelphia since 1960. He accepted the offer immediately. Mauch remained the manager of the Phillies until his dismissal 54 games into the 1968 season. He then took over the expansion Montreal Expos from 1969 through 1975, then the Minnesota Twins, and finally the California Angels on two separate occasions. In 2005, Mauch died three months before his 80th birthday.

Some of those '64 Phillies enjoyed championship success with other MLB clubs later in their careers, but their associations with the disastrous Phlop were enduring ones. During a 25th anniversary team reunion in 1989, lefthanded pitcher Dennis Bennett, who won 12 games for Philadelphia in 1964, noted, "I played on the [pennant-winning] '67 Red Sox, but people hardly ever ask me about that team. They always ask me about *this* team."[13]

Indeed, the players linked forever to the Phlop oddly seemed to embrace their place in baseball history rather than be embarrassed by it. The 1989 get-together, organized by the club and held at a Philadelphia hotel, was a surprisingly well-attended affair. (Although a few club members were absent—Jim Bunning, citing another commitment, was the most notable no-show—only one player showed any outright reluctance about coming to the event: It was Wes Covington, who, at the time, was living in western Canada and working for the *Edmonton Sun*. The outfielder, who batted .280 in 1964, refused to even acknowledge any of the several invitations he received from the Phillies.) The reunion had a charitable aspect to it, too: Open to the public, it doubled as a fundraiser to help cover the mounting medical expenses of Chris Short. He had fallen into a coma after suddenly suffering a ruptured brain aneurysm in October 1988 while working as an insurance agent in Wilmington, Delaware. He never did regain consciousness; Short died on August 1, 1991, at the young age of 53.

At that memorable reunion, Clay Dalrymple ruefully recalled the moment when the Phlop truly struck a chord with him. "I was watching the first game of the World Series on television," he recalled. "My daughter came home from the first grade and asked me, 'Daddy, how come you're not playing baseball today?' That really hurt."[14]

— 2 —

The NL Pennant Chase
The Cardinals Prevail

> "Whoever said baseball is just a game has never been to St. Louis."—Cardinals meme

Broadcaster Harry Caray simply could not control his excitement. After witnessing the unlikely batting heroics of pitcher Roger Craig connecting for a two-run double, Caray told his radio audience that their beloved St. Louis Cardinals were going to win the National League pennant that year. It was not late September or early October, however. It happened on April 17 in the second inning of a game in San Francisco—a contest the Cardinals would eventually lose to the Giants, 5–4, in ten innings. It was just the team's fourth game of the young 1964 season. Nevertheless, the amusing outburst highlighted Caray's unbridled enthusiasm about calling St. Louis Cardinal baseball games and his heartfelt desire for the team to break an 18-year championship drought.

The St. Louis Cardinals are one of the most storied and successful franchises in the history of the NL. They did not get to that level immediately, though. It took them more than three decades to become a consistently respectable outfit.

The club first began play in the NL in 1892 when they were nicknamed the Perfectos. The origin of the club's modern nickname dates back to 1899 when the team got a new set of uniforms. According to team lore, the Cardinal nickname was thrust upon the club by Willie McHale, a writer for the *St. Louis Republic*. He reported overhearing an unknown female fan say she greatly approved of the bright cardinal red shade of their stockings. When McHale started to regularly refer to the club as the Cardinals, the fans liked the term as a team moniker, so it stuck. The famous bird-on-a-perch logo would come along later.

Attractive hosiery does not produce championship baseball clubs, however. In the 38 seasons from 1882 to 1919, the Missouri club was an unsuccessful aggregation. The team mustered just five winning campaigns—and zero NL pennants during that period. In 1920, former MLB catcher Branch Rickey was hired as the team's business manager. Rickey figured the best way to turn the franchise into a winner was to have a deep farm system of minor league clubs from which to develop players. The policy was based on the premise that sheer quantity would eventually have to produce quality. It did. The team won its first NL pennant in 1926—and upset the New York Yankees of Babe Ruth, Lou Gehrig and manager Miller Huggins in that year's World Series. (Huggins had been a more-than-capable second baseman for the Cardinals for his final seven seasons as an MLB player. His SABR biographer,

Miller Huggins, in this baseball card from the 1910s, was a small but capable second baseman on the underachieving St. Louis Cardinals from 1910 through 1916 before becoming the manager of the first dynastic New York Yankees club of the 1920s (Library of Congress).

Steve Steinberg, said Huggins excelled at his position despite being one of the smallest men to ever play in the majors. Most credible sources list Huggins no taller than 5'2".) Winning became a habit in St. Louis with the likes of Rogers Hornsby, Pepper Martin and Dizzy Dean in the Redbirds' lineup. The Cardinals also took NL crowns in 1928, 1930, 1931, 1934, 1942, 1943, and 1944.

St. Louis won the NL pennant again in 1946 with a team that featured Stan Musial, Marty Marion, Harry Brecheen and Enos Slaughter. That October the Cards defeated the favored Boston Red Sox in a memorable

2. The NL Pennant Chase

Branch Rickey, shown here in 1938, was the man who created the farm system for the St. Louis Cardinals. The theory behind it—that quantity must eventually produce quality—worked wonders for the Cards, turning them into an NL powerhouse by the late 1920s (courtesy Boston Public Library, Leslie Jones Collection).

seven-game World Series. It needed to be a memorable one for St. Louis fans, because 18 long years would pass before another pennant would be won by their beloved Cardinals.

In the interim, baseball profoundly changed in 1947 with racial integration that was led, of course, by Jackie Robinson and the Brooklyn Dodgers. The Cards were among the last of the NL teams to embrace the idea. When August (Gussie) Busch bought the club in 1954, he was a hugely successful beer baron, but he only had a passing interest in America's great national pastime. He was quaintly unaware that the Cardinals had no black players on their roster until he visited his club's spring training facilities and personally noticed their absence.

There was a reason for that. In the 1950s, St. Louis was the most distant city in the major leagues. It had the most western locale—and the most southern. The Cardinals had a vast radio following via the influence of KMOX. The station's powerful signal carried their games to far-flung places within America's southwest and south. Many of these loyal listeners made annual trips to Missouri to see "their team" in action, perhaps several times per season. There was a legitimate fear that if the Cardinals recruited black players, their southern fans would rebel against the Cards. However, Gussie Busch realized that America's black population comprised the biggest segment of his Budweiser beer customers, so he feared that if the Cardinals remained a prominent, white-only fraternity, there might be a boycott of his beverages by black consumers that would negatively affect his bottom line far beyond the turnstiles of what came to be known as Busch Stadium. Accordingly, Busch calculated the pros and cons of the situation and ordered the Cardinals to integrate—and to do it quickly.

The first few black players the Cardinals reeled in and elevated to the majors were decidedly unimpressive. One pitcher, Mexican-born lefthander Memo Luna, was particularly awful. His debut game for St. Louis on April 20, 1954, versus Cincinnati also turned out to be his farewell appearance. His start lasted ⅔ of an inning. Luna gave up two hits, two walks and two earned runs to the visiting Reds before getting the hook. His career ERA is 27.00. Luna never again set foot on an MLB diamond, but he was elected to the Mexican Professional Baseball Hall of Fame.

The Cardinals eventually got the hang of signing quality black players. First baseman Bill White and outfielder Curt Flood entered the fold. Interracial relationships on the club were generally very good, but there were some obstacles in the South that were beyond the control of the players. For example, the Yankees and Cardinals both held their spring training camps in St. Petersburg, Florida. It was an annual tradition for the grateful city's businessmen to host a lavish farewell breakfast for the players—so long as they were white. Bill White rebelled against this discriminatory practice and demanded that the racial barrier be lifted immediately. It was. (Amazingly, after winning this victory, White opted not to attend the breakfast when he found out how early in the morning it would be held!)

Lodgings for the team in Florida proved more problematic. For years the black Cardinals, by law, were not allowed to register in local hotels, forcing them to board with local black families instead. These dwellings were often less than luxurious and situated far from the spring training camp. Eventually the issue was solved when a friend of Gussie Bisch bought the Skyway Motel. To bypass the law pertaining to innkeepers, he leased it to the team as a private residence for the six weeks that spring training lasted. Furthermore, another hotel was acquired to allow the players' families to be nearby their husbands and fathers, if they chose.

2. The NL Pennant Chase

Many eagerly did. It was not uncommon for the families of black and white players to openly socialize together, something rarely seen in Florida in the early 1960s.

The formerly contentious racial issue oddly became a bonding agent that unified the 1964 Cardinals. Tim McCarver and Bob Gibson slowly became great friends even though McCarver had grown up in Memphis, Tennessee—one of the most segregated cities in the South. Gibson, six years older than McCarver, enjoyed slyly testing his catcher on his racial perceptions at every opportunity. One day when McCarver informed Gibson that a "colored man" was waiting to see him outside the clubhouse, Gibson feigned surprise and asked McCarver what color the man was.

In his 1994 autobiography, *Stranger to the Game*, Gibson wrote of the '64 Cardinals,

> We would simply not tolerate any sort of festering rancor between us. We brought our racial feelings out into the open and dealt with them. I'm confident I had a lot to do with it, and so did guys like White and Flood. None of us gave an inch to racism. The white players respected that ... and in turn we respected them. Of all the teams I was on ... there was never a better band of men.

The National League's pennant race in 1964 came within one result of ending in an unprecedented three-way tie involving the Phillies, Reds and Cardinals. On October 4, the final Sunday of the regular season, had the Mets upended St. Louis for the third straight time that weekend to go along with the Phillies' 10–0 defeat of the Reds, Cincinnati, Philadelphia and St. Louis all would have finished their 162-game NL schedules with identical 92–70 records. The NL had prepared a tie-breaking procedure for such an awkward scenario, but the Cardinals rendered it unnecessary by righting their ship for the regular-season finale.

The final day of the NL calendar had not been a cakewalk for the new champions. Indeed, it had been a struggle for the Cards to post that all-important victory. The game had taken three hours and six minutes to play—a lengthy affair by 1964 standards. Bob Gibson, normally a starter, had to be summoned to the mound by Cardinal manager, 52-year-old Johnny Keane, for a rare relief appearance. Gibson replaced struggling Curt Simmons with one man out in the top of the fifth with New York ahead, 3–2. Simmons had surrendered seven hits to the New Yorkers in a shaky outing.

Thankfully for the sake of Cardinal fans, St. Louis did enough to rally and defeat the Mets, 11–5. But even the great Gibson did not finish the game; he faltered in the ninth inning and had to be rescued. Nevertheless, when the final out was made, Gibson got credit for the win, his

19th of 1964. Tim McCarver personally had a big day for the victorious home team, collecting three hits. The key blow in the game, however, was Bill White's two-run homer in the sixth inning when the Cards captured the lead for good. Not long after the final out was recorded, the Cardinals' usually laid-back manager passionately embraced his wife, Lela, atop the home team's dugout. Although it was startling, the open show of affection would not be the biggest surprise coming from Keane over the next two weeks.

The Cardinals' 1964 pennant—the tenth in the club's 73-year-history—was not really a surprise, but how they got there was a truly remarkable journey. The team had played well in 1963, finishing a very respectable second, six games behind the pennant-winning Los Angeles Dodgers. During one stretch late in that season, St. Louis won 19 out of 20 games. Their optimistic fans carried plenty of hope into spring training of 1964 that they could take the NL championship. However, the Cards certainly did not look like a championship outfit for the first 2½ months of the famous campaign. They were a sub-.500 club and had not even mustered a three-game winning streak to that point in the season. On July 9 they were in sixth place, 11 full games behind the league-leading Phillies. Anyone bold enough to predict that St. Louis would be in a tightly fought pennant race by season's end would have been justifiably ridiculed.

The team needed a spark, an infusion of life of some sort. They definitely got it midway through June thanks to a historic deal made just after the Cards had been swept in a three-game series in Los Angeles in which both Don Drysdale and Sandy Koufax shut them out. From June 16 onward, the Cardinals' best player had been 23-year-old Lou Brock, the club's major base-stealing threat. That was the date he was acquired from the Chicago Cubs in exchange for Ernie Broglio, a 28-year-old right-handed pitcher who had been the team's starter on Opening Day. He had struggled in 1964. At the time of the deal—which actually involved six players—Broglio had dropped to the fourth starter in the team's pitching rotation. He possessed a 3–5 record and an ERA hovering close to 4.00, but he was a popular man on the club and he had won 60 games for St. Louis from 1960 through 1963. (In what turned out to be his last appearance in a Cardinal jersey, Broglio had lost one of the games to the Dodgers.)

Keane was not worried about losing Broglio's arm, however. The Cards manager figured the benefits of the underappreciated Brock would far offset any deficit the team might incur on the mound. When St. Louis general manager Vaughan (Bing) Devine asked Keane about a Broglio-for-Brock deal, Keane was all for it. "If Brock gives us what I think he can," he said, "he'll win a lot of games for us."[1] The Cubs were the club that instigated the deal, however. They were going nowhere and were desperate for pitching. Brock, despite having great promise, had been a disappointment to them and was perceived as expendable. Immediately St. Louis won four straight games with Brock in their outfield. He was positioned in right field during his Cardinals debut. Broglio won only seven games for the Cubs in 2½ seasons with Chicago. By 1966, he had been demoted to AAA baseball. By the end of 1967, Broglio had retired from the sport altogether.

Brock was thrilled by the opportunity to get out of Chicago. He hated battling the sun in the Wrigley Field outfield during the 81 Cub home dates which were all played in the daytime. Furthermore, Brock was happy to escape some of the city's overly critical baseball writers. One scribe, Bob Smith of the *Chicago Daily News*, wrote, "If you have watched all the Cub home games thus far, you probably had come to the conclusion that Lou Brock is the worst outfielder in baseball history. He really isn't, but he hasn't done much to prove it."[2]

In a pre–World Series feature article, baseball journalist Milton Gross related an anecdote that may have been the turning point for the Cardinals becoming a pennant winner. "There was this night when Lou Brock doubled with a man on," Gross wrote. "But he died at second base." When he came back to the bench the following inning, he sheepishly said to manager Johnny Keane, "I wanted to go on the first pitch."[3] He mentioned that he saw the opponents' third baseman playing far back, well off the bag.

Surprised, Keane asked Brock why he did not try to steal third base. Brock said there was no steal sign flashed to him by the third-base coach. Keane responded that from that point onward Brock was free to decide for himself when he could and would steal bases. "He picked up the baton and the whole club went with him. He's been the single biggest factor in our winning this pennant,"[4] said Keane. Brock batted .348 in his two-thirds of a season with St. Louis—and stole 33 bases. He had stolen 10 bases with the Cubs, but he was batting only .251 when the trade was made. Brock was, by nature, a loner—quite the opposite of the outgoing Broglio—so the dynamics of the Cardinal clubhouse changed with his arrival. Nevertheless, by mid–July, Bing Devine ranked the acquisition of Brock as the best trade he had ever made.

Bill White, who himself made huge contributions to the success of the Cardinals in the second half of the season after a slow start, agreed with his manager about Brock. "Without Lou, we might have made sixth [place]— if we were lucky. What made Lou was that John [Keane] left him alone. We've seen him pull some boo-boos, but that hasn't mattered. A kid like him you turn loose and don't say a word."[5] At the time the Brock-Broglio trade was made, White had been a vocal critic of it.

Excluding his baserunning skills, Brock had been an excellent acquisition from a defensive standpoint, too. Keane recalled to Gross that he walked out to the outfield with his new player to deliver a message of confidence. "This is left field," Keane told Brock. "It's a big one and it's all yours. If you can do what I think you can, you ought to be able to play out here for the rest of your life."[6] Gross praised Brock by declaring, "There are some players who can play a lifetime and not do what Brock has done since the day he became a Cardinal and [the team was residing] in seventh place."[7] Brock was eventually installed as the everyday left fielder in St. Louis—the same field that had once been patrolled by Stan Musial. Keane's biographers wrote, "His terrific speed, coupled with Keane's willingness to use it to the point of recklessness, added a key ingredient of unpredictability to the St. Louis offense."[8]

"I underestimated how good this kid [Brock] could be," Keane insisted. "He's not 24 yet, but he's a real student of baserunning. He's so fast that a double for the average player is a triple for him."[9] Keane said that when Brock drew a walk, it was almost akin to him smacking a double because he was such a threat to steal second base off any pitcher/catcher duo in the NL.

Keane continued lauding Brock's talents, this time as a hitter. "I've never seen anyone hit a ball harder who weighs 168 pounds. When he hits a home run, you know it's out of the park the moment the bat hits the ball."[10] Indeed, Brock often startled NL opponents with his unexpected power. While a member of the Cubs, Brock hit a tremendous home run for a man of his slight physical stature. On June 17, 1962, at the Polo Grounds, during the first inning of the first game of a twin bill between Chicago and the expansion New York Mets, Brock drove a stunning 460-foot home run into the right-field bleachers off Al Jackson. By doing so, Brock, who had just turned 23, became only the second player to reach that section of seats at the famous old ballpark since its 1923 renovation. The first hitter to do it had been Joe Adcock of the Milwaukee Braves in 1953. In contrast, Adcock, a feared slugger who hit 336 career home runs, was an imposing physical specimen: He was 6'4" and weighed 210 pounds.

Forty-eight-year-old Bing Devine, the man ultimately responsible for the Cardinals' important acquisition of Brock, was fired about a month later by Auggie Busch when the Cardinals were still well behind the Philadelphia Phillies in the NL standings. It was widely rumored that Devine's firing was orchestrated by 82-year-old Branch Rickey, who had been brought back into the Cardinals' fold 18 months earlier as a special "management consultant." Under Rickey's large influence, the team was now "looking to go in a different direction"—a longtime sports euphemism for major personnel changes at the top of the ladder. One of Rickey's recommendations was to shake up the club's front office, including replacing

2. The NL Pennant Chase

Devine. Though nothing was official, there were also rumors flying around that Keane himself was going to be sacked after the season. His replacement would be former Cardinal manager and Branch Rickey protégé Leo Durocher. There was even scuttlebutt that Gussie Busch was secretly negotiating with him. Like everyone else close to Cardinals baseball, Johnny Keane heard these rumors and was not happy. At the end of the season, Harold Kaese of the *Boston Globe* wrote that Devine "knows how General MacArthur felt. He made victory possible ... and then was given the gate."[11] Ironically, at season's end, Devine was named MLB's Executive of the Year by *The Sporting News*. He would be rehired by the Cardinals after the 1967 season.

Although far less heralded than Brock's arrival in St. Louis, another move made by the club a month later produced unexpected dividends: It was the July recall of Mike Shannon from the team's minor league affiliate in Jacksonville and his installation as the Cardinals' everyday right fielder. Shannon had been born in St. Louis, but had grown up in nearby Clayton, Missouri. A onetime all–American high school quarterback, the 25-year-old Shannon provided superb defensive prowess for the Redbirds, day after day. Despite being of slight build, Shannon contributed additional hitting power to the club as a bonus. It was the beginning of Shannon's long association with the Cardinals—one that lasted well into the 21st century.

Bob Gibson continued to be an emerging force in the NL in 1964. He was born into dire poverty in Omaha, Nebraska, in 1935. He never knew his father, who died a few months before Bob took his first breath. Tutored in both life and sports by Josh, his much older brother, Bob Gibson was a marvelous athlete who probably should have played in the NBA. Because Gibson played collegiate hoops at little-known Creighton University—averaging more than 20 points per game—he slipped under the radar of the pro basketball scouts who were not nearly as thorough about discovering youthful prospects in far-flung locales as their baseball counterparts were. (Gibson did play with the Harlem Globetrotters for a time, but their clowning on the court ran quite contrary to the deadly seriousness of the fiery black athlete.) As a right-handed pitcher, Gibson threw hard, impressing everyone who was objective. Grunts usually accompanied every Gibson toss. Sometimes his voice became hoarse over the course of a particularly intense pitching assignment.

One person who probably was not fair in his assessments about Gibson was his first manager on the Cardinals, Solomon (Solly) Hemus. Generally captious about his players, Hemus opined that Gibson would never be a star pitcher because his off-speed deliveries were substandard and he always threw his fastballs at the same pace. Catcher Tim McCarver agreed that both points Hemus made were true, but he quickly added that Gibson's fearsome speed more than made up for its lack of variety. Gibson disliked Hemus—as did most of the Cardinals. However, he liked Johnny Keane very much when he took over the manager's job in St. Louis in July 1961, even if he was considered a prude. (When he was 21, Tim McCarver was reprimanded by Keane for missing curfew by 10 minutes because he was late arriving at the team's hotel when he was out on a date. The minor degree of McCarver's tardiness did not bother Keane, but being out late with a girl did.) Perhaps it was because Keane was a career minor leaguer as a player—and, frankly, a mediocre one—that he knew how to handle all his players' egos without angering or openly humiliating them. This was especially true of Gibson, who was quick to blow his top and was amazingly competitive at everything he did. Keane was not nearly as quick to pull Gibson from a game as Hemus had been if the pitcher got into trouble early. Gibson responded with ever-increasing double-digit win totals beginning in 1961. Gibson would win at least 11 games every year until 1975, his final MLB season.

Gibson answered to the amusing nickname Hoot. (It was the sobriquet belonging to the late popular cowboy actor of yesteryear who was born Edmund Richard Gibson in 1892.) The Cardinal hurler hated to lose far more than he liked to win. Gibson once explained to his incredulous teammates that he refused to let his young daughter win at tic-tac-toe because it would send her the wrong message about how to properly attain success in life. Gibson disliked All-Star Games because those occasions forced him to interact and be friendly with accomplished NL players who were usually his despised enemies. One scouting report the Yankees got about Gibson prior to the 1964 World Series described him as mean in its very first line. It was a fair assessment; Gibson always pitched as if he had a chip on his shoulder. Remarkably, the Yankees' pre–World Series scouting report practically ignored Gibson's blazing fastball. Instead, it described him as a pitcher who liked to nibble at the corners of the plate.

He liked to set his own pace and generally worked fast. Over the course of one game, Gibson was timed by a journalist. The data from the stopwatch was quite telling. Gibson threw a pitch, on average, every eight seconds! This quickness pleased his teammates and the umpires, but it frustrated NBC whenever the network featured St. Louis on its Saturday *Game of the Week* telecast and Gibson was the Cardinal starter. Often Gibson would sprint onto the field after the Cards had been retired, take his warmup pitches in rapid fashion, and begin the next inning while the network was still airing its commercials. Batters who stepped out of the box too frequently received his wrath. So did those who tried to bunt for base hits. (Gibson considered that tactic unsporting. Batters

2. The NL Pennant Chase

who laid down sacrifice bunts, however, were not later punished; that was an acceptable part of baseball in Gibson's opinion.) Every batter he faced seemingly represented something akin to a life-or-death struggle. Once, when Gibson was asked by Hank Aaron why he had deliberately thrown at (and struck) his teammate John Milner, Gibson seemed puzzled by the question. "I heard he could hit"[12] was the pitcher's pithy explanation. Despite his surliness, however, Gibson was also a man who possessed great comedic gifts and often elicited laughter from his Cardinal teammates with impressions of them and sarcastic remarks. By the time the 1964 World Series was contested, Gibson had not yet reached his peak as a dominating force on the mound, but he was steadily approaching it. As author David Halberstam noted in his book *October 1964*, at that point in his career, Gibson was not yet a great pitcher, but on any given day he could pitch a great game.

While Gibson and Brock were making headlines, it was another Cardinal, Ken Boyer, who won the NL Most Valuable Player Award in 1964 with his steady excellence all season long. He scored 100 runs, drove in 119 to lead MLB, and batted .295—all while playing third base solidly. (Teammate Bill White, the club's first baseman, finished third in the voting. Lou Brock and Curt Flood also did well, as they came tenth and eleventh respectively.) In 1964, Boyer hit for the cycle for the second time in his MLB career. This one occurred on June 16 versus the Houston Colts—and it was a rare "natural cycle" in which Boyer hit a single, double, triple and home run in that order. His other cycle was achieved three years earlier against the Chicago Cubs when he got five hits in a September 14, 1961, game—the final one being a spectacular walk-off home run before the hometown fans.

Boyer had the potential to be versatile, too—at least according to Bob Broeg. Despite Boyer playing the vast majority of his career at third base, the acclaimed sports journalist who covered the Cardinals for four decades for the *St. Louis Post-Dispatch* liked to tell out-of-town scribes that, if given equal pitching, a team of eight Ken Boyers would defeat a team of eight Brooks Robinsons, or eight Henry Aarons, or eight clones of any other claimant for the title of MLB's best all-around player.

Cheerful and good-natured, Boyer seldom griped about anything. Having grown up in a huge family mired in poverty in rural Missouri, Boyer fully appreciated that he was employed in a dream occupation and was a well-paid ballplayer for his era. About the only person in the Cardinal organization who seemed to dislike Boyer was the team's hugely popular radio announcer, Harry Caray, who, it was generally agreed, was overly critical of the Cards' star third baseman. (The origin of Caray's antagonism toward Boyer likely began on an afternoon when Caray experimented with broadcasting from field level and wanted to interview Boyer during the game. Boyer said no. He explained he was more than happy to do interviews before or after any game, but he drew the line at an in-game interview when he wanted to stay solely focused on playing baseball.) Caray's jabs at Boyer seemed to inspire booing from fans at home games. This angered his teammates, but neither Caray's harsh remarks nor the raspberries from the paying customers seemed to bother Boyer himself, who accepted them as part of his job. He was especially pleased by his team's dramatic charge toward the NL pennant. As the regular season approached its conclusion, Boyer gleefully told *Sports Illustrated*, "This is the closest I've been to playing in a World Series. I'd give 10 years off my life to play in one."[13]

Another key member of the 1964 Cardinals was their young catcher, Tim McCarver, who was not quite 23 years old. The son of a Memphis police officer, McCarver, a terrific athlete, had excelled in every sport he played at that city's Christian Brothers High School. He found he was especially gifted at baseball, understood the subtleties of the game better than most teenagers, and played his first MLB game at age 17. As a catcher, he was unusually swift afoot. In 1966, his 13 triples led the entire National League.

For a while, McCarver's biggest enemy was himself. He had been dominant in his short stays in the Cardinals' minor league system. His unchecked success made him short-tempered when he did not immediately do well at the major league level. Wise counselling from veteran players, such as pitcher Curt Simmons, helped McCarver channel his competitive drive into positives that benefited the entire team. Freely talkative and perhaps overly analytical, a teammate once joked that if someone asked McCarver what time it was, the loquacious catcher would go into a long and tedious monologue explaining how a clock worked. Nevertheless, McCarver was a witty and charming interview subject. In 2014, when he was asked about the tightness of the last few days of the wild 1964 NL pennant race, McCarver said with a smile, "I don't think it was magic. It was a hectic September. We happened to be the ones whose snorkels worked."[14]

Entering the 1964 World Series, the Cardinals possessed excellent pitching, batting, team speed and overall defense. Furthermore, decades later, Tim McCarver described his NL championship club as a perfect mixture of youthful and veteran players that was largely the creation of the now-departed general manager Bing Devine. What St. Louis lacked was the intangible mystique of the perennial AL champion Yankees. That was why the Cardinals were installed as the underdogs by bookmakers before Game One of the Fall Classic was played at Busch Stadium in St. Louis

2. The NL Pennant Chase

on the afternoon of Wednesday, October 7. For an intense nine days they would be on a mission to prove the baseball experts—and those who chose to bet on the favorites—wrong.

1964 National League	W	L	Pct.	GB
St. Louis Cardinals	93	69	.574	—
Philadelphia Phillies	92	70	.568	1
Cincinnati Reds	92	70	.568	1
San Francisco Giants	90	72	.556	3
Milwaukee Braves	88	74	.543	5
Pittsburgh Pirates	80	82	.494	13
Los Angeles Dodgers	80	82	.494	13
Chicago Cubs	76	86	.469	17
Houston Colt .45s	66	96	.407	27
New York Mets	53	109	.327	40

— 3 —

Another AL Pennant
The Yankees Take the Fifth

"The Yankees had been to the World Series every season since time began, it seemed, and they knew about big games. They knew how to intimidate their opponents, and somehow in a World Series, no matter where the game was played, they always managed to seem like the home team."[1]—David Halberstam

When the New York Yankees captured the 1964 American League pennant, it was their fifth in a row and ninth in ten years. It would have been unfathomable for any serious baseball fan to think they would not win another one for more than a decade. That indeed proved to be the case, though. No further pennants would fly over Yankee Stadium until 1976, a year after the old building had completed a major renovation that forced the team to play its home games at Shea Stadium, the home of the NL New York Mets, in both 1974 and 1975. In other words, the 1964 championship was the last hurrah for the most dominating team in the history of American sports. The problem was they did not realize it nor how quickly they would fall into near irrelevance.

The Yankees, like the Cardinals, were around a long time before they threatened to be a top-caliber club. They were an original AL franchise in 1901—but they were a reincarnation of the Baltimore Orioles. The club stayed in Maryland through 1902, but moved to the greener attendance pasture of New York City for the 1903 season. They were called the Highlanders until 1912 and played their home games at Hilltop Park, a small venue in the Washington Heights section of New York City. The quaint and cozy ballpark could only seat 16,000 paying customers. For the 1913 season, the AL team relocated to the much more spacious Polo Grounds in Manhattan. The club was a mere tenant there; the NL New York Giants

3. Another AL Pennant

owned the ballpark. Their lack of success on the field made the Yankees little more than a mediocre sideshow. They routinely lagged behind the Giants in popularity, attendance, and newspaper coverage.

Things changed for the club almost overnight, however. The Yankees ushered in the Roaring Twenties spectacularly. They garnered national media exposure beginning on January 5, 1920, when the Yankees officially announced they had acquired Babe Ruth, the two-time AL home run champion, from the Boston Red Sox in a cash deal. Once the 1920 campaign got underway, Ruth began to smash home runs at an astonishing clip, easily shattering his old seasonal record of 29 and upping it to 54. Interest in the team skyrocketed, of course. The Yankees' home attendance at the Polo Grounds more than doubled that season from what it had been in 1919 as close to 1.3 million people eagerly passed through the ballpark's turnstiles to watch the most talked about man in all American sports. Newspapers could not get enough of the Babe whose colorful exploits were bigger than life. With Ruth as its kingpin, New York's American League club won the 1921 AL pennant—its first in franchise history—and drew more than 1.23 million fans. Baseball in New York no longer solely meant John McGraw and his New York Giants, who attracted 973,477 paying customers that same season. It was enough to lead the NL, but it was only about four-fifths of the Yankees' total. That statistic did not please the Giants nor McGraw. The NL club grew to resent the Yankees' success and evicted them after the 1922 campaign. That development forced their AL rivals to speedily build cavernous Yankee Stadium in the Bronx which opened in time for the 1923 season. Nearly 100,000 fans turned out to try to watch the Yankees-Red Sox game on Opening Day on April 18. To their great disappointment, some 25,000 of them could not gain admission to the impressive new venue and thus missed New York's comfortable 4–1 win over Boston.

Slowly but steadily, the positions of the Giants and Yankees changed in the hearts and minds of New York City's sports fans. By the end of the 1920s, a decade in which the Yankees won six pennants, they were an almost unstoppable dynasty. Certainly, they had rivals. The Philadelphia Athletics returned to greatness and championship form for three seasons, besting New York from 1929 through 1931. Even Washington finished first in the AL once and Detroit did it twice during the 1930s. Overall, those victories by interlopers were mere outliers in the Yankees' long-term domination of the Junior Circuit. Five more AL pennants were won by New York with a mostly different cast of characters in the 1930s, with Lou Gehrig being the superb and tragic link between the two eras after Ruth left the team in 1934. Even the manpower shortages of the Second World War did not really interrupt the string of Yankee pennants. Five more were secured

A long-distance photograph of Yankee Stadium, taken during the season it opened: 1923 (Library of Congress).

in the 1940s, usually accompanied by World Series titles. The apex of Yankee power was achieved in the 1950s. They won eight pennants when television began to showcase them in all their October glory. Fans in other AL cities were understandably bitter about New York's endless string of championships. Mike Royko, a Pulitzer Prize-winning newspaper columnist from Chicago, was among them. He once wrote, "Hating the Yankees is as American as pizza pie, unwed mothers, and cheating on your income tax."

But television would indirectly result in the empire's demise. The tube impacted the sport greatly as fewer and fewer people bothered to attend minor league games. Why pay to see an inferior product when MLB was available on TV on a semiregular basis? Slowly but steadily, minor pro leagues contracted and shut down as their parent MLB clubs became increasingly money conscious. Only the St. Louis Cardinals, who pioneered the farm system as a way to sift quality players from sheer quantity, could rival the breadth of the Yankee farm system when it was at its apex. New York, however, allowed its feeder system to gradually wither away. For most of the 1950s, the Yankees bought or traded their way to a glut of AL pennants, acquiring key veterans or promising youngsters from rival teams struggling with cash flow problems. Roger Maris was just one example. Buying proven players from have-not teams was more efficient than running money-losing teams in out-of-the-way places that did not guarantee the likes of another Mickey Mantle. The cellar-dwelling Kansas City Athletics were such frequent sellers to the Yankees that many baseball writers kidded that the A's were merely a glorified farm team for New York's illustrious pinstripe crew.

By the time the 1964 season rolled around, the Yankees were still the Yankees. However, their core stars were starting to show their age. Whitey Ford, Mickey Mantle and Roger Maris were all in some stage of decline. Elston Howard arguably was too. Players such as Tony Kubek, Bobby Richardson, Tom Tresh, Clete Boyer and Joe Pepitone were present to bolster the Yankee lineup—but there was no longer an endless supply of prospects eagerly waiting and available if their MLB counterparts faltered. Pepitone, at age 23, was the youngest of the regulars.

The Yankees, like most AL teams, were slow to sign black players. The Yankees reign of five consecutive World Series wins from 1949 through 1953 came without a single black player in the regular lineup. Meanwhile, the NL freely signed blacks and benefited from the aggressive style of running game they brought with them from the dying Negro Leagues. When the Yankees finally did sign catcher Elston Howard in 1955, Casey Stengel joked to the media that his club's front office had handed him a rarity: a black ballplayer who could not run well. (Despite his lack of footspeed, Howard was voted AL MVP in 1963.) Howard was never one to draw attention to himself, but his mere presence on the club made him a conspicuous figure. He usually roomed alone on road trips as the Yankees preferred not to arrange for a white player to share hotel accommodations with a black man. In 1961, Al Downing, a diminutive black pitcher from Trenton, New Jersey, joined the Yankees for a time. By 1964 he had been a regular on the MLB club for two seasons.

The biggest change entering the 1964 AL season for the Yankees was that Lawrence Peter (Yogi) Berra, arguably the greatest MLB catcher of all time, had been elevated to the team's manager. He was replacing Ralph Houk, the military man who had replaced Casey Stengel after the team's upset loss in the 1960 World Series. Houk was moving up in the Yankee hierarchy as the team's new general manager. His was a tough act to follow. In his three years as New York's manager, "The Major," as Houk was often called, had won three AL pennants and two World Series. Berra had never managed at any level prior to 1964. In fact, he had still been an active player in 1963, retiring once the Dodgers had swept the Yankees in that year's World Series.

Berra was a beloved figure to Yankee fans; that was his greatest asset in the eyes of the club's management. His skills in calling a game from behind the plate were unparalleled, but it was his personality that won people over. His observations on baseball and just about everything else

Yogi Berra (left) poses in 1955 with Elston Howard, the man who would succeed him behind the plate as New York's regular catcher (courtesy Boston Public Library, Leslie Jones Collection).

in life were quotable tidbits of joy to be savored—even if he did not really say all of the things he was supposed to have said. But was he a good fit to manage the team he had played on since the late 1940s? Berra knew the game thoroughly; that was beyond question. While he was playing, many knowledgeable baseball people believed Berra would someday make an excellent manager—when the time came. (In some respects, he had been Casey Stengel's understudy and aide for years.) But Berra had no managerial résumé whatsoever in 1964. So why was he hired in to manage MLB's most storied franchise while other candidates who possessed far more credentials were passed over?

The answer was probably that the Mets, founded in 1962, had remarkably surpassed the Yankees in popularity in New York City by 1964. The Mets were lovable castoffs with the quotable and comical Casey Stengel managing them—when he wasn't occasionally napping during games. The Mets' record was dismal but that did not deter the people of Gotham from supporting them beyond all sense of reason. Met fans were a combination of disenfranchised ex–Giant and Dodger fans who had suddenly lost their teams after 1957 when their owners moved them 3,000 miles westward to California; and youngsters and fans new to the sport who were looking for something other than the predictable, dynastic Yankees to root for. To many fans, the Yankees symbolized the arrogance of unbridled success and corporate greed. The Mets, in contrast, were a fun outfit, free from pomposity and any burdens of tradition and excellence. For example, a fan could not buy a replica Yankee cap (never mind a jersey or warmup jacket) at Yankee Stadium in 1964. Tradition was not for sale there. Such a thing would devalue the real caps and jerseys worn by the players on the field, it was reasoned. But the Mets sold caps and other paraphernalia by the thousands at Shea Stadium. In the Mets' first season at their modern new ballpark, they drew more than 1.7 million fans. The Mets, as in the previous two seasons, were still a last-place club in the 10-team NL. The Yankees were pennant winners, of course, but the perennial AL champions were considerably in arrears of the Mets at the turnstiles with 1.3 million patrons attending their home games in 1964 at what was MLB's most famous baseball palace. That figure was about three-quarters of what the lowly Mets drew in 1964.

The Yankee hierarchy presumably considered Berra to be their homegrown version of Stengel—an entertaining manager whose good humor and likable presence would breathe new interest into a franchise that had steadily grown dull in the public's mind because of its repeated successes. Mickey Mantle respected Berra, but he was skeptical of his former teammate's ability to lead the players he so recently had as colleagues on the field. "I think we can win in spite of it,"[2] the Yankee superstar commented to the press about the Yankees' managerial change before the 1964 season began. Mantle meant it to be an insincere, funny remark, but there was likely a great deal of honesty embedded within those few words. Didn't the Yankees always win? Did the name of the manager on the lineup card really matter very much? Berra surprisingly insisted on just a one-year contract, although he could have asked for and likely gotten a longer deal, because he himself was initially not quite sure he was a good fit for the job. Berra would later regret that selfless decision. He told *The Sporting News*, "I didn't know for sure if I could manage. That's why I didn't sign the two-year contract they offered me. I wanted to make sure I could do the job first. I didn't want to stick anybody with a flop for two years."[3]

Another lesser known but perhaps equally important change in the 1964 New York Yankees was the dismissal of pitching coach Johnny Sain. An Arkansas-born right-hander, Sain gained immortal baseball fame for his connection with the 1948 NL champion Boston Braves ("[Warren] Spahn and Sain and two days of rain!" was the fans' mantra for the otherwise pitching-poor team that somehow won 91 times and comfortably captured the pennant by 6½ games that season in what proved to be the Braves' last hurrah in Boston.) Sain had contributed 24 of those 91 victories in 1948. He had been traded to the Yankees midway through the 1951 season as the Braves' fortunes began plummeting along with his effectiveness on the mound.

When Sain's playing career ended in 1955, he coached the lackluster Kansas City A's for a short time. Hearing good things about him, New York snatched him away from the A's and put him on the club's payroll. In his own very independent-minded way, Sain became hugely important to the careers of several prominent New York hurlers. Jim Bouton, Ralph Terry, and Al Downing all swore by his methods and advice. (Ned Garver loved his approach. Garver said, "If [Sain] had an idea that he thought could be of value to you, he would tell you about it to try to help you. But by the time he finished visiting with you about it, you would think that you'd thought of it yourself."[4]) Sain's final MLB job was as a pitching coach with the 1978 Atlanta Braves.

Not only was Sain gifted in spotting and correcting mechanical flaws in pitchers' deliveries, he was also quite adept as an amateur psychologist. New York's pitchers were always mentally prepared for their outings. Whenever trouble brewed in a game, Sain would emphasize the strengths of whoever was on the mound and tell him to focus on what he already knew and had mastered. However, Sain and then–Yankee manager Ralph Houk did not get along well. Both were stubborn, strong-minded individuals. When Houk even mildly questioned Sain about any aspect of his coaching—even something trivial—Sain would terminate the conversation by asking Houk how many games he had pitched in the major leagues. Houk had been a tough-as-nails Army major during the Second World War. He was not used to insolence from an underling. When Houk became the Yankee GM after the 1963 season, the 46-year-old Sain's days with the club were numbered. He was not offered a contract for 1964. During his coaching career, Sain was fired twice in midseason by MLB teams. On both those occasions, the manager was fired not long afterward when the quality of the team's pitching declined.

Sain would happily go to great lengths—and heights—to help his pitchers. "The project that best epitomizes Sain at work has to be Denny McLain," wrote Jan Finkel, Sain's SABR biographer about his time with the Detroit Tigers. "Learning that McLain was working to obtain a pilot's license, Sain helped him prepare for the required tests, and even went up in the air with him. From that basis, the two moved to McLain's pitching so smoothly that he was the best pitcher in the American League in 1968 and 1969, winning 55 games, a Most Valuable Player Award, and two Cy Young [Awards]."[5]

3. Another AL Pennant

In 1964, Mickey Mantle, at age 32, was still the marquee face of the Yankees and still carried clout and popularity, although chronic injuries had reduced his playing time severely in 1963. He was, in many respects, one of the most remarkable athletes ever to grace the American stage. As a youngster he could run faster than anyone in baseball. The first time he saw Mantle, Casey Stengel was utterly flabbergasted by the youngster's speed, declaring him to be faster than Ty Cobb ever was. People who witnessed his running motion compared Mantle's legs to the spokes of a bicycle wheel in motion. They moved so fast you merely saw a blur—not the individual legs hitting the ground. The Yankees did not emphasize the stolen base much in their heyday or else Mantle's base stealing totals would undoubtedly be impressive. Years later when ballplayers became acclaimed for achieving pioneering feats of 20/20 or 30/30 seasons (ratios of home runs to stolen bases), Mantle chuckled and said he could have done that too—if such a feat was even thought about during his MLB days. But it was his bat that Mantle was most known for. Bill Dickey, the great Yankee catcher from the 1920s and 1930s who became a New York coach, seldom engaged in hyperbole. However, upon seeing the teenage Mantle's power from both sides of the plate combined with his speed, an impressed Dickey told anyone who would listen that Mantle had the potential to be the greatest baseball player who ever lived.

Bill Dickey, the great Yankee catcher from the Ruth-Gehrig era (and pictured here in 1937), tutored Yogi Berra in the finer points of calling a game. He also was one of the club's first coaches to predict greatness for Mickey Mantle (courtesy Boston Public Library, Leslie Jones Collection).

Fans love home runs, and Mantle set out to please them. In Ken Burns' terrific *Baseball* documentary, Mantle commented that when he was asked if he deliberately tried to hit home runs, he replied, "Every time." He succeeded 536 times in his 18 MLB seasons. Mantle ushered in the era of the "tape-measure home run" when he belted a 565-foot homer in Washington in the first week of the 1953 season. (The ball would have traveled farther if its flightpath had not caused it to deflect off a large billboard beyond the bleachers.) Mantle had a legitimate chance at surpassing Babe Ruth's lifetime record of 714 round-trippers had he stayed healthy and/or taken better care of himself. Be that as it may, Mantle always took delight at those homers that sailed far into the distance. They were special to him.

He arrived in the big leagues as something of a country hick from Oklahoma, but he quickly caught on to the lifestyle benefits of being a celebrity in New York City in the 1950s. He and teammate Whitey Ford became great friends and world-class carousers. Casey Stengel once joked that the twosome must not be able to tell time accurately because they did not know the difference between midnight and noon. Certainly, Stengel did not like their boozing and sleepless nights, but the two of them were his best players—and the Yankees won eight AL pennants from the time Mantle joined the club in 1951 and Stengel's dismissal after the 1960 season—so the great Yankee manager was not able to argue that their social schedules were tangibly detrimental to the team's success. Mantle came from a family whose males had histories of dying young. Hodgkin's disease was a common killer of Mantle men. (Mantle's father died at age 39.) Mantle openly told concerned friends that he was going to live life hard and fast because he did not expect to live long. When Mantle attained his fiftieth birthday and beyond, he commonly joked that he would indeed have taken better care of himself had he known he would get so old.

Once Joe DiMaggio retired after the 1951 season, Mantle eventually became the dominating presence in the Yankee clubhouse, a place he loved because it was secluded and he was naturally shy around strangers. Unlike DiMaggio, Mantle was gregarious with those he knew and trusted, and almost always fun to be around. (He was notoriously surly when he was in a batting slump, however.) He told jokes, many of them ribald in nature, laughed at his own shortcomings, and treated newcomers to the team very well. Mantle usually asked a surprised rookie to dine with him both as an act of kindness and as a privacy buffer. (He figured his restaurant meals were less likely to be interrupted by autograph-seekers if he brought along a dining companion.)

By 1964, Mantle's fragile legs were heavily taped before just about every game and he was playing right field more often than center field because the former required less agility than the latter. Numerous operations had removed nearly all the cartilage in his knees. The bandaging became a common sight to his teammates, but other AL players who saw him dress and undress at All-Star Games were genuinely shocked at the ordeal Mantle had to go through every single day to prepare himself simply to play baseball. Joe Pepitone once noted that Mantle may have been the only big-name athlete in American history who was more admired by his teammates than by his adoring fans.

And Mantle was adored. He was the hero of every baseball-loving schoolboy who followed the Yankees. Stories abound about middle-age men weeping with joy when they finally got to meet their all-time favorite MLB player. Bob Costas admitted to carrying a Mantle baseball card in his wallet well into adulthood. Actor Billy Crystal, at age 29, was visibly shaking and overwhelmed when Dinah Shore arranged for him to meet Mantle on her daytime talk show in 1977. Costas and Crystal would both be present at Mantle's funeral in Dallas in 1995 where the sportscaster delivered a superb eulogy. Crystal described Mantle as "a great big American hero" in Ken Burns' excellent *Baseball* documentary. Few sports fans who grew up in the 1950s would argue the point.

The Yankees did not get off to a flying start in 1964 as injuries became a recurring problem. They were 1–4 after five games and sitting at the bottom of the 10-team AL standings. However, by Mother's Day, the Yankees had risen to a tie for first place. The first week of June saw New York drop to fifth spot with a 22–18 record, but after June 18 the club was never below third place for the rest of the 1964 campaign.

New York and the Chicago White Sox had emerged as the two teams most likely to vie for the AL pennant. The White Sox were thought by many to have a superior pitching staff. (Baltimore was in the hunt for a while, too. The Orioles' fabulous third baseman, Brooks Robinson, would be named the AL MVP for 1964. Their slugging first baseman, 23-year-old Boog Powell, missed 28 games due to injuries. Many writers who covered the Junior Circuit figured if Powell had stayed healthy, the Orioles would have taken the franchise's first pennant since 1944 when they were the St. Louis Browns.)

Within the New York clubhouse, Berra's leadership abilities were mildly questioned sometimes, but one incident tested it severely. On Thursday, August 20, the Yankees lost 5–0 to the ChiSox at Comiskey Park. That result gave the Chicagoans a four-game series sweep and dropped the Yankees into third place, imperiling their pennant chances. Berra was understandably not in a light-hearted mood when the team boarded a bus to take his club to O'Hare Airport from where they would fly to Boston for their next series. Reserve infielder Phil Linz, who had not played in the last game in Chicago but had three hits and two runs scored in the second one, seemed unconcerned about the losing streak. He casually pulled a harmonica from his pocket ... and began to play "Mary Had a

Little Lamb." An angry Berra ordered him to stop the music. Linz did not quite hear Berra's command. When he asked Mickey Mantle what Berra had said, the Yankee superstar—a notable prankster—reputedly told him, "Play it louder." So Linz did. Berra angrily stormed to the rear of the bus and knocked the harmonica out of Linz's hand, or perhaps Linz threw it at him. (Accounts of the incident vary.) The two men then exchanged a few heated words. Linz was eventually fined $200 by the club for his impudence. In 1964 it was common for the Yankee beat writers to travel with the team, so there were plenty of witnesses to the peculiar Linz-Berra confrontation. The scribes dutifully reported the oddball story in their columns.

Accordingly, the "harmonica incident" became widely circulated around the American League and in newspapers throughout North America. It became mainstream news. Johnny Carson, who was not much of a baseball fan, referenced it in his *Tonight Show* monologue. Carson joked that Linz would be performing a harmonica solo on that night's program with the first selection being "Who's Sorry Now?" (Humorously, Linz got an endorsement deal from the Hohner Harmonica Company—most certainly a first for an MLB player—which paid him either 25 or 50 times the amount he had to fork over to the Yankees in fine money.) Sales of the pocket instruments apparently soared. When the Yankees played their next series at Fenway Park, several harmonicas were tossed onto the field near the Yankee dugout over the four games. After the first game of the series (which the Red Sox won), Bob Holbrook of the *Boston Globe* wrote in his Saturday column,

> Local fans went armed with harmonicas to Fenway Park to serenade the Yankees. Linz is not even an accomplished harmonica player and only purchased the troublesome instrument in Chicago. And while we're talking about sour notes, did these Yankees impress you as the old Yankees did?[6]

The team rallied around Berra, however, and began to win. From September 16 to 26, the Yankees won 11 consecutive contests to assume a four-game lead in the AL standings. The White Sox eventually whittled the difference to just one game, but they got no closer. On the second-last day of the regular-season, New York's 99th win of 1964—an 8–3 home win over Cleveland—secured the 29th pennant in the club's illustrious history and their fifth consecutive trip to the World Series. The Yankees had been the victors in 20 prior Fall Classics.

Berra himself cited two big wins in Minnesota as the turning point in the Yankees' difficult 1964 campaign. They occurred on Labor Day and the night after. "While we were doing that, the two clubs on top of us [in the AL standings] weren't doing so good [sic]," he recalled. "The White Sox lost two [games] to the Senators and Baltimore split with the Athletics. That put us almost even in the loss column, but we were on our way. We split in Detroit, then we came home and things kept going good [sic] for us."[7]

The day after the regular season ended, Harold Kaese, also of the *Boston Globe*, drew a few conclusions about the winners and still champions of the American League. He penned that the Yankees had proven the following points:

1. They could win in a year ending in "4." [Authors' note: That had never happened before in the six-decade, storied history of the club.]
2. They could win even though Phil Linz played a harmonica on a bus.
3. They could win despite most of their best players having bad seasons.

> And now they have won with most of their regulars playing like Yankees ONLY in September [when they were 21-7]. All this proves is that the Yankees are so good—or their opponents so inferior—that they can win with one hand tied behind their back.[8]

Decades later, in an essay about the demise of the Yankee franchise in the mid–1960s, author Al Featherston noted,

> When the Yankees surged from behind to win the 1964 American League pennant in the final weekend of the season, it was perceived at the time as just another monotonous triumph by the greatest dynasty in American sports.
>
> Indeed, the big story at the time was how close they had come to *not* winning—not that they had won their 14th pennant in 16 years.[9]

For whatever it was worth, this aging Yankee team, one that had struggled mightily to finish atop the AL in 1964, would once again proudly carry the league's banner into the annual World Series, as it had done so many, many times before. The question remained: Could new manager Berra be as successful in the World Series as his predecessors Casey Stengel and Ralph Houk had been?

1964 AL Standings	W	L	Pct.	GB
New York Yankees	99	63	.611	—
Chicago White Sox	98	64	.605	1
Baltimore Orioles	97	65	.599	2
Detroit Tigers	85	77	.525	14
Los Angeles Angels	82	80	.506	17
Cleveland Indians	79	83	.488	20
Minnesota Twins	79	83	.488	20
Boston Red Sox	72	90	.444	27
Washington Senators	62	100	.383	37
Kansas City Athletics	57	105	.352	42

— 4 —

A World Series Without Mel Allen

"Hello there, everybody. This is Mel Allen..."

Usually, a World Series is recalled because of the people who were there. The 1970 World Series was Brooks Robinson's; the 1977 Fall Classic was Reggie Jackson's, and so on. However, in 1964, the opposite was true. Longtime baseball fans recall the obvious absence of broadcaster Mel Allen, a man who had certainly become a fixture at MLB's showcase event. Beloved by Yankee fans, disliked passionately by others who hated anything remotely connected to MLB's longtime dynasty, a World Series broadcast always meant that Mel Allen was on hand seated behind a microphone. That tradition came to a sudden conclusion in October 1964.

For a quarter-century, Allen was the omnipresent voice of sports broadcasting in America. He was an absolute institution within the nation's sports radio/television industry. The oldest of three children, Mel Allen Israel was born to Russian immigrants in Birmingham, Alabama on February 14, 1913. Allen was truly a natural behind the microphone. Biographer Curt Smith commented in a 2023 interview, "A florist must have decorated [Mel Allen's] voice: Southern, deeply-voweled, and dramatic."[1] It was first widely noticed when Allen was the public-address announcer at University of Alabama football games in 1933. Allen was quickly promoted to calling the team's games over WBRC radio in Birmingham. (His famous catchphrase "How about that?" began there.) Upon graduating with a law degree, Allen visited New York City in 1937, boldly walked into CBS' office, asked for a tryout, and was quickly hired by the network. Early in his tenure there, Allen had the solemn task of interrupting Kate Smith's program of songs to announce the fiery crash of the *Hindenburg*. By 1943, Melvin Israel had legally changed his surname to Allen, the middle name belonging to both himself and his father.

4. A World Series Without Mel Allen

Mel Allen, the "Voice of the Yankees," calling a game for New York City's WPIX-TV in 1955 (Library of Congress).

Allen's versatility and ability to fill in dead air with some sort of compelling commentary got him a job as the analyst for the 1938 World Series radio coverage—which happened to be a CBS property. He did such an outstanding job that one of the Series sponsors, Wheaties, strongly suggested the Washington Senators hire Allen for a broadcasting vacancy the club would have for the 1939 season. Owner Clark Griffith declined, opting to hire former pitcher Walter Johnson instead. As luck would have it, a spot suddenly opened in mid–1939 in the New York Yankees' booth. (One of the team's two broadcasters was abruptly fired for twice mispronouncing the team's major sponsor Ivory Soap as "Ovary Soap.") Allen was called upon to fill that vacancy. He was on the Yankees' payroll for the next 25 years. Allen's 1996 obituary in the *New York Times* noted that his tenure with the team ran "from the last days of Lou Gehrig to the last gasp of the Yankee empire." Indeed, shortly after accepting employment with the defending AL champions, Allen served as the official emcee for Lou Gehrig Appreciation Day at Yankee Stadium on July 4, 1939. He bled pinstripe blue, at least figuratively, and welcomed radio listeners with his trademark greeting atop this chapter.

The pace of a baseball game perfectly suited Allen's folksy delivery. Although he was seldom seen, Allen's absolutely distinct voice could be regularly heard at the World Series, the MLB All-Star Game, the Rose Bowl, and other marquee events on the sports calendar. He called NFL games and NCAA football as well—once the baseball season had concluded. At the apex of his fame, he was hired by Movietone Newsreels to do voiceovers for sports and other events the company had filmed and edited for theatrical showings. It was estimated that some 80 million American moviegoers viewed these newsreels each week. In 1955, *Variety* magazine rightfully listed Allen among "the world's 25 most recognizable voices." (Others who made the list were Frank Sinatra and Winston Churchill.) Those aforementioned events were all mere accessories on his sports announcing résumé. Allen's daily job during the baseball season was calling New York Yankees games, both home and away. Biographer Curt Smith declared, "Mel's gold standard was the Yankees. He became their Voice in 1940 [sic]."[2]

Allen also greatly benefited from the dominance the Yankees held over the American League for a generation. When NBC held the rights to the World Series from 1947 to 1976, the network hired the main broadcaster from each of the two participating teams to call the games. It was a smart idea. The local broadcasters knew the players' strengths and weaknesses in detail along with many interesting anecdotes pertaining to them and their club. Between 1949 and 1964, the Yankees failed to win the AL pennant just twice! Allen, therefore, became forever linked with the World Series and widely known nationally to millions of baseball fans. According to Smith, once when Allen was hailing a cab in Omaha, Nebraska, he simply said to the driver, "Sheraton, please." From hearing just those two words, the cabbie instantly realized he had the famous Mel Allen as his passenger—and almost drove off the road in surprise.

Allen was often accused, with some justification, of being a "homer" by those rooting for New York's opponents. It was a charge that Allen never really denied. He did try his best, however, to maintain some standards of professional impartiality. Allen enjoyed telling an amusing story from the 1957 World Series between the Yankees and Milwaukee Braves. Sometime around the third inning of one game, he received a brief telegram that read, "Shut up you Yankee homer and let me enjoy the game." Allen was taken aback and made a concerted effort not to get too excited about anything positive New York did on the field. Late in the game he reread the missive and noticed its time stamp. The message had been telegraphed well before the game even began.

Then, suddenly, in 1964, the famous and familiar "Voice of the Yankees" was fired at the relatively young age of 51. That is about the time in life when veteran broadcasters often attain the high point of their craft. At the time of his unexpected termination, Allen was likely at his peak as an American institution. "He gave the Yankees his life and they broke his heart,"[3] Red Barber once commented.

Curt Smith noted,

> In fall 1964, Allen expected the Yankees to extend his contract. Instead, in December they released him without even an announcement, ignoring Mel's honor, chary tenderness, and reluctance to offend. To America, Allen vanished overnight, ceasing to exist, for reasons he never grasped nor

4. A World Series Without Mel Allen

understood. "The Yankees never held a press conference. They left people to believe whatever they wanted—and people believed the worst."[4]

Indeed, *Sports Illustrated* later declared, "Allen became a victim of rumors. It was as if he had leprosy."[5] Allen certainly became something akin to a pariah. His gigs with the Rose Bowl and Movietone were swiftly terminated too.

Many years later, Allen told Smith the Yankees had abruptly fired him under mounting pressure from Ballantine Ale & Beer, the team's longtime sponsor. According to Allen, his dismissal was merely a cost-cutting move by Ballantine, which had been experiencing declining sales for years. (The brand would eventually be sold and discontinued in 1969.) However, Allen's broadcasting partner, Phil Rizzuto, was retained for 1965. Joe Garagiola, already a well-known baseball announcer, was brought aboard to replace the well-paid Allen. Therefore, if the firing of Allen was indeed a budget-related measure, the Yankees did not save a whole lot of money by hiring Garagiola to work alongside Rizzuto. "Garagiola didn't come cheaply,"[6] wrote baseball scribe Stan Isaacs in debunking money as a possible reason. Combined with Allen suddenly losing his other occasional jobs, this seems to prove that something greater than the Yankees' Ballantine beer sponsorship agreement was working against him.

Of course, the absence of any official explanation from Yankees ownership led to considerable conjecture about the driving reason behind Allen's dismissal. There were plenty of theories. None was flattering to Allen's reputation.

Larry Israel, Mel's brother, believed Mel's dislike of and dissatisfaction with the last statistician assigned to him by the Yankees was a little-known but key factor. His name was Bill Kane. According to Mel's sibling, Kane had a slight limp, but he milked it for sympathy, and he may have been hired solely out of pity rather than anything close to merit. Whenever he gave Allen data for a broadcast that turned out to be inaccurate—apparently a frequent occurrence—Allen would gently flick Kane with his scorecard and give him a disapproving glance. Kane supposedly took great offense at these chidings and reported Allen for being a tyrant in the broadcast booth.

Longtime *New York Post* journalist Maury Allen (no relation to Mel) recalled a minor incident that occurred on September 8, 1964, when the Yankees were in Bloomington to play a two-game series versus the Minnesota Twins. The ballpark's press room was crowded before a game. In one end of the room, Yankee general manager Ralph Houk and a Twins attendant were attempting to have a pleasant conversation. At another end, the powerful voice of Mel Allen started booming. The acoustics of the room were such that no one could hear anyone else speaking over the broadcaster's voice. For some reason, Houk took unusually great offense at Allen's noisy presence. Houk angrily shouted an obscenity at Allen, walked out of the press room, and promptly phoned Yankee owner Dan Topping to complain. According to that story, it was at this point that Topping decided to terminate Allen's services at season's end. The trivial incident hardly seems serious enough to justify discharging such a longtime and faithful employee as Allen was to the Yankee franchise. Was it just the last straw for Topping?

The most persistent, whispered explanation was that Allen had been axed by the Yankees because he was rumored to be a homosexual. There is not a scintilla of evidence that ever surfaced to prove that Allen was a gay man. It was only speculation because he was a loner who never was known to have had a romantic relationship with anybody. (Certainly, had the gossip of homosexuality been true, it would have been a career-ending admission during Allen's heyday.) Writer Stan Isaacs agreed that those rumors had no substance, noting that Allen was merely "a mama's boy. She just wanted him to get married, just to no one in particular."[7] In a 1974 interview, Allen disagreed somewhat. He claimed he was on the verge of wedlock three or four times, but his parents strongly disapproved of each potential wife, effectively vetoing those potential marriages. One sympathetic writer suggested to Allen that it might be wise to go on record and refute those unsavory rumors about his sexuality. Allen completely disagreed with that idea. He thought it would be totally counterproductive to deny an accusation about him that had never been publicly made in print or over the airwaves. Nevertheless, in a 1957 interview, Allen sort of addressed the issue in a roundabout way by jokingly noting, "Everybody in [my] family seems to spend most of their waking hours trying to marry me off. I think I must be at the point where most girls would consider me too old ... for anything but a rocking chair."[8]

Other harsh rumors claimed Allen had become addicted to heroin or that he was a drunk. No proof exists of either of those things being true. However, Allen undoubtedly took numerous pills every day which had an effect on him that was plainly noticeable to others by the early 1960s. Allen was apparently something of a hypochondriac who allegedly travelled around the American League circuit with a satchel full of pills among his belongings. The scuttlebutt is that Allen became addicted to them to help him maintain his very hectic schedule. One broadcasting colleague, Bud Blattner, recalled, "Mel [would] take a pill to get up, a pill to fall asleep. He'd do a game, jet somewhere [to voice] an ad, then tape a Movietone newsreel. I'd say [to him], 'You don't need this. Slow down.' He wouldn't."[9] Away from the microphone, by the early 1960s Allen occasionally seemed "spaced

4. A World Series Without Mel Allen

out" to people close to the baseball broadcasting industry. A keen listener in 1964 could hear that Allen's speech was slightly slurred and a smidgen slower than it had been in past seasons. Allen's personal physician was Max Jacobson, who was known in New York celebrity circles as "Dr. Feelgood" because of the pills he frequently and often recklessly prescribed to his famous clients. (Jacobson would have his medical license revoked by the state of New York in 1975.) Biographer Curt Smith figures this pill-induced decline was the main reason behind Allen's dismissal. A closely related firing theory is that Allen directed Mickey Mantle to Dr. Jacobson with disastrous results—and the club dismissed him as punishment.

Something was certainly wrong with Allen during the 1963 World Series, which proved to be the beginning of the end for baseball's most recognizable broadcaster. During Game Four of the Los Angeles Dodgers' surprising sweep of the Yankees, Allen was calling the second half of the game on the NBC television broadcast. However, he froze at the microphone in the eighth inning and was unable to continue. It was said to be an untimely attack of laryngitis. His partner, Vin Scully, immediately saw that something was amiss with Allen. He coolly stepped in and gently said, "That's alright, Mel." Allen left the booth. Scully finished the game solo, explaining to his audience that Allen had taken ill. No one really knows what happened that day, as the laryngitis explanation was not and is not universally believed. (Yankee-haters were quick to joke that Allen was terribly unnerved at the unthinkable prospect of New York losing the Fall Classic in four straight games. Indeed, the Dodgers won the final contest, 2–1, to complete the sweep. New York scored just four runs in their four-game defeat.) Be that as it may, it was an inglorious and totally unfitting way for Allen's illustrious World Series career to conclude.

On September 21, 1964, Allen was quietly informed—and greatly stunned—that his annual contract with the Yankees would not be renewed for 1965. Even so, Allen should have broadcast the 1964 World Series for NBC as he was the lead announcer for the Yankees who were once again the AL champions. However, the Commissioner's Office agreed with the team's strong suggestion that Phil Rizzuto, the former Yankees shortstop and Allen's broadcast partner, get the prestigious assignment because Allen would not be returning to the club. Millions of fans were puzzled by Allen's conspicuous absence from the Cardinals-Yankees 1964 Fall Classic as his firing would not be made public until December 17. It was the first World Series in which Allen did not work in some capacity since 1943 when he was in the army during the Second World War. The United Press International story that announced Allen's dismissal in mid–December was very brief—and wrongly claimed Allen had been with the Yankees for 18 years. It was actually 25.

With Allen out of the picture, MLB announced the World Series broadcast teams for 1964: Curt Gowdy of NBC would be coupled with Harry Caray, the St. Louis announcer, as one pair while Phil Rizzuto and Joe Garagiola (then of NBC) would be the other twosome. Gowdy and Caray would be the TV announcers for the games in St. Louis (1, 2, 6 and 7) while Garagiola and Rizzuto called the action for the radio audience. The twosomes would switch media when the Series moved to New York City for Games 3, 4, and 5.

Allen worked sporadically for the Milwaukee Braves in 1965 (the team's last season in Wisconsin before relocating to Atlanta) and for the Cleveland Indians in 1968. Oddly, Allen maintained an unexpected loyalty to the team that had dumped him so callously in September 1964. (When George Steinbrenner bought the Yankees in 1973, he made a point of reconnecting Allen with the club.) He often made appearances at Yankee Stadium to emcee special events such as old-timers' games and jersey-number retirements. He routinely received tremendous applause whenever he stepped onto the field to perform these duties. Allen himself is honored at Monument Park in Yankee Stadium with a marker that proclaims him, quite accurately, as "The Voice of the Yankees."

By 1976, whatever possessed the Yankees to dismiss their famous Voice was apparently water under the bridge. That season, Allen returned as a special host of pregame

A youthful Phil Rizzuto is shown in his Yankee uniform in 1949. A highly skilled shortstop in his day, Rizzuto gained even more fame in later years as an enthusiastic baseball announcer. The 1964 World Series was the first Fall Classic he worked behind the microphone (Library of Congress).

and postgame shows on their cable TV broadcasts and, once in a while, even did play-by-play. Allen remained with the team in that capacity through 1985. As a publicity stunt, Allen called one game in 1990 on WPIX to make him the first man to call games in seven different decades. (Vin Scully equaled that feat in 2010.)

In the last two decades of his life, Allen's career was fully resurrected. His talents were exposed to a new audience as the host of *This Week in Baseball*, a hugely popular syndicated MLB highlights show. It was must-see viewing for fans of the National Pastime, especially before the advent of 24-hour sports channels. Allen narrated the 30-minute program from its inception in April 1977 until shortly before his death in June 1996. Stories abound about people being pleasantly surprised to once again hear Allen describing baseball for the first time in a decade—and by younger fans who quickly became enamored with his voice. Curt Smith recalled the delight his mother showed in 1977 when she heard the famous voice from yesteryear emanating from the family TV set. She was only a casual baseball fan, but even she readily realized who was doing the talking. "I can't believe it!" she exclaimed with excitement, "Is that Mel Allen?"[10] Upon Allen's death, Warner Fusselle capably took over as *TWIB*'s narrator, but the show's decline was inevitable. When *TWIB* was relaunched after a one-year hiatus, in a strange homage to the late Allen, it used a Claymation version of him to open and close the program until 2002. The gimmick received mixed reviews.

Many fans thought *TWIB*'s terrific popularity was largely because of Mel Allen's excellent narration week after week. Smith concurred. He wrote, "[Its] success was due to him. Allen had all, lost all, and improbably, came back. There is still no sportscasting precedent for his rise, ruin, and return—and no parallel since."[11]

A full decade after his passing, a 2006 retrospective on Allen's life and career published in the *Washington Times* concluded, "When Mel Allen died of a heart attack at his home in Greenwich, CT, on June 16, 1996, we may assume he was a happy man. He had been watching a ballgame."[12] Mel Allen was 83 years old.

— 5 —

Before the First Pitch
Anticipating the Series

"The idea of waiting for something makes it more exciting."—Andy Warhol

The city of St. Louis was celebrating its bicentennial in 1964. The residents of "The Gateway to the West" could not have asked for a better way to conclude the festivities than their first Fall Classic in 18 years.

World Series mania was in full swing in St. Louis as Game One approached on Wednesday, October 7—and had been since the final out was made against the New York Mets to clinch the NL flag on Sunday. Shortly thereafter, enthusiastic fans began camping outside the Busch Stadium ticket offices in hopes of buying tickets for the Cardinals' home games. Only bleacher seats remained available.

"St. Louis' Series-starved citizens," wrote the alliteration-loving Joseph Reichler, "who have waited since 1946, were all agog over the Cardinals impending meeting with the Yankees. Many thousands of fans were crying for tickets, which were about as hard to get as hotel reservations in town. And that's impossible."[1] According to Reichler, scalpers were asking and getting $100 for a pair of $12 box seats. Due to pre–Series ticket sales, a sellout of 32,000 was assured for the first two Series games three days before the Cards had even clinched the NL pennant. The official capacity of Busch Stadium in 1964 was only 30,500.

Baseball may have been the most popular sport in America in 1964, but betting on baseball must have been a close second. As Game One at Busch Stadium approached, a UPI story projected an estimated $600 million would be bet on the upcoming World Series. The figure was quoted by John Scarne, a gambling expert, author and lecturer who was presently employed as a consultant for casinos in the United States and in Caribbean countries. That sum, if it proved to be accurate, would surpass the $500

5. Before the First Pitch

million bet four autumns before on the 1960 Pirates-Yankees World Series. "This 1964 World Series has captivated the nation," Scarne explained, "because both teams had to come from behind in home-stretch runs [to win the pennant]. In addition ... a month of unprecedentedly heavy betting on professional football games has actually stimulated speculation on baseball."[2] In legal betting venues, Las Vegas casinos liked the Yankees' chances. New York was typically listed as the 9:5 favorite to win the Series, and at even shorter odds, 7:5, to take the opening game.

A Philadelphia-based computer also picked the Yankees to triumph. It foresaw a seven-game series, however. Officially named Big Magic and located at the Franklin Institute, the machine "said" the Yankees had a 65 percent chance to win baseball's biggest prize. The Honeywell 1400 computer was fed the stats from all the players and simulated 100 games between the Cardinals and Yankees to generate the data to make its bold prediction. Furthermore, Big Magic broke down the stats to calculate that, in any given game, the Yankees had a 57 percent chance of emerging victorious.

St. Louis manager Johnny Keane thought little about prognosticators' opinions whether they came from computers or human beings. At least that was his public statement. He said, "It's useless to try to predict the outcome in such a short series, but I think the two teams are about evenly matched. I know my boys are ready for the Yankees. The pressure is off. There was more pressure in our last four regular-season games."[3] Keane, in a reflective moment, told reporters he had been at the first World Series game ever played in St. Louis on October 5, 1926, as a 14-year-old spectator. He recalled standing in line for six hours to obtain a bleacher seat at Sportsman's Park. Keane saw the Cardinals beat the Yankees 4–0 that day. Jesse Haines, a 33-year-old righty, threw a five-hit shutout against Babe Ruth and his teammates.

All wagering aside, the Yankees were the favorites of the baseball journalists covering the Series by a considerable margin. A poll of 51 sports writers and broadcasters found exactly two-thirds of them (34) predicted a New York triumph. As for the number of games it would take, six was the most common response from those who favored Yogi Berra's AL squad. Only one person polled thought the Yankees would finish off the Cardinals in a four-game sweep. Of those 17 respondents who liked the Cardinals' chances, not a single one of them thought St. Louis would take four straight contests from New York.

After due consideration, Red Smith, one of America's most widely read sports columnists, favored the Cardinals. He wrote,

> The Yankees are by no means a team of sluggers, and they will be opposed by professional batsmen who have been through the fire. Though this is St. Louis'

first pennant in 18 years, the Cardinals are no callow kids quailing before a challenge. After what they've been through, they must believe they can beat anybody, against any odds.[4]

Smith noted that the Cardinal infielders—Bill White, Julián Javier, Dick Groat and Ken Boyer—were all starters for the NL in the 1963 MLB All-Star Game in Cleveland. He placed special emphasis on shortstop Groat. (Four years earlier, shortstop Groat had been the 1960 NL batting champion and Most Valuable Player while a member of the Pittsburgh Pirates. A fine, multi-sport athlete, Groat was so skilled at collegiate basketball that he had his #10 jersey retired by Duke University in 1952—the first Blue Devil hoopster so honored.)

First baseman Bill White may have been the most intelligent man on the Cardinal roster—which was no small feat. Once, when playing under fiery manager Eddie Stanky in the minor leagues, Stanky took umbrage at a book of crossword puzzles that White possessed. He rudely suggested to White that his time would be better spent reading a baseball rule book. Without missing a beat, White retorted that if he read the rule book thoroughly, the club would have no need for Stanky's services. That cutting comment promptly ended further discussion on the topic. White was both a terrific fielder and an excellent batsman. He once got 14 hits in two consecutive doubleheaders versus the Chicago Cubs.

Smith also readily complimented Tim McCarver as being "a hustling catcher with good power." The renowned scribe was also impressed by the entire Cardinal outfield as a threesome. "Curt Flood is a brilliant ballplayer," Smith penned. "Lou Brock is the reason they're in the Series. The other outfielder is Mike Shannon, the kid who caddied for Stan Musial last year and inherited his job." Indeed, Musial, a thoroughly beloved figure in St. Louis, had retired after the 1963 season, missing a trip to the Fall Classic by one year. Stan the Man had been the last remaining Cardinal on the roster to have played in their most recent World Series appearance before 1964. As Smith put it, Musial had been "the heart and kernel"[5] of the Cardinals in all the club's non-championship years since 1946.

Before the World Series began, two St. Louis scouts, Mo Mozzali and Mike Ryba, addressed the Cardinals to inform them that the team's overall speed might be their greatest weapons against the fabled Yankees. The New York outfielders, the twosome reported, might be especially vulnerable. An aging Mickey Mantle had been moved from center to right field because he was no longer as mobile as he had once been. His agility when he suddenly had to move sideways quickly was now in question. Furthermore, the scouts said, Mantle was not used to playing right field, and his perspective on the game had changed. He was not especially

5. Before the First Pitch

Prior to a 1946 World Series game at Boston's Fenway Park, Rudy York of the Red Sox (left) poses with Stan Musial of the Cardinals. That Fall Classic, Musial's final one, was also the last one not televised and the last for the Cards until 1964 (courtesy Boston Public Library, Leslie Jones Collection).

good at judging where he had to run to track down slicing fly balls. Roger Maris, now playing center field, was, however, very good in his defensive coverage, but he still had the arm of a big-league right fielder—not a center fielder—the scouts emphasized. When the Cardinals observed the first practice the Yankees held in Busch Stadium, they saw for themselves that the two scouts were correct: Mantle was indeed struggling with his new outfield position.

Harold Kaese of the *Boston Globe*, a man well-versed in baseball history, saw some parallels between the 1964 Cardinals and the 1960 Pittsburgh Pirates who upset the Yankees in that year's thoroughly wild Fall Classic. "The Cardinals are a lot like the Pirates who beat the Yankees in seven games," he wrote. "[They have] good hitting, modest power, and fair pitching. But smaller Busch Stadium favors the muscular Yankees much more than Forbes Field did."[6]

An obvious point of interest in the Series was that two brothers would be facing each other. Ken Boyer was with St. Louis while Clete was on the New York roster. Each man was the starting third baseman for his respective club. (It was not the first time a World Series had pitted siblings against each other, but the last time it had happened was in the early 1920s. In 1923, the Meusel brothers faced each other for the third straight October! Bob played for the Yankees while Emil—more commonly known by his nickname "Irish" due to his pale skin and red hair—toiled for the New York Giants. Irish's team won two out of those three encounters.) There were seven Boyer brothers altogether, and every one of them had played professional baseball at some level in their lives. An older brother (Cloyd) had reached the majors, too. He was a pitcher who won 20 games for the Cardinals and Kansas City Athletics between 1950 and 1955. In 1964, a pair of Boyer brothers vying against each other in the World Series spotlight was considered such a novelty that they appeared jointly as mystery guests on the popular panel show *What's My Line?* It was a live broadcast on the evening of Sunday, October 11, when the Series was in New York City. To avoid confusing himself and his readers, Roger Birtwell of the *Boston Globe* liked to refer to their individual strong points. Clete was "The Boyer with the Glove" while Ken was "The Boyer with the Bat." In their youths, those two Boyer brothers from rural Missouri had, more than once, faced a baseball team from nearby Commerce, Oklahoma. Its star player was a youngster named Mickey Mantle.

American Airlines had prepared for the World Series in its own special way. It announced that a select number of its most modern passenger aircraft would be equipped to show pictures of the action as it happened. The airline's newfangled "Astrovision" sets had been wired to pick up NBC's live television coverage of the games—including slow-motion replays—on flights linking New York, Boston and Washington with Dallas, San Francisco and Los Angeles. Some flights departing from Chicago's O'Hare Airport would also have the luxury of an Astrovision hookup. On those American Airline flights not equipped with the modern technology, stewardesses were instructed to relay updated scores frequently via information gathered by flight captains. The men flying the airplanes fully expected to be apprised of the baseball action from their communications with baseball-loving air-traffic controllers.

The Yankees were less than thrilled by the quality of the infield at Busch Stadium during their first visit to the NL champions' ballpark. During a light practice, its hardness was a point of concern—especially to the New York infielders. The team's veterans rated it even worse than the infield at Forbes Field in Pittsburgh on which they had played the 1960 Fall Classic. "The infield in Pittsburgh was hard underneath but it had a layer of sand on top," recalled second baseman Bobby Richardson. "This one is hard all the way."[7] Third baseman Clete Boyer agreed with

5. Before the First Pitch

his teammate, calling it the worst infield the New Yorkers had set foot upon all season.

Scribe Harold Kaese recalled that the Pittsburgh infield four Octobers before "was harder than a concrete highway and produced a high bounce that caused [New York shortstop] Tony Kubek acute tonsilitis and cost the Yankees the deciding game."[8] Kaese was alluding to a famous mishap from Game Seven of the 1960 World Series when what looked like a double-play grounder from the bat of Bill Virdon took a famously bad hop in the eighth inning of a tight game and struck Kubek solidly in the throat. Gagging and unable to talk, he was forced to leave the diamond. Instead of having two outs with nobody on base, the Pirates now had two runners on base with nobody out. They rallied to tie—and eventually win—the game. Kubek was on his way to the hospital for examination when Bill Mazeroski hit his famous walk-off home run for the Pirates in the ninth inning.

Kubek, the AL Rookie of the Year in 1957, was one of Casey Stengel's favorite players, as is apparent from this 1960 quotation: "Now this man Kubek has improved tremendously as a fielder and a batter," said Stengel. "He is determined, ambitious, and the leading young player on my club. Is he the best shortstop in the business? No. But he can play at any of five positions on this ball team."[9] Kubek was still New York's starting shortstop in 1964, but he would miss the entire World Series with a badly sprained wrist. (It was a silly, self-inflicted wound. During a September 20 home game versus Kansas City, a frustrated Kubek punched a dugout door, thinking it was constructed of plywood. It was not; rather, it was made of metal sheeting.) Of a more serious long-term concern was Kubek's ailing back which was giving him major troubles. Kubek always believed it was the result of a football injury—a *touch football* injury!—he sustained while playing with some fellow soldiers when he was serving in the army in 1961. He was upended on one play and landed very awkwardly in an upside-down position.

The man who would be the Yankee shortstop for the Fall Classic was not in Kubek's class. (Some writers considered Kubek to be the best overall shortstop in the AL despite his lack of flashiness.) However, Phil Linz was a highly competent replacement who did not lack experience. He had played in 112 games for New York in 1964, six more than the injury-plagued Kubek had. Linz was already on the Yankees' World Series roster. The man actually replacing Kubek for the Fall Classic was 22-year-old Mike Hegan. His father, Jim, was the Yankee bullpen coach. Jim had been a catcher on the 1948 Cleveland Indians, a club that had won the AL pennant and World Series that year.

Another Yankee who would be conspicuously absent from the 1964 World Series was pitcher Pedro Ramos. The veteran Cuban pitcher, who answered to the nickname Pete, was acquired by New York late in the season from Cleveland in exchange for two players to be named later. They turned out to be Ralph Terry and Bud Daley. The Yankees hoped to bolster their shaky bullpen with the move. Ramos had spent his entire MLB career as a starter for dismal teams, so his transition to a reliever's role might have been a problem for him. Instead, it proved to be the total opposite. Ramos, finally playing for a competitive team, thrived in the bullpen, giving New York more than solid support as they battled for the AL pennant. In fact, according to his SABR biographer Peter C. Bjarkman, "It turned out to be one of the best deals ... that the Yankees ever made." He continued,

> Ramos experienced a new life in his transformation into a bullpen stalwart. He suddenly was able to produce some of the best and most consistent pitching of his career. Now a workhorse reliever instead of a workhorse starter, Ramos made 13 appearances in the final month for New York, striking out 21 [men] in 22 innings without walking a single batter. It was a brilliant performance ... which proved to be New York's salvation during the stretch run.[10]

Altogether, Ramos picked up eight saves for New York and compiled a strong 1.23 ERA in the month since his arrival. He was on the mound for the final three outs when the Yankees clinched the AL pennant on the penultimate day of the season. Their opponents that afternoon were the Cleveland Indians—the MLB team Ramos had last pitched for before moving to New York. Their manager, Birdie Tebbets, had bluntly told Ramos he would not be desired by any team in either major league. When the last out was made on a foul popup in the Yankees' 8–3 win, Ramos made eye contact with Tebbets—and then gave him the finger with great emphasis.

Sadly, for both Ramos and the Yankees, he joined the team after September 1—by rule too late to be eligible for World Series play. The 29-year-old Cuban Cowboy (a nickname Ramos earned because of his fondness for donning flashy western apparel) would be a mere spectator when his new club clashed with the NL champion Cardinals for the championship of MLB.

An Associated Press story said the often-injured Mickey Mantle, who was paid an enormous $100,000 a season, declared himself fit and "feeling great" for the upcoming World Series—despite wrapping "seemingly endless rolls of tape around his battered legs."[11] Mantle, the most famous of all New York ballplayers in 1964, cautioned reporters by saying, "You have to remember one thing, though. I felt pretty good last year [versus the Dodgers] and didn't do much. But I played well up to [this year's] Series and things could be different."[12] Mantle managed just two hits in 15 at-bats versus Koufax, Drysdale and company in 1963. One of those hits was his

5. Before the First Pitch

record-tying 15th homer in World Series play. He now shared the all-time mark with Babe Ruth.

The traditional six-man umpiring crew, common in October baseball, would oversee the 1964 World Series. As usual, it was evenly comprised of three American League and three National League arbiters. Unlike previous Fall Classics where only the four umpires stationed on the infield rotated for each game, MLB tried something new in 1964: all six men would rotate positions. Thus, if the Series lasted six games, six different men would call balls and strikes. A seventh game would have the crew repeat their assignments from Game One. For the October 7 opener at Busch Stadium, Frank Secory was behind the plate, Bill McKinley was stationed at first base, Ken Burkhart was at second base, and Hank Soar was positioned at third base. Down the outfield lines Vinnie Smith was assigned left field while Al Smith (no relation to his colleague in blue) monitored right field. Two of the men in blue had played in the majors. Secory was an outfielder with the Cubs, Tigers and Reds from 1940 to 1946. Burkhart was a pitcher at about the same time who had been on the roster of the 1946 Cardinals as a 29-year-old, but he did not appear in any World Series games that autumn versus the Boston Red Sox.

In his pre–World Series assessment piece for the October 5 edition of the *Boston Globe*, columnist Harold Kaese made one thing perfectly clear in his conclusion. He sincerely meant it when he wrote, "Alas, [even if] it may be the greatest Series ever played, it will never obscure the [baseball] story of the year—the collapse of the Phillies."[13]

— 6 —

Game One
October 7

"The key game is the first. Johnny Keane must play for time, trusting Ray Sadecki and his good relief pitchers to give Whitey Ford an argument while Bob Gibson and Curt Simmons rest."[1]—Sports columnist Red Smith

Before an official paid attendance of 30,805 excited spectators, Game One of the 1964 World Series, the sixty-first of the modern era of Major League Baseball, opened at St. Louis' Busch Stadium in the afternoon sunshine on Wednesday, October 7. The weatherman called for a high of 70 degrees and pleasant weather. He actually underestimated the heat as the temperature was 72 degrees at the ballpark when the first pitch was thrown. It would be an abnormally windy day in St. Louis. As it was an even-numbered year, the NL champions hosted the first two games plus Game Six and Game Seven, if either or both of those contests were necessary. Yankee Stadium would host the third, fourth and fifth games Saturday through Monday with no day off there, as long as the weather cooperated.

Before the game there was a comical incident that would become famous in Cardinal lore. Backup catcher and first-rate team clown Bob Uecker was shagging fly balls in the outfield. Not too far away, three different Dixieland bands were taking turns entertaining the gathering crowd with a selection of upbeat tunes. While one of the bands was on a break, Uecker picked up a discarded tuba. At first, he attempted to play the large horn but gave up. Then, the comically inspired Uecker decided to use the instrument as a funnel to catch baseballs. He succeeded only about 50 percent of the time, but his teammates and the fans in the bleachers thought the stunt was hilarious. (However, the tuba's owner certainly did not think so and later billed the Cardinals $250 for the repairs needed to fix it.) Looking at the silliness, the Yankees thought the Cardinals had to be crazy. Be that as it may, the wacky incident proved the home team was definitely a loose bunch entering Game One. A tuba had united the NL champs. In contrast, a harmonica had caused friction among their AL counterparts.

The Cardinals also set a precedent with their gleaming home-white World Series uniforms. Each player's surname appeared on his jersey above the number. That was a first in Fall Classic history. The Yankees, sticklers for tradition, had numerals only on their plain grey uniforms.

Although it was a weekday afternoon, some 40 million people were tuned into NBC's television broadcast of Game One. In his opening remarks to the network's national radio audience, Joe Garagiola—a one-time Cardinal catcher who grew up in St. Louis—made a point of noting that balls rolling along the infield and outfield were moving swiftly during pregame warmups thanks to a recent mowing by the ballpark's groundskeepers. "The infield here in St. Louis is known to be fast," stated Garagiola, "so you'll see some balls scoot right through."[2]

Garagiola said that the two managers, the umpiring crew, and MLB Commissioner Ford Frick had earlier toured the field together to go over the ground rules for the games at Busch Stadium. Yogi Berra got a huge round of applause when he was spotted by the early-arriving fans in the crowd, even if he was clad in a gray uniform of the visiting team. The great ex-catcher, now the first-year Yankee manager, was born in St. Louis on May 12, 1925, and was always proud of his connection to the city. His rival manager, Johnny Keane, took his first breath in St. Louis too, on November 3, 1911. Neither man had ever played an MLB game for either the Cardinals or the now-departed Browns, however.

Singers Monty Bronson and Vikki Carr performed the national anthem as a duet. (Bronson was a well-known media personality in the St. Louis area.) Fittingly, the much-beloved Stan Musial was called upon to make the ceremonial first pitch. He shared the spotlight alongside a 4½-year-old poster boy for a local charity, who threw a ball to Cardinal catcher Tim McCarver as well. The youngster made a surprisingly strong toss and was heartily cheered for it.

Left-hander Ray Sadecki was on the mound for the Cardinals. A much-sought-after amateur pitcher from Kansas, Sadecki had gotten a $50,000 signing bonus from the Cardinals not long after graduating from high school. While he was throwing his warmup tosses to catcher Tim McCarver, Phil Rizzuto noted on NBC radio that Sadecki was a mere fourth-grade pupil when his mound opponent for the Series opener, New York's veteran Whitey Ford, had pitched his first Fall Classic game in 1950 for the Yankees. Sadecki was in his fifth season in the majors. It had been spent entirely with the Cardinals. The 1964 campaign had been his most fruitful to date. Sadecki won 20 games and lost 11. He compiled a passable 3.68 ERA in 220 innings of work for the NL champion Redbirds. In his last regular-season outing on October 3, however, Sadecki had looked quite shaky in a dreadful 15–5 loss to the last-place New York Mets. In that game he lasted just one inning.

Phil Linz, the Yankee shortstop, got things underway when he stepped into the right-handed batter's box to face Sadecki. Linz, born in Baltimore, was a third-year player with New York. He had appeared in 112 games in 1964 and batted .250. Of his 92 hits, three were triples and five were home runs, so Linz was not perceived as much of a power threat. He grounded out to third baseman Ken Boyer. It was a trickier play for Boyer than it probably should have been, as the bounding ball struck his chest. However, the third-sacker for the home team recovered in time to throw out Linz at first base. Umpire Bill McKinley made the signal with his right fist. The first out of the 1964 World Series had been recorded.

The Cardinal defense had another adventure on their hands with Bobby Richardson, the Yankee second baseman, who batted in the number-two spot for the AL champions. He hit a high infield popup, but the 60-mile-per-hour wind blew the ball into the shallow part of right field. What looked like a routine play for St. Louis second baseman Dal Maxvill quickly turned into trouble. Maxvill had to suddenly backpedal and lunge for the ball. Nevertheless, he caught it for the second out as the home crowd gasped at its unexpected difficulty.

Next up was Roger Maris. He became the game's first baserunner when he drew a walk on a full count. Mickey Mantle, remarkably playing in his twelfth World Series, batted cleanup behind Maris. A switch-hitter, Mantle hit right-handed versus the left-handed Sadecki. The speedy Cardinal outfielders played straight away without any sort of shift. (Joe Garagiola commented that center fielder Curt Flood had moved considerably deeper with Mantle at the plate, joking the outfielder and the Yankee slugger were "a $1.35 cab ride apart."[3]) Flood did not need to worry. Mantle's high fly ball to shallow right field was easily tracked down by Mike Shannon to end the top of the first inning with New York failing to score.

Edward Charles (Whitey) Ford, who would turn 36 years old not long after the Series ended, was on the mound for the AL champions from New York. Even in 1964, no one was quite sure how he got the nickname Whitey, except that it was hung on him as a minor leaguer. It was virtually a tradition for the pinstripe crew to have Ford start Game One of the Fall Classic. He had 10 World Series wins for the Yankees on his pitching résumé. Despite aging and injuries, Ford was 17–6 in 1964 with an excellent ERA of 2.13.

6. Game One

Curt Flood led off for the Cardinals in the bottom of the first inning. On the second pitch from Ford, Flood grounded out to Yankee third baseman Clete Boyer. On a full count, Lou Brock singled into right field where it was retrieved by Mickey Mantle. With a huge stolen base threat on first base, the crowd immediately became excited. There was no stolen base however, because Dick Groat also singled into right field on the first pitch he saw from Ford. Brock easily advanced to third base standing up. (Years later Brock told author David Halberstam that he intended to test Mantle's arm at every opportunity. St. Louis' scouts had categorized Mantle as a defensive liability. The Cardinals noted that Mantle did not even attempt to fire the ball to third base.) The underdog home team had runners on the corners with Ken Boyer, batting fourth, coming to bat. Boyer wasted no time launching a fly ball into right field. The wind played havoc with this ball too. Mantle, by Phil Rizzuto's estimation, had to drift 20 feet from where he first positioned himself to make the catch. Brock scored on the sacrifice fly as Mantle's throw went to second base to keep Groat at first. St. Louis had quickly vaulted into a 1–0 lead. On the basis of four St. Louis hitters, the usually masterful Ford looked very beatable.

Ford, who had a terrific pickoff move, nearly caught Groat leaning. In fact, Phil Rizzuto thought Groat had been picked off and said so in his broadcast. Indeed, several Yankee infielders shouted their disagreement with umpire Bill McKinley's safe call. (McKinley was a familiar face to the Yankees as the 54-year-old was an AL arbiter who had the second most seniority in his league. He was not especially popular with the players; a common joke around the Junior Circuit was "They shot the wrong McKinley!"—an allusion to the assassination of U.S. President William McKinley in 1901.) Unperturbed, Ford proceeded to whiff Bill White to end the inning and limit the damage done by the Cardinals to a single run.

Elston Howard led off the top of the second inning for New York. He ripped a hit past shortstop Dick Groat that benefited from the fast infield. Yankee outfielder Tom Tresh came up next and blasted a home run over Curt Flood's head. The third Fall Classic homer in Tresh's career, it was a virtual line drive that landed in the Busch Stadium bleachers in left-center field. Suddenly the favored Yankees had assumed a 2–1 lead in Game One.

Ray Sadecki was reeling. Joe Pepitone followed Tresh by grounding to second baseman Dal Maxvill for the first out of the inning. Clete Boyer, the New York third baseman, was the next batter to face Sadecki. Boyer had batted just .218 in 1964, but he was in the visitors' lineup because he was invaluable defensively, always a consideration by the AL champs. Nevertheless, Boyer blooped a broken bat single that dropped into the outfield. Pitcher Whitey Ford, a .119 hitter during regular-season play with eight hits in 67 at-bats, batted next. Ford faked a bunt and Boyer stole second base. (Boyer had swiped just six bags all season, a total he would never exceed in his MLB career.) Ford productively hit a well-placed grounder that bounded over first base and into right field. It was an RBI single that extended New York's lead over the Cardinals to 3–1 as Boyer scampered home. Yankee shortstop Phil Linz drew a walk to add to Sadecki's woes. Ford, wearing a warmup jacket while on base, advanced ninety feet to second base. Relief pitchers began to loosen up in the home team's bullpen in case the roof caved in on Sadecki.

The Yankees attempted to pile on more runs, but Lou Brock and Ken Boyer combined to make a big out. Bobby Richardson lined another New York hit into left field. However, third baseman Ken Boyer subtly faked out Ford, who was approaching the bag, into thinking the ball had been caught. Ford hesitated momentarily before advancing to third and then trying to score. A perfect throw by Lou Brock nailed the Yankee pitcher at home plate for a huge second out of the inning. National League umpire Frank Secory correctly signaled out—and there was no argument from Ford. "Holy Cow! Did he throw a strike!"[4] gushed Phil Rizzuto in the NBC radio booth. On the fine play, Linz got no further than second base while Richardson was at first base. Sadecki managed to whiff Roger Maris on a called third strike to end an awful inning in which he allowed five New York hits and surrendered a base on balls.

Mike Shannon, a .261 batter, led off for St. Louis against Whitey Ford to begin the bottom of the second inning. Shannon promptly lined a hit into left field. Tim McCarver, a left-handed hitter who batted .288 in 1964, followed Shannon. His at-bat was wasted as he popped up to Clete Boyer in foul territory. Second baseman Dal Maxvill made a full swing but the ball dribbled in front of the plate. Ford fielded it and nipped Maxvill at first base with a strong, accurate throw to Joe Pepitone who was covering the bag. Shannon moved to second base on the fielder's choice. Pitcher Ray Sadecki helped himself with a timely base hit to right field combined with a throwing error committed by Mickey Mantle in right field. His throw to the plate to try nail Shannon was high and far off the mark. It sailed over catcher Elston Howard's head and bounced into the box seats. Shannon scored and Sadecki advanced to third base on the overthrow rule. There he stayed as Curt Flood grounded out to shortstop Phil Linz to end the bottom of the second. The Yankee lead had been narrowed to 3–2. Phil Rizzuto confidently predicted, based on the way the first two innings had gone, that the 1964 Fall Classic looked to be a hitters' series.

Mickey Mantle struck out swinging on a Ray Sadecki breaking pitch to start the top of the third frame for New York. Elston Howard walked on four pitches, but Tom Tresh promptly grounded into a 6–4–3 double play that ended the mild New York threat.

6. Game One 61

Lou Brock led off the bottom of the third inning for St. Louis. He was warmly greeted with loud applause by the home crowd for his throw that had retired Ford earlier in the game. Brock meekly grounded out to second baseman Bobby Richardson. The second out was made when Richardson caught Dick Groat's infield popup with little trouble. Ken Boyer drew a four-pitch base on balls from Ford. Bill White hit a ground ball to Joe Pepitone near first base. Pepitone made the inning-ending putout, but he had to apply a tag on White to do so. At the end of three innings, the score remained 3–2 in favor in the Yankees.

Joe Pepitone led off the top of the fourth inning. Joe Garagiola commented that Pepitone had numerous different crouching batting stances that he used depending upon which pitcher he was facing. Rizzuto somehow estimated the total to be 45. Pepitone apparently did not choose the correct one as he hit a high fly ball that was caught by Mike Shannon in right field. Clete Boyer was up next and grounded out to shortstop Dick Groat for the second out. Whitey Ford was the third Yankee batter of the inning. He walked on a full count. It was the fourth base on balls surrendered by Ray Sadecki. The crowd began to show its disapproval when Sadecki fell behind the next Yankee batter, Phil Linz. However, the Cardinal pitcher got out of a potential mess when Linz was ruled out at first base on a grounder to third baseman Ken Boyer who made a fine backhanded play to knock the ball down. Boyer scrambled to pick it up in foul territory and make an accurate throw to first baseman Bill White who was stretched to the maximum length. The play was close. Umpire Bill McKinley's emphatic out call was hotly disputed by Linz, New York manager Yogi Berra, and first-base coach Jimmy Gleeson. McKinley's call stood, of course. Many daily newspapers carried an argument-settling photo of the play the following day. (The *Montreal Gazette* ran the photograph prominently, three columns wide.) The image showed Linz's foot was clearly on the bag before the ball had reached White's glove, proving the Yankees indeed had a legitimate gripe. Regardless of the accuracy of the call, Phil Rizzuto stated that Boyer's play was one of the best defensive gems he had ever seen in a World Series game. While it was a fine play, that statement was likely hyperbolic.

The bottom of the fourth inning began with Phil Linz catching Mike Shannon's popup in foul territory behind first base. The next Cardinal batter, Tim McCarver, ended up on third base courtesy of a blast to the outfield. The ball eluded Roger Maris in right-center field, but no error was charged as McCarver was credited with a triple. Dal Maxvill followed McCarver in the batting order for the home team. He failed to lay down a bunt—a costly miscue—and eventually struck out. St. Louis pitcher Ray Sadecki, batting ninth, was the next Cardinal to come to the plate. He looked bad in striking out on three pitches. McCarver's triple was wasted. He was stranded on third base as the Yankees retained their 3–2 edge after four full innings of Game One had been completed.

Bobby Richardson led off the fifth inning for the visitors. Cardinal third baseman Ken Boyer nicely corralled his bounding ball and threw out Richardson at first base with plenty of time to spare. Roger Maris grounded out to pitcher Ray Sadecki for the second out. Mickey Mantle batted next. He drove a bullet past Ray Sadecki's head that landed in center field for a single. Elston Howard hit a sinking drive toward a diving Mike Shannon in right field. The ball was in his glove momentarily, but it was jarred loose when Shannon fell to the outfield grass. Right field umpire Al Smith decisively correctly signaled "no catch." Howard stopped at first base, but Mantle, running on the play, advanced to third base. Busch Stadium's hard infield undoubtedly affected the following play. Tom Tresh hit a ground ball toward Ken Boyer that bounced clear over the third baseman's head. Mantle scored easily, Howard moved to third base, and Tresh stood on second base with a double and his third RBI of the day. New York's lead was now 4–2. Joe Pepitone ended the inning by flying out to Curt Flood in center field. In revisiting the game 30 years later, historian David Halberstam wrote, "That was normally a good lead to hand to Whitey Ford midway through a World Series game."[5]

Flood led off the bottom of the fifth inning for St. Louis. The Cardinals asked plate umpire Frank Secory to examine the ball for any irregularities. Nothing odd was found. Joe Garagiola told his NBC radio audience that Ford had been occasionally accused of throwing spitballs, but he defended the renowned Yankee hurler by saying, "He's just a good pitcher."[6] Flood hit a bouncing ball toward Clete Boyer at third base. Boyer made an excellent defensive play to retire the swift-footed Flood. "The Boyer brothers are putting on quite an exhibition!"[7] exclaimed the impressed Garagiola. Lou Brock was the next batter. His shallow fly ball was a bit of an adventure and looked to cause confusion, but left fielder Tom Tresh took charge of the situation well and made the catch for the second out of the inning. Dick Groat batted next and grounded out to Clete Boyer. It was the first inning in the game in which no runner reached first base.

Busch Stadium's grounds crew replaced all the bases before the top of the sixth inning began. Joe Garagiola mentioned the batter's boxes were now enveloped in shadows. The number-eight hitter for New York, Clete Boyer, put a scare into the home fans with a long drive. Curt Flood had to drift back to the center field wall, but he made the catch. Whitey Ford followed Boyer to the plate. He walked for the second time in the game. It was the fifth base on balls that Ray Sadecki had allowed. Phil Linz gently flied out to Lou Brock in the outfield for the second out. Bobby Richardson was the next Yankee batter. Garagiola mentioned that the Yankee second baseman had 679 plate appearances in 1964. He joked to his listening audience, "That might not mean much to you, but that was my career total."[8] Richardson's routine-looking popup to Dick Groat became a juggling act for the shortstop, but he got a handle on it before it hit the dirt. The startled crowd gasped, but the third out was safely recorded.

To lead off the bottom of the sixth inning for the home side, Ken Boyer singled into left field. With Bill White batting, a passed ball was charged to catcher Elston Howard as Boyer moved to second base. White struck out swinging on a Whitey Ford breaking ball, but it was the last effective pitch that the Yankee starter threw in Game One—or any other postseason contest.

Moon Man batted next for the home team. That was the nickname that his Cardinal teammates had given St. Louis right fielder Mike Shannon due to his eccentricities. Shannon blasted a home run on Ford's 1-0 curveball—a Ford pitch the Cards had noticed was clearly flat in Game One. It was a tremendous shot. Yankee left fielder Tom Tresh retreated a step or two, but he soon ruefully realized he could only watch the ball sail far over his head. It was a no-doubter for the Cardinal right fielder. Some reporters estimated its *height* to be 500 feet. It solidly smacked into the huge scoreboard at the rear of the left field stands to tie Game One at four runs apiece. By happenstance, the ball squarely struck the "B" in a Budweiser advertising sign, drawing attention to the beverage produced by the team's owner's family. Estimates put the homer's distance at 450 feet. The fans at Busch Stadium roared their approval. After the game, Cardinal manager Johnny Keane said it was the longest home run he had ever witnessed at his club's ballpark. Ford, his voice tinged with disgust, told reporters he knew it was a tremendous home run the second the ball left Shannon's bat.

The following day a photograph appeared on the front page of one of the St. Louis dailies showing Shannon's home run swing and an arced dotted line showing the ball's path to the distant Busch Stadium scoreboard. (The image was reprinted in *The Sporting News*.) Upon his retirement, when Shannon became a restaurateur, he had a large copy of the image on display in his eatery. He asked Whitey Ford to sign it. The Yankee pitcher complied, but he was not exactly overjoyed about doing the task.

Catcher Tim McCarver followed Shannon's extra-base hit with one of his own—a long double—and the audible anticipation of the hometown rooters intensified further. Second baseman Dal Maxvill was the next scheduled hitter for St. Louis, but manager Johnny Keane opted to pinch hit for him. He brought in Charlie James to do the job. That provoked a counter move from Yankee manager Yogi Berra, who replaced the tiring

Ford on the mound with Al Downing, a young left-hander with a strong fastball. Ford left the mound at Busch Stadium with great pain in his left arm and a partial loss of feeling, but, for the good of his team, he did a masterful job of hiding it. It was later learned that Ford's arm was so bad that, for a time, he had trouble using cutlery during meals.

James was ineffective versus Downing as he popped up to second baseman Bobby Richardson. Carl Warwick, a 27-year-old right-handed hitter who threw lefthanded, was then summoned to bat for pitcher Ray Sadecki. Warwick promptly singled into left field. It was the beginning of a very auspicious Fall Classic for Warwick as a pinch hitter. Tom Tresh's throw to the plate was cut off by Clete Boyer who threw to second base to try to put out batter-runner Warwick. However, Warwick safely slid into second base—and the home team now led this very entertaining game, 5–4.

The Cardinals were not done scoring in the home half of the sixth inning. Julián Javier pinch ran for Warwick at second base. Curt Flood launched another ball in Tom Tresh's direction. It was not a homer, but it hit the bottom of the outfield wall. (Joe Garagiola speculated that Tresh may have lost the ball in the sun. Tresh confirmed as much after the game when he was questioned about the important play. Indeed, the official MLB highlight film of the 1964 World Series shows Tresh completely lost in trying to find the ball in the sky. He moved a step forward when he should have continued toward the wall.) Javier crossed the plate to make the score 6–4 for St. Louis. Flood was credited with a triple on a ball that really should have been caught. Lou Brock tried to surprise the Yankees with a bunt, but Clete Boyer fielded it well and threw it in time to Joe Pepitone at first base. There was a minor collision between Brock and the Yankee first baseman, but Pepitone maintained control of the ball to record the third out.

Right-handed knuckleball artist, the balding 38-year-old Barney Schultz, entered the game to replace Ray Sadecki on the mound for St. Louis in the top of the seventh frame. Accordingly, catcher Tim McCarver donned a much larger glove to handle the often-elusive delivery. ("It doesn't have an autograph on it; it has a license plate,"[9] kidded Garagiola about the huge size of the catcher's mitt.) Schultz's presence was a feel-good story for sports fans. He had largely toiled in the minor leagues for 18 different teams—some more than once—over 20 seasons and he was now pitching in the World Series in the twilight of his baseball career. (He even got one vote for NL MVP in 1964.) Julián Javier stayed in the game as the new Cardinal second baseman. Roger Maris popped out to Curt Flood in shallow center field to lead off the inning. Mickey Mantle hit a drive off the outfield screen in right field but it was played well by Mike

Shannon and Mantle was forced to hold at first base. New York's catcher Elston Howard was also retired on a fly ball to Curt Flood. Tom Tresh followed Howard. Tresh managed to hold his swing on a full count and drew a walk. Mantle advanced to second base. He and Tresh were stranded on base when Joe Pepitone struck out swinging.

Dick Groat, who batted .292 in 1964 and had one hit so far in the game, batted first in the bottom of the seventh inning. Al Downing was still on the mound for New York. Groat grounded out to second baseman Bobby Richardson. Ken Boyer got an extra enthusiastic round of applause from the appreciative fans when he followed Groat to the plate. It did not help him. He struck out swinging. Joe Garagiola commented on the Yankee pitcher's velocity, "A guy like Downing will break in a [catcher's] new glove in about three innings."[10] The next batter was Bill White, who was hitless in three prior at-bats and had suffered two strikeouts. He put the ball in play this time, but Richardson had no trouble fielding it and throwing White out at first base to complete the home half of the seventh. St. Louis still held a 6–4 advantage over New York in Game One.

Clete Boyer was the leadoff hitter for New York in the top of the eighth inning. He grounded out to shortstop Dick Groat. Johnny Blanchard batted for pitcher Al Downing as the Yankees were rapidly running short of outs. With a full count, Blanchard doubled into right field. He was very nearly put out by Mike Shannon's excellent and accurate throw. Blanchard safely made a head-first slide into second base, described by Garagiola as a "half-gainer."[11] Mike Hegan replaced Blanchard as a pinch runner. Phil Linz grounded to Ken Boyer, the third baseman. Boyer looked Hegan back to second base and coolly threw to first baseman Bill White for the second out of the inning. On an 0–2 pitch from Barney Schultz, Bobby Richardson bounced a hit past Ken Boyer at third base. Hegan scored on the play. The Yankees now trailed just 6–5 and had the potential go-ahead run at the plate in the person of Roger Maris. The dangerous Maris got an infield hit that eluded the grasp of pitcher Schultz. Julián Javier fielded the ball but Maris beat his throw to first. Now Mickey Mantle was batting. He hit a grounder straight at Javier and was easily retired to end the frame. (That play ended Javier's 1964 World Series; he did not appear in another game.) New York had gotten within a run of the Cards, however.

A new pitcher entered the game for New York in the bottom of the eighth: Roland (Rollie) Sheldon, a 28-year-old righthander. Leadoff batter Mike Shannon knocked a hit past Clete Boyer at third base. There was some delay in ruling it an error. The scoreboard first flashed hit, but that was properly amended to "E5." On a passed ball, Shannon moved to second base while Tim McCarver batted. McCarver eventually walked. Pitcher Barney Schultz smacked a broken-bat line drive to the pitcher. Sheldon caught it. After hesitating for a moment, he threw to first baseman Joe Pepitone to double off McCarver who had run on contact. Bob Skinner was called up to pinch hit for Julián Javier, but Skinner was intentionally walked. Jerry Buchek ran for Skinner. Pete Mikkelsen then replaced Rollie Sheldon on the mound. "The wheels are really turning here at Busch Stadium,"[12] declared Joe Garagiola.

Curt Flood was next to bat for St. Louis. He drilled a line-drive single off Mikkelsen into left field to knock home Shannon. The home team suddenly enjoyed a bit more breathing room with its 7–5 lead. Lou Brock, the next Cardinal hitter, drove in two runs with a double to left field. Buchek and Flood both scored as the home team increased their advantage to a comfortable 9–5. Dick Groat walked to keep the rally alive, but Ken Boyer, the Cardinal cleanup hitter, weakly made an out with a foul popup to Clete Boyer at third base. The home fans roared their approval over the productive home half of the eighth. New York had one inning left to erase the four-run lead accrued by St. Louis.

Buchek remained in the game as the new Cardinal second baseman. He saw no action defensively as the Yankees went down very quietly to Barney Schultz and his knuckleball in the top of the ninth. Catcher Elston Howard grounded out to St. Louis shortstop Dick Groat. Tom Tresh popped up to Ken Boyer at third base. The game ended with Joe Pepitone flying out to Curt Flood in center field. Judging by their huge smiles and general body language, both Flood and right fielder Mike Shannon, who was in close proximity, seemed delightfully surprised that their team had won the Series opener. The last out came two hours and 42 minutes after the game's first pitch. The Cardinals could take heart in the fact that the team that had won the opening game in each of the past four World Series had gone on to win the Fall Classic.

Starter Whitey Ford took the Game One loss for New York. Such decisions were becoming familiar to him. Ford had now dropped four of his last five World Series decisions. At one time, not so long before, Ford was nearly invincible in Fall Classic games. His World Series record now stood at 10–8. It had been a substandard outing for an all-time Yankee great. Few people, however, would have thought that the 5⅓ innings Ford tossed in Game One of the 1964 World Series would be the last postseason appearance of his marvelous career.

It was not an easy one to pinpoint, but Boston baseball scribe Roger Birtwell claimed to have found an obscure common denominator in the Cards' success in Game One: It was the club's minor league affiliate in Jacksonville, Florida. "Jacksonville yesterday defeated the Yankees," according to Birtwell's report in the *Boston Globe*. "Mike Shannon, up from Jacksonville, in July, clubbed the Yanks with his bat. Barney Schultz, up from Jacksonville in August, fought them with his knucklers. And so, the underdog St. Louis Cardinals surged from behind and defeated the Yankees 9–5 in the opener of the World Series."

Birtwell continued with his report with an allusion to Irish geography. He wrote, "Whitey Ford, pitching king of the Yankees, was leading southpaw Ray Sadecki of the Cardinals, 4–2, going into the last of the sixth. It looked for all the world like the old story—another victory for the Yankees. Then the River Shannon started flowing."[13]

The home team's dressing room was a surprisingly subdued place after the 9–5 win. Some reporters noted that the members of the media were more boisterous than the victorious Cards. Manager Keane said the attitude was a reflection of his team's professionalism. "We played methodical ball today," Keane told a writer. "Our team came through when they had to. The Yankees were tough but we rose to the occasion."[14]

Keane said he was proud of his team for doing so well in the glaring spotlight of a World Series. For most of the manager's charges, it was a new experience for them. "The longer the game went, the better we got," Keane insisted. "Our younger players were very cool. [Being in a World Series game] didn't bother them at all."[15] Certainly a few Cardinals were awestruck at the end of Game One when an army of media people descended to the St. Louis clubhouse and proceeded to ask hundreds of questions.

Plaudits went to relief pitcher Barney Schultz who allowed just a single run to the visitors in his three innings of work to preserve the home team's win. Schultz, who earned a save for his efforts—a pitching statistic rarely mentioned in 1964—admitted he was slightly worse for wear than when he entered the game in the seventh inning. "There's a small blister under my nail," he told one scribe, "but it doesn't bother me much. However, it might have some effect if I have to pitch a lot of innings. You see, I dig my first two fingers in the ball when I throw the knuckler." Baseball writer Bob Addie labelled the well-traveled Schultz as "the gypsy of America's diamonds."[16] He was certainly a forthright and witty interview subject. When Schultz was queried over who had taught him to throw baseball's most unpredictable pitch, he promptly replied, "Barney Schultz."[17]

Yogi Berra was asked if he wished he had Pedro Ramos, his terrific late-season reliever, to summon from the bullpen. Berra dismissed the question by noting, "But we don't have him!"[18] Ramos, of course, was not permitted to be on the Yankees' World Series roster because the Cuban right-hander had been acquired by New York from Cleveland past the World Series eligibility deadline of August 31. Berra also said that the Cardinals got timelier hits on the day than his club. Both teams had the same total: 12, but it seemed like St. Louis had more than New York. There was good reason for thinking that. Eleven of the Cardinals' 12 hits put runners in scoring position. The teams' combined 24 hits tied the World Series record for most ever in an opening game. The Yankees and Brooklyn Dodgers each got 12 hits in the Opener of the 1953 World Series, too.

Doing well in a World Series opener was a rarity for St. Louis. This was the Cardinals ninth trip to MLB's premier event, but it was only the second time they had won the opening game. The only previous occasion in which they had started the Fall Classic with a victory was in 1934 versus Detroit. Dizzy Dean had thrown a complete game for an 8–3 Cardinal win three decades earlier.

The Cardinals were also sounder defensively in Game One than the Yankees had been. St. Louis played error-free baseball while the Yankees made two fielding blunders. The fielding error by Clete Boyer was particularly a rarity for New York's sure-handed third baseman. (He had made just 13 all season for a respectable .955 fielding average.) Catcher Elston Howard also had two passed balls charged to him.

Home run hero Mike Shannon, not surprisingly, claimed his mammoth home run was the highlight of his MLB career so far. He did note that it was not his longest in professional baseball, citing more prodigious blasts he had hit in both Pittsburgh and Dublin. Shannon was not referring to the famous Irish city. He meant Dublin, Georgia, population 13,000. It had a minor league baseball club.

An Associated Press article that ran in the next day's *Montreal Gazette* accurately noted that New York's Game One defeat continued an unusual post-season losing streak for the storied franchise. The unnamed reporter, who seemed to enjoy the Yankee setback, stated, "A standing-room throng of 30,805 at St. Louis' first Series game since 1946 savored the spectacle of the proud Yankees losing their fifth straight. The favored American League champions went crashing down four times in a row to the Los Angeles Dodgers last fall."[19]

Generally overlooked in the Cardinals' triumph was Tom Tresh's excellent day at bat for the losing Yankees. He drove in three of New York's five runs with a home run and a double. As AP scribe Jack Hand noted, "St. Louis' finishing kick negated an outstanding performance by the Yankee outfielder."[20]

Due praise was also splashed on Carl Warwick who had an important pinch-hit single in the sixth frame when the Cardinals retook the lead for good. Warwick, a 27-year-old from Dallas, had not played an inning of baseball since September 27 after he was struck in the face by a line drive during a St. Louis batting practice. Hand reported that Warwick stepped to the plate in Game One "with a scar on his right cheek and a throbbing in his head"[21]—and still had a productive at-bat for his club at a crucial point in the opening contest.

6. Game One

There was some speculation among St. Louis writers and others familiar with the home team that substitute second baseman Julián Javier was not at 100 percent for Game One. Jack Hand was one of those skeptics. "The condition of Javier, the Cardinals second baseman, remained doubtful," Hand penned. "He went into today's game as a pinch runner and scored a run, but he could not come in fast enough to handle a routine ground ball that went for a hit by Richardson in the eighth inning. Dal Maxvill ... probably will start [in Game Two]."[22]

It was reported that Las Vegas sports betting venues had the Yankees listed as 17:10 favorites to win the Series before it began. St. Louis' win, however, significantly altered that landscape for gamblers. After Game One, both clubs were now considered "11:10 pick 'em" bets to take home the championship.

Mike Shannon heard through the grapevine that his monstrous home run had significantly damaged the Budweiser advertising sign—and the estimated repair bill would be no less than $4,000. Aghast, Shannon felt the need to apologize to team owner Gussie Busch for the unexpected expense. Prior to Game Two, he walked to Busch's box seat and did just that. Busch just laughed it off, telling Shannon that he was more than welcome to hit the sign a couple more times if he could manage the feat. All monetary concerns aside, Shannon would always recall the towering blast as his most memorable moment of his MLB career. "That homer gave me the biggest thrill of my life. I was a hometown boy in front of the hometown crowd, and I hit a home run off Whitey Ford in the World Series. You can't hardly top that."[23]

The Cardinals later revealed that their scouting report on the Yankee pitchers had advised them to swing early in the count against Whitey Ford. Ray Sedecki, Carl Warwick and Mike Shannon all compiled RBIs on either the first or second pitches they saw from him.

Runs were plentiful in Game One, but one St. Louis player thought it would not be that way for the rest of the World Series. Relaxing by his locker, Dick Groat told a reporter from *Sports Illustrated* he figured the offensive outburst by both teams in Game One was just a fluke. "Every Series, just like every season," Groat explained, "is decided by pitching. I refuse to believe this one will not be."[24]

Game One Box Score
New York Yankees 5, St. Louis Cardinals 9
Game played on Wednesday, October 7, 1964, at Busch Stadium I

New York Yankees	ab	r	h	rbi	St. Louis Cardinals	ab	r	h	rbi
Linz ss	4	0	0	0	Flood cf	5	1	2	2
Richardson 2b	5	0	2	1	Brock lf	5	1	2	2

World Series '64

New York Yankees	ab	r	h	rbi	St. Louis Cardinals	ab	r	h	rbi
Maris cf	4	0	1	0	Groat ss	4	0	1	0
Mantle rf	5	1	2	0	Boyer 3b	3	1	1	1
Howard c	4	1	2	0	White 1b	4	0	0	0
Tresh lf	4	1	2	3	Shannon rf	4	3	2	2
Pepitone 1b	5	0	0	0	McCarver c	3	1	2	0
Boyer 3b	4	1	1	0	Maxvill 2b	2	0	0	0
Ford p	1	0	1	1	James ph	1	0	0	0
Downing p	0	0	0	0	Schultz p	1	0	0	0
Blanchard ph	1	0	1	0	Sadecki p	2	0	1	1
Hegan pr	0	1	0	0	Warwick ph	1	0	1	1
Sheldon p	0	0	0	0	Javier pr,2b	0	1	0	0
Mikkelsen p	0	0	0	0	Skinner ph	0	0	0	0
Totals	37	5	12	5	Buchek pr,2b	0	1	0	0
					Totals	35	9	12	9

```
New York    0 3 0   0 1 0   0 1 0 - 5 12 2
St. Louis   1 1 0   0 0 4   0 3 x - 9 12 0
```

New York Yankees	IP	H	R	ER	BB	SO
Ford L (0-1)	5.1	8	5	5	1	4
Downing	1.2	2	1	1	0	1
Sheldon	0.2	0	2	0	2	0
Mikkelsen	0.1	2	1	0	1	0
Totals	8.0	12	9	6	4	5

St. Louis Cardinals	IP	H	R	ER	BB	SO
Sadecki W (1-0)	6.0	8	4	4	5	2
Schultz SV (1)	3.0	4	1	1	1	1
Totals	9.0	12	5	5	6	3

E—Mantle (1), Boyer (1). DP—New York 1, St. Louis 1. PB—Howard 2 (2). 2B—New York Tresh (1,off Sadecki); Blanchard (1,off Schultz), St. Louis McCarver (1,off Ford); Brock (1,off Mikkelsen). 3B—St. Louis McCarver (1,off Ford); Flood (1,off Downing). HR—New York Tresh (1,2nd inning off Sadecki 1 on, 0 out), St. Louis Shannon (1,6th inning off Ford 1 on, 1 out). SF—Boyer (1,off Ford). IBB—Skinner (1,by Sheldon). SB—Boyer (1,2nd base off Sadecki/McCarver). IBB—Sheldon (1,Skinner). U-HP—Frank Secory (NL), 1B—Bill McKinley (AL), 2B—Ken Burkhart (NL), 3B—Hank Soar (AL), LF—Al Smith (AL), RF—Vinnie Smith (NL). T—2:42. A—30,805.

— 7 —

Game Two
October 8

> "In seasons that followed, as he watched Gibson intimidate opposing hitters, Tom Tresh thought the Yankees had been relatively lucky in the sense that they were new to Gibson. They were battling only his skills ... instead of having to battle both that and his reputation...."[1]
> —David Halberstam

Veteran baseball journalists assigned to the World Series were not only having trouble comprehending the fact that the favored Yankees were upended in Game One, but that they had now lost five straight games in the Fall Classic dating back to their humbling sweep at the hands of the Los Angeles Dodgers the previous autumn. "The holes the Dodgers punctured in the once-invincible New York Yankees' machine continued to spring leaks here [in St. Louis yesterday] afternoon," Al Abrams wrote in his daily sports column for *Pittsburgh Post-Gazette*.

It was all quite un-Yankee-like, scribes and fans seemed to agree. Yet the Cardinals had played confidently and efficiently. Accordingly, they did not celebrate their opening game triumph with any great gusto. One could sense that the victors in Game One felt they rightfully belonged on the same field with the most decorated club in MLB history.

The wind was still strong at Busch Stadium on the afternoon of Thursday, October 8 when Game Two began. During pregame batting practice it was noticeably pushing fly balls to deep right field, so the left-handed hitters in both teams' lineups were a happy bunch. NBC's radio duo of Phil Rizzuto and Joe Garagiola reported that the skies were slightly overcast which meant that the fielders could see the baseball clearly. Though chilly at 58 degrees, it was still a good day in St. Louis to play a World Series game. Another crowd of 30,805—exactly the same number that had been officially tabulated for the first game—filled the ballpark for the second encounter between the Cardinals and Yankees.

Entering the game there was some doubt if St. Louis pitcher Bob Gibson, a 19-game winner during the regular season, had been given enough rest since his relief outing in the pennant-clinching game versus the Mets on Sunday. Certainly, he had a shaky start in his World Series debut. The surly right-hander's first five pitches were all called balls by plate umpire Bill McKinley—and the Busch Stadium fans quickly became upset by their team's pitcher's inaccuracy. Phil Linz, who went 0–4 at the plate in Game One, drew a four-pitch walk to start Game Two. The wildness did not last long as Gibson faced Yankee second baseman Bobby Richardson. He became a strikeout victim. New York's third batter of the game, Roger Maris, nearly got an extra-base hit to left field—where he seldom hit—but it dropped about a foot foul down the outfield line. St. Louis left fielder Lou Brock was relieved because he was playing the left-handed Maris almost in center field because of Maris' habit of pulling the ball. (Joe Garagiola jokingly opined that if the ball landed fair, Maris could have run for a day and a half.) Instead, Maris struck out swinging for the second out. Cleanup hitter Mickey Mantle also went down swinging at a Gibson fastball. The fickle St. Louis fans were now loudly cheering Gibson who recorded three strikeouts in retiring the Yankees.

Mel Stottlemyre, a 22-year-old, six-foot-one right-hander from tiny Mabton, Washington, was on the mound for New York. (How small was Mabton? When Stottlemyre graduated in 1959, his high school baseball team had just 10 players on its roster.) A rookie who had spent most of the season with the Yankee AAA affiliate in Richmond, Stottlemyre had posted a terrific 1.42 ERA to lead the International League. He had unusually small hands, but a very flexible right wrist. Stottlemyre's specialty was his ability to produce ground-ball outs from his array of sinkers. Since his call-up to the Yankees, Stottlemyre had won nine games and thrown two shutouts in his 12 starts for the perennial AL champions, but starting the second game of the 1964 World Series was obviously the biggest moment of his baseball life to date. Stottlemyre knew that if he were to be successful in Game Two, he had to avoid being awed by the occasion. He watched Bob Gibson warm up. Stottlemyre recognized quality immediately and saw Gibson's fastballs whistle into the catcher's glove, but he realized that he should not try to match the Cardinal starter's power. That would be a huge tactical error. He had to stay within his own boundaries. Stottlemyre was a sinkerball pitcher—and that was what had gotten him from a small town in Washington to the 1964 World Series.

Speedy center fielder Curt Flood was the first Cardinal batter Stottlemyre faced. Flood struck out on a 3–2 curveball. Up next was Lou Brock

7. Game Two 73

who hit a bouncer back to the mound where Stottlemyre fielded it without much difficulty. His calm throw to Joe Pepitone efficiently retired Brock at first base. Bill White was called out on strikes to end the home half of the first. Stottlemyre's debut inning under the scrutiny of a massive World Series TV audience and media coverage had gone just splendidly. Combining Stottlemyre's total with Gibson's, five of the game's first six outs had come via strikeouts.

Catcher Elston Howard led off the top of the second inning for New York. Joe Garagiola noted that Howard preferred to wield a 38-ounce bat—something of a fossil in MLB. Garagiola and his broadcast partner Rizzuto agreed that the typical MLB player in 1964 swung a far lighter 31-ounce piece of lumber. The extra weight certainly did not help Howard against Bob Gibson. He struck out—the fourth Yankee in a row to do so. First baseman Joe Pepitone batted next. He made good contact, but his line drive was snared by Ken Boyer beside third base with an athletic leap. The home crowd applauded the play enthusiastically. Outfielder Tom Tresh batted next. He struck out too. "It's early, but there's a strong indication that both pitchers have good stuff today,"[2] Garagiola suggested. The score of Game Two was 0–0 after an inning and a half.

Ken Boyer faced Mel Stottlemyre and bounced out to Yankee shortstop Phil Linz. Dick Groat was next up and promptly grounded out to Clete Boyer at third base for the second out. Garagiola noted that Stottlemyre's sinkers produced a large portion of ground-ball outs for him. Cardinal catcher Tim McCarver hit a ground ball as well that challenged Linz's glove, but he deftly fielded it. His throw to first baseman Joe Pepitone nipped McCarver who had unusual speed for a catcher. The game remained scoreless after two innings.

Clete Boyer had one hit in four at-bats in Game One for New York, but he failed to reach base against Bob Gibson. Boyer grounded to second baseman Dal Maxvill for the first out of the top of the third inning. Mel Stottlemyre came to bat next. The pitcher had gotten nine hits in 34 at-bats in the regular season, but Gibson overpowered him, striking out his mound opponent with ease for the second out of the inning. The Yankee bats came to life shortly thereafter, however. Phil Linz hit a single to right-center field. For a moment, it looked like Linz was considering trying to go to second base, but he thought better of it and retreated back toward first. On NBC radio, Joe Garagiola said that Linz, throughout the 1964 regular season, had gained a reputation as a daring baserunner. Bobby Richardson followed with a double to left field. Linz moved to third base on the two-base hit. The visitors' threat died when Roger Maris grounded out to shortstop Dick Groat. Zeroes were still on the scoreboard at Busch Stadium.

Mike Shannon led off the bottom of the third inning for St. Louis. He was greeted by an appreciative roar from the crowd for his Game One heroics. On the first pitch Shannon saw from Stottlemyre, he stroked a single into left field. Dal Maxvill, the next Cardinal batter, did exactly the same thing. Shannon stopped at second base. Pitcher Bob Gibson, batting ninth, was up next. He laid down a beautiful sacrifice bunt that was fielded by Elston Howard. The catcher's only play was to first base where second baseman Bobby Richardson was properly positioned to cover the bag. It was a close play at first base. Gibson's footspeed almost got him a base hit on the play. The sacrifice put two Cardinal runners in scoring position with just one out. With the home team back at the top of their batting order, Curt Flood broke the scoreless tie with an infield out. His ground ball to shortstop Phil Linz was an RBI-fielder's choice as Shannon scored and Maxvill moved to third base. Lou Brock hit a rocket back to pitcher Stottlemyre. The crowd gasped as the Yankee pitcher knocked the ball down and made an easy out to first base to conclude the inning, but the home team now held a 1–0 lead in Game Two.

Mickey Mantle led off the top of the fourth inning for New York. Gibson got two strikes on Mantle, then threw three consecutive balls to the Yankee slugger. Following a foul ball, Mantle took a called third strike. It was Gibson's seventh whiff of the game. Elston Howard batted next. Howard got a side-armed pitch from Gibson and drove a double into left field. Joe Pepitone, the New York first baseman, came to bat. He blooped a hit between left fielder Lou Brock and shortstop Dick Groat. Howard was frozen at second base as he was unsure if Brock would make the catch. He did not. The ball fell to the outfield grass just in front of Brock's reach. Groat, fairly deep in the outfield, picked it up as Howard advanced to third but no further as third-base coach Frank Crosetti emphatically gave Howard the stop sign. However, Pepitone was running on the play and beat Groat's throw to second base. "That's a bit of an oddity," declared Garagiola. "There were two doubles and nobody scored."[3] This time it was the Yankees who had runners at second and third with one man out. With first base open, an intentional walk was issued to Tom Tresh to load the bases in hopes of turning a double play. It did not work out that way for St. Louis. Clete Boyer flied out to center field deep enough to drive in Elston Howard with the tying run. Pitcher Mel Stottlemyre followed Boyer to the plate. He ran the count to 3–1, but Gibson rallied to strike him out. The score was tied, 1–1, heading to the home half of the fourth inning.

Bill White challenged the Yankee infielders to make a good defensive play on the first pitch of the bottom of the fourth inning. He hit a ground ball that forced Joe Pepitone to move far to his right to field it. Pitcher Mel Stottlemyre alertly covered the now vacated first base and received the throw in time to retire White. It was a textbook play. "They practice that play for hours on end in spring training," noted Joe Garagiola. "You wonder why they do it. Then you see it done as well as the Yankees just did it, and then you know why."[4] Stottlemyre finally got a fly ball out, but it was an extremely dangerous one. A long fly ball by Ken Boyer sent Roger Maris back to the center field fence near the 400-foot marker to make a fine catch for the second out of the inning. Maris made the play look relatively simple, which caused Phil Rizzuto to state that the slugging New York outfielder was very underrated defensively. Broadcast partner Joe Garagiola concurred. Perhaps the long out rattled Stottlemyre because the next St. Louis hitter, Dick Groat, drew a walk—but not before painfully fouling a ball off his foot. It was the first base on balls surrendered by the Yankee pitcher. Tim McCarver, a left-handed hitter, made shortstop Phil Linz move far to his left to collect his ground ball, but Linz was up to the challenge. McCarver was retired at first base to end the inning. The two teams remained level at a run apiece.

The fifth inning began with Phil Linz batting for New York. Linz was put out on a play quite similar to the one he had made on McCarver a few minutes earlier. Dick Groat moved to his left nicely to gather Linz's bouncing ball. Groat's throw required a stretch from first baseman Bill White, but the out was made. Groat made an even better play on Bobby Richardson for the second out. With his back towards home plate, Groat chased down a popup in shallow outfield that was going to fall in front of left fielder Lou Brock. The Cardinal shortstop made an excellent over-the-shoulder catch. An impressed Phil Rizzuto likened Groat to Lou Boudreau, a shortstop from an earlier era, who wasn't blessed with great speed, but had terrific hands and instinctively knew how to position himself for each hitter. On this play, Groat got a good jump on Richardson's ball which made all the difference. Roger Maris batted next. He hit a gentle fly ball to Brock in left field for the third out. Halfway through the game, the score was still tied, 1–1. It was a compelling contest.

Phil Rizzuto took over as the NBC radio play-by-play man for the second half of the game. Mike Shannon led off the bottom of the fifth inning for the home team. He grounded out to second baseman Bobby Richardson. Dal Maxvill was the next man to face Mel Stottlemyre. He quickly bounced out to Clete Boyer at third base. Pitcher Bob Gibson was the third Cardinal batter of the inning. He got aboard by hitting a single off the end of his bat that fell into shallow center field. Curt Flood grounded to Bobby Richardson. The ball took a tricky short hop, but it did not fool the second baseman. He stepped on his base to force out Gibson and end the inning.

Mickey Mantle drew a walk off Bob Gibson to start the sixth inning. Mantle got ahead in the count and was given the green light to swing on a 3–0 pitch. He fouled the pitch off, and then got a fourth ball on the next Gibson offering. Dal Maxvill made the defensive fielding play of the game with a spectacular, leaping grab off Elston Howard's sizzling line drive. Mantle did well to scramble back to first base in time to avoid being doubled up.

After the most beautiful play of the game came the most controversial: Joe Pepitone was allegedly hit on his shirt sleeve by an inside curveball on a check swing—at least that's what Phil Rizzuto told the NBC radio audience. (Later it was learned that Pepitone was allegedly hit on his thigh.) "Wait a minute! It hit him!"[5] bellowed Rizzuto, who clearly was as surprised by the decision as the home team was. The call was made by plate umpire Bill McKinley, the same official who had made two controversial calls at first base in Game One. McKinley's call was delayed—and thoroughly unpopular with the Cardinals and their supporters. McKinley was besieged by catcher Tim McCarver and Gibson. McCarver was convinced the ball had nicked Pepitone's bat—not his thigh. Tim McCarver would later tell the press, "A pitch on the thigh doesn't sound like wood unless he has a wooden leg."[6] Cardinal manager Johnny Keane told a collection of baseball writers afterwards, "It may have hit him, but we heard it hit his bat first." (By rule, such an occurrence is a foul ball.) Keane continued, "Tim McCarver saw it, Gibson saw it, the whole Cardinal bench saw it."[7]

As the debate grew more heated, Dick Groat intervened to make sure that Gibson did not get ejected for arguing. It was a legitimate concern. Gibson was overly intense at the best of times—and he was not particularly fond of umpires at any time. Manager Keane joined the discussion too. "Protests are usually kept to a minimum in Series play," wrote an unnamed scribe from the *Boston Globe*, "but Cards catcher Tim McCarver and manager Keane raged at McKinley."[8] They tried to enlist first base umpire Ken Burkhart to help overturn the call, but he was in no position to agree or disagree with his colleague. No amount of bickering was going to get McKinley's decision changed, however. Pepitone was awarded first base which advanced Mantle to second base.

The Yankees seemed to have caught a break—and they took full advantage of it. With just one out, on the very next pitch, Tom Tresh singled to center field past a diving Dick Groat, scoring Mantle while Pepitone stopped at second base. It was Tresh's fourth RBI of the World Series. The Yankees were ahead, 2–1. Gibson retired the next two Yankees who came to the plate. Clete Boyer flied to Mike Shannon in right field and Stottlemyre's ground ball to Ken Boyer made for an easy force out at third base. However, the damage was done. When the inning concluded, a huge chorus of boos rained down on umpire McKinley, who was certainly the most conspicuous man in blue so far in the 1964 World Series.

7. Game Two

The now-trailing Cardinals had Lou Brock leading off the bottom of the sixth inning. There was a humorous moment when Brock backed away from an inside 0–2 pitch prompting many Cardinal fans to facetiously lobby umpire McKinley for a hit-by-pitch call. On a full count, Stottlemyre was hit by a line drive that struck both the palm of his pitching hand and his torso. (It was the third time in the game that a sharply hit ball had been driven toward Stottlemyre on the mound.) The Yankee pitcher managed to throw out Brock at first base, but Stottlemyre required a little bit of attention to his pitching arm. After a few, light warmup tosses, Stottlemyre casually pronounced himself fit to continue. Bill White came up next and drove a long fly ball to left field. The crowd roared in anticipation, but Tom Tresh tracked it down and made the catch. Third baseman Ken Boyer, the next batter, thought he had drawn a walk. On a close 3–1 pitch, Boyer took a couple of steps toward first base, but plate umpire Bill McKinley called it a strike—to the displeasure of the partisan crowd. Boyer struck out on the next pitch to end the inning, further angering the paying throng of customers.

Phil Linz led off the top of the seventh inning for New York with a single off Bob Gibson, his second hit of the game. This one was hit into left field. Bobby Richardson followed Linz to the plate. On the second pitch, Richardson squared around to bunt as Linz broke for second base. On what was ruled a wild pitch, Gibson's pitch got by catcher Tim McCarver, allowing Linz to go all the way to third base with nobody out. Richardson then got a break, literally, when he plopped a broken-bat single into center field. On NBC radio, Joe Garagiola noted that the largest portion of the shattered bat nearly traveled as far as the baseball did. The Yankees had extended their lead to 3–1. Shortly thereafter, Roger Maris batted and added to the Yankees' rally by slapping a ground ball that took a severe bounce far over the head of Bill White, St. Louis' first baseman, and into right field for a base hit. Phil Rizzuto immediately blamed the rock-hard infield for turning a routine out into a single. Whatever its cause, it was the third straight single by the Yankees in the seventh inning without an out being recorded—and Mickey Mantle was stepping into the batter's box. He grounded to Dal Maxvill at second base who had some difficulty fielding the ball. Maxvill's only play was to first base to retire Mantle. Richardson scored on the fielder's choice and Maris moved to second base. New York's lead was now 4–1. Elston Howard grounded to shortstop Dick Groat. Howard was put out at first base as Maris took third. Joe Pepitone was up next for New York. He was perceived as the villain of the day by the home fans and was roundly booed throughout every pitch of his at-bat. He drove Curt Flood close to the center field fence with a long fly ball, but Flood made the catch. Heading to the seventh-inning stretch, the home team trailed the AL champs by three runs in Game Two.

Dick Groat batted first for St. Louis in the home half of the seventh. Groat hit a line drive off Mel Stottlemyre but the ball went directly to fellow shortstop Phil Linz who was positioned perfectly. Linz made the easy catch for the first out. Roger Maris robbed Tim McCarver of an extra base hit with a terrific running, stretching catch in right-center field. "It was a cinch double," opined Joe Garagiola, "maybe a triple or an inside-the-park home run."[9] Even the partisan Cardinal supporters in Busch Stadium politely applauded the fine play by the Yankee outfielder. The third out came quickly thereafter as Mike Shannon grounded out to Linz. With seven full innings in the book, the score remained 4–1 in favor of New York.

Left fielder Tom Tresh, who had singled home one of the four New York runs, led off the eighth inning for the visitors. Bob Gibson was still on the mound for the home team. He looked very fresh. New York went down in order without much resistance. Tresh grounded out to Dal Maxvill at second base, Clete Boyer bounced out to brother Ken Boyer for the second out, and Mel Stottlemyre struck out for the third time in the game to end the uneventful inning for the Yankees.

The bottom of the eighth inning began with Dal Maxvill scheduled to bat, but St. Louis manager Johnny Keane sent in Carl Warwick to pinch hit just as he had in Game One. The result was the same: Warwick came through for the Cardinals with a single. Another pinch hitter, Bob Skinner, hit a double that landed directly on the right-field foul line, according to umpire Al Smith who was in perfect position to make the correct call. The ball veered right and bounced into the stands for a ground rule double. The result of the play was baserunners at second and third base for St. Louis with nobody out. Manager Keane opted to replace Skinner at second base with pinch runner Jerry Buchek. The crowd, sensing a dramatic comeback, was in an uproar as Curt Flood came to bat. His turn in the batter's box, however, was wasted: Flood grounded out the third baseman Clete Boyer. The runners were compelled to remain on their respective bases as Boyer threw out Flood at first base. Lou Brock grounded sharply to Yankee shortstop Phil Linz. Brock was retired at first, but Warwick scored on the fielder's choice. (Buchek stayed put at second base.) Game Two's score had now narrowed to 4–2 in favor of the Yankees. Despite the high drama, pitcher Mel Stottlemyre looked remarkably composed on the mound as if it were a spring training game, not a World Series affair. Bill White batted next. A pitch eluded Elston Howard. It was ruled a passed ball, allowing Buchek to move to third base. White eventually drew a walk—just the second one Stottlemyre had permitted in Game Two. For White, it was the first time in the World Series he had reached base safely. Ken Boyer followed White in the batting order, but he too hit a ground ball at Phil Linz. The New York shortstop deftly scooped it up and tossed it accurately to Bobby Richardson at second base to force out White. A hugely promising inning for the Cardinals had resulted in just a single run for the home team.

Jerry Buchek stayed in the game as the Cardinals second baseman as the Yankees came to bat in the top of the ninth inning holding a two-run advantage. A new pitcher was on the mound for St. Louis, however, as Bob Gibson had been replaced by a pinch hitter the previous inning. Knuckleballer Barney Schultz, who had a wonderful outing in Game One, took over the pitching duties. Phil Linz, who already had a good claim at being the MVP of Game Two, had a long at-bat versus Schultz featuring many foul balls. At one point, shortstop Dick Groat chased a foul ball to an area near the third-base field boxes. To his chagrin, as he stood at the base of the barrier, the wind blew the ball back over the playing field. It dropped to the grass, just out of Groat's reach. Although it was not recorded in the books as an error, it was a wasted opportunity to retire Linz. Given a second life, Linz powered a home run into the left field seats. The delivery was not a Schultz knuckleball; it was a fastball. The Yankees led 5–2.

Bobby Richardson batted next and made a quick out, grounding to shortstop Dick Groat. Roger Maris came up next and smacked a single. The Yankees' tenth hit of the game prompted Johnny Keane to make another pitching change. The fans gave Schultz a polite round of applause. Left-hander Gordon Richardson—no relation to Bobby Richardson of the Yankees—was handed the ball. The first New Yorker he faced was Mickey Mantle. New York's famous #7 promptly doubled, his hit landing squarely on the left-field foul line. (Mantle later told his teammates that he was upset that he had only connected for a two-bagger off Richardson. He figured he should have driven the pitch for a home run.) Roger Maris raced all the way home to increase the Yankees' edge to 6–2. Elston Howard was given an intentional walk. Joe Pepitone belted a line-drive single into right field. Mike Shannon did well to hold Pepitone to a single, but Mantle scored the Yankees' seventh run. Howard advanced to third base on the play. Left fielder Tom Tresh hit a sacrifice fly to deep right field to score Howard. Pepitone advanced to second base as Shannon launched a desperate throw toward catcher Tim McCarver. It was a terrific toss, but Shannon had no chance to nail Howard. Keane chose to make yet another mound move. Roger Craig, one of just three Cardinals with previous World Series experience, was brought in to stop the New York rally. He got Mel Stottlemyre to whiff for the fourth time in the game. This time the Yankee pitcher was caught looking at strike three. The hometown Cardinals were in deep trouble, trailing 8–2 heading to the bottom of the ninth inning.

Mel Stottlemyre was hoping to secure a complete game when he took the mound for the bottom of the ninth inning. For defensive purposes, the Yankees replaced Mickey Mantle in right field with Hector Lopez. Dick Groat led off for St. Louis with a triple to right field. Not long afterward, Tim McCarver singled Groat home. The score was now 8–3 for New York with no one out in the bottom of the ninth. Yankee manager Yogi Berra made a trip to the mound, but he had no intention of removing Stottlemyre at this point in the game. The visit was just to remind him to keep his pitches down and to stay focused. The little chat seemed to work. Any hints of a St. Louis rally were quashed when the next Cardinal batter, outfielder Mike Shannon, grounded into a 6–4–3 double play. The crowd became silent in a hurry. Johnny Keane made one final strategic move. It was an obvious one. Charley James batted for pitcher Roger Craig. He struck out swinging to end Game Two. The game had taken two hours and 29 minutes to play. Mel Stottlemyre, the acclaimed sinkerball specialist, had recorded 16 outs on ground balls.

Stottlemyre had a complete-game victory in his World Series debut—a terrific achievement for a young man who had spent a few months after the 1963 season working in a fruit plant to supplement his income. More importantly, the Series had been leveled at a game apiece. The 1964 Fall Classic was heading to New York City and cavernous Yankee Stadium where Games Three, Four and Five (which was now guaranteed) would be contested on Saturday, Sunday and Monday so long as the weather cooperated. A travel day on Friday insured the teams would arrive well rested.

The 8–3 win ended an embarrassing five-game losing streak in World Series play for New York which was technically their longest in club history. However, the Yankees lost the final three games of the 1921 World Series, went winless in 1922 (although Game Two ended a tie), and lost the opener in 1923. (All three of those Fall Classics were versus their crosstown rivals, the New York Giants.) That meant the Yankees had once played nine consecutive World Series games without a win.

"The whole story of the Yankee victory today is a simple combination of good hitting and pitching," said Joe Garagiola in his brief postgame remarks to the NBC radio audience. "Mel Stottlemyre really set the Cardinals down."[10] Indeed, Stottlemyre had only been in serious trouble in the eighth inning when St. Louis' first two batters, both pinch hitters, singled and doubled. "One more hit and he would have been [removed],"[11] Yogi Berra told a scrum of reporters afterwards. The young Yankee pitcher remained thoroughly poised, however, and limited the potential Cardinal rally to just one run. Stottlemyre was backed up by 12 Yankee hits, many of which were of the timely variety. Stottlemyre had allowed seven hits to the home team.

"The Cardinals had won Wednesday's opener, 9–5, with a late-inning explosion, but New York supplied all the closing fireworks today before 30,805 chilled fans in Busch Stadium,"[12] was how the Associated Press summary of Game Two began.

At the conclusion of Thursday's game, the major talking point was, of course, the alleged hit-by-pitch suffered by Joe Pepitone in the seventh inning that was indirectly responsible for New York's second run of the game. Everyone agreed it had been a momentum-changer. Maury Allen, who was covering the World Series for the *New York Post*, thought it had been a pure acting job on Pepitone's part. According to Allen, as the Yankee first baseman sat in the clubhouse after the game, Pepitone was inconsistent about which thigh Gibson's pitch had supposedly struck! When asked by different scribes where the ball supposedly had hit him, the leg he showed them varied regularly. In the next day's newspaper, Allen penned, "Each time he showed reporters the spot on his leg, he banged his thigh with his hand and it grew redder and redder. Both legs had the same mark."[13] Pepitone said that when the ball went past him, he said to umpire Bill McKinley that it had hit him. The arbiter agreed, declaring that Pepitone had checked his swing, and was therefore entitled to first base. Pepitone also said that he heard St. Louis shortstop Dick Groat complain that he [Pepitone] had given no indication that he had been hit by the pitch. "What was I supposed to do," the Yankee first baseman asked rhetorically, "roll around in pain?"[14] At least the *Post*'s punny headline writer had a chance to be creative. Allen's story ran under the banner, "Pepitone's 'Hit Me' Blackjacked Cards."

Following the Pepitone hit-by-pitch, the second major topic of conversation was Stottlemyre being struck on his pitching hand by Lou Brock's drive in the sixth inning—and staying in the game until the finish. During the NBC radio broadcast, it was reported that the ball had struck Stottlemyre's wrist, but afterwards the pitcher said the ball had struck the palm of his hand. He was extremely fortunate the ball missed his fingers by a couple of inches. If that had been the case, catcher Elston Howard told reporters, "[Stottlemyre] would have been out of there."[15]

"The hand was numb and I wasn't sure if I could continue,"[16] Stottlemyre admitted to the curious scribes surrounding his cubicle in the visitors' clubhouse. He also told the media, "It wasn't my best game of the season, but it certainly was my biggest victory."[17]

Elston Howard was quite impressed by the hurler from tiny Yakima Junior College in Washington. "He has more poise than any young pitcher I have ever caught," declared the Yankee backstop. "He keeps the ball down and never lets a base hit rattle him. He keeps coming back."[18] Howard also recalled that he figured the unknown rookie would make the Yankees roster after watching him for just a short time in spring training.

Calling Stottlemyre "a pitching lifesaver,"[19] Jack Hernon of the *Pittsburgh Post-Gazette* praised the winning hurler for tossing a masterful game in which the heart of the St. Louis batting order came up completely dry all afternoon. Indeed, no one in the Cardinals' one to four spots got a hit off him in Game Two.

Ken Boyer marveled at Stottlemyre's outing. "That kid was more effective when he got behind on our hitters than when he was ahead of them," he noted. "And he got hit hard twice by balls hit back at him. He never got rattled. That's what impressed me the most. It had to impress anybody."[20] Author David Halberstam wrote of Stottlemyre, "He did not look like someone who had been pitching in Richmond only a few weeks earlier; if anything, he looked like he had been dealing with pressure as long as Whitey Ford had."[21]

Yogi Berra told the gentlemen of the press that his biggest concern during Game Two had nothing to do with his young pitcher being in the World Series spotlight for the first time. Instead, it was something he could not control: the early dominance of Bob Gibson. "He had me worried when he was striking everybody out,"[22] Berra said.

Ken Boyer of the defeated Cardinals was quick to praise the youngster who had given him a fruitless 0-for-4 day at the plate. "The kid's got the best sinker and curve I've seen," said the man who would be named the 1964 NL MVP. "There isn't a pitcher in the National League with this kind of stuff."[23]

Despite the World Series being on level terms after Game Two, the *Boston Globe* reported, "The Yankees remain the heavy favorite to win the Series against the lighter-hitting Cardinals who are not expected to find the spacious confines of [Yankee Stadium] tailored to their type of baseball."[24] According to a United Press International story from Las Vegas, the casinos' bookmakers now had the Yankees listed as 21:10 favorites to win the World Series and 8:5 to win Game Three on Saturday.

Berra also had the best impromptu line about Game Two. When 23-year-old Joe Pepitone, a member of the 1963 Yankees who had been swept by the Dodgers, loudly exclaimed, "Hey! This is my first World Series victory!" Berra, the smiling rookie Yankee manager who had *played* in more Fall Classic games than anyone in baseball history, could not resist a rejoinder. He promptly piped in, "Mine too."[25]

Game Two Box Score
New York Yankees 8, St. Louis Cardinals 3
Game played on Thursday, October 8, 1964, at Busch Stadium I

New York Yankees	ab	r	h	rbi	St. Louis Cardinals	ab	r	h	rbi
Linz ss	4	2	3	1	Flood cf	4	0	0	1
Richardson 2b	5	1	2	1	Brock lf	4	0	0	1

7. Game Two

New York Yankees	ab	r	h	rbi	St. Louis Cardinals	ab	r	h	rbi
Maris cf	5	1	2	0	White 1b	3	0	0	0
Mantle rf	4	2	1	2	Boyer 3b	4	0	0	0
Lopez rf	0	0	0	0	Groat ss	3	1	1	0
Howard c	4	2	1	0	McCarver c	4	0	1	1
Pepitone 1b	4	0	2	1	Shannon rf	4	1	1	0
Tresh lf	3	0	1	2	Maxvill 2b	2	0	1	0
Boyer 3b	3	0	0	1	Warwick ph	1	1	1	0
Stottlemyre p	5	0	0	0	Schultz p	0	0	0	0
Totals	37	8	12	8	Richardson p	0	0	0	0
					Craig p	0	0	0	0
					James ph	1	0	0	0
					Gibson p	1	0	1	0
					Skinner ph	1	0	1	0
					Buchek pr,2b	0	0	0	0
					Totals	32	3	7	3

```
New York   0 0 0   1 0 1   2 0 4  -  8 12 0
St. Louis  0 0 1   0 0 0   0 1 1  -  3  7 0
```

New York Yankees	IP	H	R	ER	BB	SO
Stottlemyre W (1-0)	9.0	7	3	3	2	4
Totals	9.0	7	3	3	2	4

St. Louis Cardinals	IP	H	R	ER	BB	SO
Gibson L (0-1)	8.0	8	4	4	3	9
Schultz	0.1	2	2	2	0	0
Richardson	0.1	2	2	2	2	0
Craig	0.1	0	0	0	0	1
Totals	9.0	12	8	8	5	10

E—None. DP—New York 1. PB—Howard (3). 2B—New York Richardson (1,off Gibson); Howard (1,off Gibson); Pepitone (1,off Gibson); Mantle (1,off Richardson), St. Louis Skinner (1,off Stottlemyre). 3B—St. Louis Groat (1,off Stottlemyre). HR—New York Linz (1,9th inning off Schultz 0 on, 0 out). SF—Boyer (1,off Gibson); Tresh (1,off Richardson). HBP—Pepitone (1,by Gibson). IBB—Tresh (1,by Gibson); Howard (1,by Richardson); Boyer (1,by Richardson). SH—Gibson (1,off Stottlemyre). WP—Gibson (1). HBP—Gibson (1,Pepitone). IBB—Gibson (1,Tresh); Richardson 2 (2,Howard,Boyer). U-HP—Bill McKinley (AL), 1B—Ken Burkhart (NL), 2B—Hank Soar (AL), 3B—Vinnie Smith (NL), LF—Frank Secory (NL), RF—Al Smith (AL). T—2:29. A—30,805.

— 8 —

Game Three
October 10

> "Barney Schultz was to pitch the ninth, and the Cardinal players were pleased because he had become their invincible man that season. Somehow, when Barney came in, the game was a lock."[1]—David Halberstam

On Saturday, October 10, an overcast day greeted the St. Louis Cardinals and New York Yankees for the third game of the 1964 World Series on Saturday, October 10, at Yankee Stadium. In his pregame comments, NBC radio's Curt Gowdy informed his listening audience that the temperature in New York City that afternoon had turned chilly within the past couple of hours. It was in the high fifties on the Fahrenheit scale. There was a 15-mile-per-hour wind blowing from third base to first base within the famous ballpark where in excess of 67,000 fans were on hand to see which team would pull in front in the best-of-seven clash. (Gowdy and his broadcast partner Harry Caray from the Cardinals had swapped duties with Joe Garagiola and Phil Rizzuto. The latter pair of gentlemen had moved to the network's television coverage where Gowdy and Caray had been working when the first two games of the Fall Classic had been played in Busch Stadium in St. Louis.)

"In every game so far in this Series, the breeze has been a factor," Gowdy noted. "It's going to cause trouble today on fly balls and popups. Batters who get the ball up in the air in right field are going to get a big boost."[2]

Veteran pitcher Curt Simmons was on the mound for St. Louis. At age 35, the left-handed Simmons was old enough to have been on the roster of the pennant-winning 1950 Philadelphia Phillies, although he did not play in that World Series that autumn versus the Yankees due to his military commitments. Like the vast majority of the Cardinals, the 1964

Curt Gowdy (left) emcees an on-field ceremony at Fenway Park with Joe Cronin; Red Sox coach Rudy York (third from left) and pitcher Bill Monbouquette are in the background. Before he became nationally known as a broadcaster for NBC, Gowdy called Red Sox games on radio and TV for 15 seasons (courtesy Boston Public Library, Leslie Jones Collection).

World Series was his MLB postseason debut. Born in Egypt, Pennsylvania, Simmons made his big-league debut with the Phillies back in 1947 as an 18-year-old call-up. Simmons' lone appearance that year—the last game of the season on September 28—was quite impressive. It was a complete-game five-hitter in which he allowed just a single run to the New York Giants. He struck out nine men and went 1-for-2 at the plate. Simmons had been with the Cardinals since 1960. He was aging like fine wine, though, as 1964 saw him win 18 games—the highest total in his fine MLB career. Over the course of his pitching days, Simmons changed from being mostly a fastball hurler to being a very effective purveyor of junk. His screwball was especially effective. His off-speed offerings combined with a herky-jerky delivery vexed Hank Aaron to no end. Once, during a 1965 Braves-Cardinals game, Aaron literally ran at a Simmons slow delivery and connected for an apparent home run, but he was called out by umpire Chris Pelekoudas for being out of the batter's box when he made contact with the pitch.

Simmons' mound opponent for Game Three was right-hander Jim

Bouton. The 25-year-old Yankee hurler from New Jersey was in his third MLB season and, in the opinion of Curt Gowdy, had stuff as good as any pitcher in the American League. Bouton too had won 18 games in 1964. His fastball and overhead curve were especially effective. A bit of an oddball when it came to pregame rituals, Bouton liked to warm up twice before his starts. He threw 30 minutes before a game, after which he rested, and then threw again for another 10 minutes just before the game started. Bouton had pitched in the 1963 World Series for New York, losing a 1–0 heartbreaker to Don Drysdale in Game Three at Dodger Stadium. He was a young man who was sure of his talents and his value to his club. Before the 1964 season began, Bouton engaged in a well-publicized holdout before finally re-signing with the Yankees for the princely wage of $18,000 for the season.

Tony Martin sang the national anthem before Game Three. Harry Caray, who had been the St. Louis Cardinals broadcaster for 20 seasons, called the first half of the game for NBC's radio audience while Curt Gowdy did color commentary. Halfway through the scheduled nine innings, they would switch tasks.

Curt Flood, who was 2-for-9 thus far in the 1964 World Series, led off for St. Louis against Jim Bouton. He flied out to Mickey Mantle in deep right-center field. Lou Brock, also 2-for-9 over the first two games was the second batter in the top of the first inning for the visitors. He was fooled with a changeup and popped out to Clete Boyer at third Base. Bill White, 0-for-7 in the Series thus far, batted third for the Cardinals. Because of his strong, overhand delivery, Bouton accidentally knocked the cap off his head on his first pitch to White. Caray told fans this would be far from a rarity. Accordingly, Caray decided to keep a running total of how often it occurred. (Caray's last report on the subject said Bouton lost his cap eight times.) White lined out to Tom Tresh in left field to end the first half of the opening inning.

Shortstop Phil Linz led off the home half of the first inning for New York. Third baseman Ken Boyer made a sparkling defensive play at third base to deprive Linz of a base hit. Boyer threw out Linz at first base. Bobby Richardson grounded to second baseman Dal Maxvill for out number two. On Curt Simmons' first pitch to Roger Maris, the slugger checked his swing but he made enough contact to send a soft popup to Maxvill for the third out.

Ken Boyer, who was 1-for-7 in the Series, was the first St. Louis batter to confront Bouton in the second inning. Broadcaster Harry Caray noted that Boyer led the NL with 119 RBIs during the regular season. Boyer popped out to first baseman Joe Pepitone. Shortstop Dick Groat, batting fifth for the Cardinals, followed. He scared the Yankee fans with a long

8. Game Three

foul ball that drifted wide of the foul pole. He struck out on the next pitch, rung up by NL plate umpire Ken Burkhart. Groat disagreed with the call, thinking the pitch was high. Tim McCarver drew a walk to become the first baserunner of the game. Mike Shannon fell behind 0–2 in the count, but he singled to center field, sending the swift-footed McCarver to third base. An audible contingent of St. Louis fans cheered their delight, but the rally produced nothing. Dal Maxvill popped out to Joe Pepitone on first base.

Mickey Mantle, 3-for-9 in the World Series, led off the bottom of the second frame. He grounded out to shortstop Dick Groat. Elston Howard was the next Yankee to face Curt Simmons. He was not fooled by a change-up and hit it into center field for a single. It was Howard's fourth base hit of the Series. Outfielder Tom Tresh, a right-handed hitter whose father Mike had been an MLB catcher, fouled off several pitches before he popped out to Ken Boyer in foul territory near third base. Joe Pepitone was sent sprawling with the first pitch Simmons threw. The second pitch almost hit him as well. Harry Caray speculated it was a form of payback for the controversial HBP from Game Two. Pepitone drew a four-pitch walk which sent Howard to second base. Clete Boyer was up next and doubled an 0–2 offering into left field. (Ahead in the count, Simmons had attempted to waste a pitch, but had gotten it too close to the plate.) Howard scored and Pepitone stopped at third. Jim Bouton flied out to Lou Brock in left field to end the inning, but the Yankees were ahead, 1–0, after two complete frames.

Behind by a run, the Cardinals batted in the top of the third inning. The sky had become so overcast that the lights at Yankee Stadium had been turned on before Curt Simmons stepped into the batter's box to face fellow pitcher Jim Bouton. Many fans, including Cardinal owner Gussie Busch, were seen donning overcoats as the temperature continued to drop. Simmons went down swinging as Elston Howard squeezed a foul tip with two strikes. St. Louis center fielder Curt Flood flied out to deep left-center field where Roger Maris pulled the ball in for the second out of the top of the inning. Left fielder Lou Brock bounced out to Yankee shortstop Phil Linz. He threw out Brock with a strong toss to Bill White at first base as Brock made the play surprisingly close with his speed. The game remained 1–0 in favor of the home team.

A sensational play by Cardinal shortstop Dick Groat robbed New York's Phil Linz of a hit as the bottom of the third inning began. Groat had to sprawl for the ball. He ended up face down on the infield with the ball, but he rose quickly to throw out Linz at first base by a full step. Linz was not a slow-footed runner, which made the play even more terrific. Bill White caught a foul popout to retire Bobby Richardson on one pitch.

Roger Maris made out number three of the inning with a ground ball to Cardinal first baseman Bill White. White gently tossed the ball to Curt Simmons who had alertly covered first base.

The first Cardinal to bat in the top of the fourth inning did not bat for long. Bill White, hitless in eight World Series at bats thus far, flied out on the second pitch to Tom Tresh in left field. Ken Boyer also hit a routine fly ball. This one was caught by Roger Maris in center field. St. Louis had had just one base hit to this point in Game Three. "Jim Bouton is the master of the situation so far,"[3] declared Harry Caray to his radio listeners. In recognition of his fine fielding the previous inning, Cardinal shortstop Dick Groat received a polite round of applause from the New York fans when he batted. He popped out to second baseman Bobby Richardson to conclude the inning.

Bright sunshine returned to Yankee Stadium when Mickey Mantle stepped into the right-handed batter's box the face the left-handed Simmons to lead off the bottom of the fourth inning. He walked on five pitches. It was the second base on balls given up by Simmons. Elston Howard batted next and promptly hit into an easy 4-6-3 double play. Outfielder Tom Tresh hit a sharp ground ball to Ken Boyer at third base. The ball hit Boyer's chest, but he picked it up quickly and threw to first baseman Bill White in plenty of time to retire Tresh. Four innings had been completed in the swift-moving game. New York was in front, 1-0.

Catcher Tim McCarver, who led off the top of the fifth inning, was one of only two Cards to reach base thus far in Game Three. He slapped a ball into right field for a single, but he ended up standing on second base when the ball bounded through Mickey Mantle's legs. The play was ruled a hit and an error on Mantle. Mike Shannon launched a line drive into right field, but Mantle was positioned perfectly. He hardly had to move to catch the ball for the first out. Dal Maxvill, the number-eight Cardinal batter, was the next hitter for St. Louis. He bounced a grounder to second baseman Bobby Richardson. The fielder's choice putout at first base sent McCarver to third base for the second time in the game. Pitcher Curt Simmons helped his own cause. To the delight of the small but noisy contingent of Cardinal rooters in Yankee Stadium. Simmons smacked a ball that nicked lunging third baseman Clete Boyer's glove, but it ended up in left field. It was an RBI single for the Cardinal pitcher that tied Game Three at 1-1. Curt Flood, the leadoff hitter for the visitors, batted next. His ground ball to Phil Linz resulted in Simmons being forced out at second base to end any further threat of St. Louis breaking the deadlock. "Boy, we've got ourselves a honey of a ballgame!"[4] exclaimed Harry Caray as he handed off the NBC radio play-by-play duties to partner Curt Gowdy.

As first baseman Joe Pepitone strode to the plate to lead off the

8. Game Three

bottom of the fifth inning for New York, Curt Gowdy informed his listeners that both Joe DiMaggio and Stan Musial were present at Yankee Stadium in a special VIP box. Pepitone was promptly brushed back again by Simmons, prompting boos from the Yankee Stadium faithful. Pepitone hit a grounder to first baseman Bill White who had to make a throw to Simmons at first base for the putout. A bounding grounder from Clete Boyer to his brother Ken at third base resulted in an easy putout throw for the second out. Pitcher Jim Bouton came to bat with two outs. He popped out to St. Louis catcher Tim McCarver to end the inning. The score of Game Three was still 1–1.

Lou Brock failed to reach base when he led off the top of the sixth inning for St. Louis as he grounded out to Bobby Richardson at second base. First baseman Bill White, who was a miserable 0-for-9 so far in the World Series, came to bat hungry for a hit. He got it, but it was not spectacular. White was credited with an infield hit as his high chopper to Clete Boyer was airborne long enough for White to beat the third baseman's throw to first baseman Joe Pepitone. It was St. Louis' fourth hit of the game. Ken Boyer then flied out to Tom Tresh in left field for the second out. Dick Groat, the subsequent Cardinal batter, hit a line drive that fell beyond the reach of Tresh. It resulted in a double. However, Tresh's hustle on the play saved a run as he quickly corralled the ball. His quick throw to the infield forced White to hold at third base. The hot-hitting Tim McCarver received an intentional walk from Jim Bouton to load the bases. The Yankees' strategy worked as Mike Shannon sent a ground ball to shortstop Phil Linz. He threw to Bobby Richardson for the force play on McCarver at second base. An excellent scoring opportunity for the Cardinals had been wasted. Game Three remained deadlocked.

The pitchers' duel continued. New York shortstop Phil Linz was the first Yankee hitter to face Curt Simmons in the bottom of the sixth. Simmons coaxed a ground ball back to the mound for an easy first out of the inning. Bobby Richardson also hit a pitch right back towards Simmons. The St. Louis pitcher could not react to it fast enough, however, and it bounced into center field. Roger Maris made the second out when he flied out to Mike Shannon in right field. Mickey Mantle came up, again batting right-handed. Curt Gowdy told his listeners that Mantle's batting average in 1964 while hitting from that side was a remarkable .424. On a 3–0 pitch, Mantle was given the green light by Yogi Berra to hit away. The great Yankee slugger responded by driving a double into right field that sent Richardson to third base. In a scenario identical to the previous half inning, Elston Howard was intentionally walked to load the bases with two out. Tom Tresh, a switch-hitter batting right-handed, failed to break the tie. He popped up the first pitch he saw to St. Louis first baseman Bill White.

Game Three, an excellent ballgame, was two-thirds over with the score even at 1–1.

The top of the seventh inning saw Dal Maxvill lead off for the visitors with a double into left center field off a high changeup. "That gives the Cardinals a rousing start in the seventh inning,"[5] declared Harry Caray. Curt Simmons bunted down the line toward third base. Clete Boyer fielded it and threw to first base for the out, but the sacrifice moved Maxvill to third base with one out. Curt Flood's high pop fly into very shallow center field was caught by an onrushing Roger Maris. It was not deep enough for Maxvill to even attempt to score. It was a huge out for Bouton. Lou Brock failed to drive Maxvill home as well as his bounding ball to Yankee third baseman Clete Boyer was handled cleanly. Boyer threw to Pepitone at first base for the third out.

The bottom third of the New York order came to bat in the bottom of the seventh inning and was dismissed swiftly. Joe Pepitone led off. His foul popup was caught by Bill White near the Yankee dugout for the first out. The second Yankee to go down was Clete Boyer. He was struck out on a screwball making him Simmons' first whiff of the afternoon. Pitcher Jim Bouton hit a fly ball directly at Lou Brock in left field which was easily snagged. After seven full innings, Game Three was still a 1–1 tie—just as it had been since the top of the fifth inning.

In the top of the eighth frame, St. Louis sent Bill White to the plate to lead things off for the visitors. He hit a Jim Bouton changeup toward Bobby Richardson. First baseman Pepitone had tried to field the ball, so Bouton had to leave the mound to cover the bag. It was done correctly as Richardson accurately flung the ball to the pitcher for the first out. Ken Boyer hit another changeup and hit a high fly ball to Tom Tresh in left field. Quickly there were two outs for the Cardinals. Shortstop Dick Groat grounded to Clete Boyer at third base. The sure-handed Boyer made the routine throw to first baseman Joe Pepitone to retire the Cardinals.

Yankee fans tried rhythmic clapping to inspire their team as the bottom of the eighth inning began. It paid no dividends. Shortstop Phil Linz hit a long fly ball that Curt Flood caught with ease in center field. Second baseman Bobby Richardson hit a ground ball to Dick Groat. The shortstop's throw was not ideal; Bill White had to stretch to haul in the slightly high throw, but he did it successfully for the second out of the frame. Roger Maris, batting .250 in the Series, was the third batter of the inning—and he made the third out on a called third strike by umpire Ken Burkhart, who was quietly having a good game behind the plate. Maris was upset at the call and tossed his bat away in anger. Game Three, a terrific contest by any measure, headed to the top of the ninth inning deadlocked at 1–1.

Tim McCarver was the first batter for St. Louis in the visitors' half

8. Game Three

of the ninth. He drove a ball right through the legs of shortstop Phil Linz. "That was a real croquet shot!"[6] roared Curt Gowdy about the obvious error. The next Cardinal up, Mike Shannon, laid down a sacrifice bunt toward first base. Joe Pepitone fielded it and had to chase Shannon for a couple of steps to apply a tag as the St. Louis batter/runner retreated toward the plate. With McCarver standing on second base with one out, St. Louis manager Johnny Keane sent pinch hitter Carl Warwick into the game to bat for weak-hitting Dal Maxvill. He drew a walk from Jim Bouton. Keane rolled the dice again as he sent in Bob Skinner to pinch hit for Curt Simmons. He hit a long fly ball to deep right-center field. The ball was chased down and caught by Roger Maris for the out. McCarver tagged up and moved to third base with two outs. Warwick remained planted at first base. Leadoff hitter Curt Flood batted next. The Yankees caught a huge break when Flood hit a chopper down the third base line. Clearly, there was no chance for anyone to make a play on the ball to throw out the speedy Flood—which would have scored McCarver—so catcher Elston Howard and third baseman Clete Boyer opted to let it roll and hope for the best. Their gamble worked: It eventually rolled into foul territory. Flood flied out gently to Mickey Mantle shortly thereafter to end the top of the ninth inning.

Keane's pinch-hitting maneuvers had forced Simmons out of the game. Replacing him on the mound was 38-year-old Barney Schultz, the knuckleballer who had already made two appearances thus far in the World Series. Schultz had masterfully saved the first game, but he had only lasted a third of an inning in relief in Game Two. Jerry Buchek also came in to play second base for St. Louis in place of Dal Maxvill. There was some confusion as to which Cardinal substitute was going into which vacancy in the lineup, so it had to be sorted out by plate umpire Ken Burkhart with Johnny Keane—and the information relayed to Yogi Berra—before the inning could begin.

Mickey Mantle led off the bottom of the ninth inning batting left-handed against the right-handed Cardinal reliever. When Mantle was introduced by public-address announcer Bob Sheppard, the crowd roared in anticipation. They were a prescient bunch. Whenever Mantle batted lefty, his swing was more of an uppercut than when he batted righty. Mantle had been told by scouts that the best Schultz pitch to hit was likely going to be the first one delivered. It was harder and straighter than a true knuckleball in order for Schultz not to fall behind in the count. Mantle was ready for it when it came.

"Forget about it! It is gone! The ballgame is over!"[7] declared Curt Gowdy with absolute certainty. Mantle hammered the first pitch he saw into the fourth row of seats in the third deck in Yankee Stadium's right-field bleachers to give the home team a 2–1 victory in Game Three—and a similar lead in the 1964 World Series—in the most dramatic of ways. It was the 16th World Series home run for Mantle, putting him one ahead of the late Babe Ruth atop the all-time list. Joyful Yankee third-base coach Frank Crosetti ran alongside Mantle for the last 90 feet of his journey to home plate. Yogi Berra excitedly ran out of the home team's dugout to aggressively slap Mantle on the back several times as he circled the bases. Losing pitcher Schultz knew immediately that he had surrendered a game-ending four-bagger. He merely shrugged and walked slowly to the visitors' clubhouse.

In an interview years later, Mantle said that before he stepped into the batter's box, he saw teammate Elston Howard, the next batter in the Yankee lineup, crouching in the on-deck circle. Mantle told him he might as well go back to the dugout because he was going to end the game with a home run. Howard confirmed the conversation.

The term "walkoff homer" (where the last pitch of a baseball game is hit for a home run) had not yet been coined in 1964. Be that as it may, Mantle's was just the fifth to occur in World Series history. Three of the previous four instances also involved the New York Yankees. Remarkably, there were none from the Fall Classic's inception in 1903 through 1948. Beginning with the next autumn, they began to occur—and occur somewhat frequently. Tommy Henrich's in Game One of the 1949 Series was the first. It gave the Yankees a 1–0 win in nine innings over the Brooklyn Dodgers. Five years later, in 1954, Dusty Rhodes did it for the New York Giants at the Polo Grounds against the Cleveland Indians to win Game One of that World Series in the tenth inning. Eddie Mathews also belted a tenth-inning homer in Game Four of the 1957 World Series to upend the Yankees at Milwaukee's County Stadium. Most famously, Bill Mazeroski did it in the ninth inning of Game Seven of the 1960 World Series at Forbes Field to give the Pittsburgh Pirates a memorable triumph over the New York Yankees.

"Mickey Does It" was the banner headline atop the next day's *New York Daily News*, pushing the heart-attack death of beloved entertainer Eddie Cantor to the middle pages of the tabloid.

In the *Boston Globe*, Roger Birtwell wrote, "The Cards lost because they had a scoring opportunity."[8] Birtwell was referring to the substitutions that St. Louis manager Johnny Keane made when Tim McCarver reached first base in the top of the ninth inning on Phil Linz's egregious fielding error. One move saw Curt Simmons, who had been excellent on the mound for the visitors, forced from the game when pinch hitter Bob Skinner batted for him.

"We had to go for the run," Keane explained to reporters, who generally agreed with his situational strategy. "It was the top of the ninth, and if we scored, we only had to stop them for one inning."[9] Although McCarver eventually advanced to third base, he failed to score the go-ahead run for his team—and St. Louis had lost Simmons' services for the rest of the game. When the home half of the ninth came around, the rest of the game turned out to be just one pitch.

"It was a good pitch," insisted Cardinal catcher Tim McCarver. "It dipped the same way it's fooled lots of batters. You have to give credit to Mantle."[10] Schultz himself was understandably not in a talkative mood. He sat slumped forward in his stool in the St. Louis clubhouse, barely moving for a lengthy period of time. "It's a shame to have to throw one pitch like that,"[11] the slouching, losing pitcher mumbled to several baseball writers situated near his cubicle.

For every dramatic winner, of course, there must be a dramatic loser on the other side of the coin. According to *Sports Illustrated*'s poignant account of New York's big win, the victimized pitcher "stood on the mound, looking toward home plate for a long moment, and then he slowly walked to the dressing room, sat down and cried."[12]

Curt Simmons did not see the home run—he only heard the tremendous tumult from inside the Cardinals' clubhouse. From the roar of the crowd, he could tell right away what had happened. It was not the type of cheer that followed a base hit or even a double. Simmons instinctively knew Mantle had homered. He was not angry or bitter that his fine effort had not produced a victory for his team. He had finally pitched in a World Series—something that he had been deprived of back in 1950—and had pitched extremely well.

Even though Mantle was the obvious hero, Birtwell marveled at Jim Bouton's sensational, complete-game win for New York. "Bouton held the Cards to six hits," he penned, giving him the credit he deserved. "Now he's pitched two World Series games and only yielded two runs. In the other, he bowed, 1–0, to Don Drysdale of the Dodgers last October."[13] Bouton, however, preferred to direct the plaudits to his famous right fielder seated across the room. "There's your hero,"[14] he said as he pointed his finger in Mantle's direction.

Both Mantle and Linz chuckled that the ball that rolled between Linz's legs for an error, in a roundabout way, got Schultz on the mound in the ninth inning in place of Simmons who had done so well through eight innings against the Yankee batters. Linz admitted he casually let McCarver's ball play him instead of charging it. Mantle said, "I'm a better right-handed hitter than I am lefty. But I sure am happy the way things turned out."[15]

New York manager Yogi Berra claimed he had an inkling that Mantle would end the game as he did with his at-bat in the ninth inning. "I'm going to stand in the runway," Berra said to his right fielder as he selected a bat, "to get a head start to the clubhouse once you hit it."[16]

When Mantle was informed by a reporter from United Press International that he had surpassed Babe Ruth's record for World Series home runs, Mantle modestly commented, "I guess that adds something to it, but it would have been a big thrill anyway."[17]

Elston Howard was not reluctant to use a superlative to describe Game Three. He told *Sports Illustrated*, "I've been a Yankee for 10 years and this is my ninth World Series covering I don't know how many games. But this was the most exciting one I've ever seen, because of the way it was played and the way it ended."[18]

Whitey Ford attempted to exploit Mantle's home run for a little fun and profit at the expense of his surprisingly gullible carousing confrere. In the Yankee clubhouse, Ford told Mantle that his home-run ball had fallen from the fourth deck, and luckily for posterity, Ford had the good fortune to be situated in precisely the right spot to pick it up. It was certainly a historic MLB artifact since it had won a World Series game and gave Mantle the lifetime lead in Fall Classic home runs. Accordingly, Ford offered to sell Mantle the ball for $1,000. Mantle, without much fuss at all, agreed to his friend's price. Not long afterward, a disheveled and bedraggled fan named John Mazzarella who had been seated in the upper deck was escorted into the room by ballpark security. He possessed the *real* home run baseball—and he had the torn clothing, plus assorted cuts and bruises to prove it had taken a violent scuffle for him to secure it. He had been granted access to the Yankee clubhouse to personally present the treasure to Mantle. Despite suddenly being deprived of $1,000, Ford laughed loudly at the unexpected turn of events—as did all the other Yankees within earshot. The injured pitcher was forced to admit the ball he had tried to sell to his great friend was indeed nothing more than a fake. The amusing prank, combined with the happy faces of the winners, indicated the Yankees were now the looser of the two teams competing in the 1964 World Series.

Game Three Box Score
St. Louis Cardinals 1, New York Yankees 2
Game played on Saturday, October 10, 1964, at Yankee Stadium

St. Louis Cardinals	ab	r	h	rbi	New York Yankees	ab	r	h	rbi
Flood cf	5	0	0	0	Linz ss	4	0	0	0
Brock lf	4	0	0	0	Richardson 2b	4	0	1	0
White 1b	4	0	1	0	Maris cf	4	0	0	0
Boyer 3b	4	0	0	0	Mantle rf	3	1	2	1
Groat ss	4	0	1	0	Howard c	2	1	1	0

8. Game Three

St. Louis Cardinals	ab	r	h	rbi	New York Yankees	ab	r	h	rbi
McCarver c	2	1	1	0	Tresh lf	3	0	0	0
Shannon rf	3	0	1	0	Pepitone 1b	2	0	0	0
Maxvill 2b	3	0	1	0	Boyer 3b	3	0	1	1
Warwick ph	0	0	0	0	Bouton p	3	0	0	0
Buchek 2b	0	0	0	0	Totals	28	2	5	2
Simmons p	2	0	1	1					
Skinner ph	1	0	0	0					
Schultz p	0	0	0	0					
Totals	32	1	6	1					

St. Louis	0	0	0	0	1	0	0	0	0	– 1	6	0
New York	0	1	0	0	0	0	0	0	1	– 2	5	2

St. Louis Cardinals	IP	H	R	ER	BB	SO
Simmons	8.0	4	1	1	3	2
Schultz L (0–1)	0.0	1	1	1	0	0
Totals	8.0	5	2	2	3	2

New York Yankees	IP	H	R	ER	BB	SO
Bouton W (1–0)	9.0	6	1	0	3	2
Totals	9.0	6	1	0	3	2

E—Linz (1), Mantle (2). **DP**—St. Louis 1. **2B**—St. Louis Groat (1,off Bouton); Maxvill (1,off Bouton), New York Boyer (1,off Simmons); Mantle (2,off Simmons). **HR**—New York Mantle (1,9th inning off Schultz 0 on, 0 out). **SH**—Simmons (1,off Bouton); Shannon (1,off Bouton). **IBB**—McCarver (1,by Bouton); Howard (2,by Simmons). **IBB**—Simmons (1,Howard); Bouton (1,McCarver). **U-HP**—Ken Burkhart (NL), **1B**—Hank Soar (AL), **2B**—Vinnie Smith (NL), **3B**—Al Smith (AL), **LF**—Bill McKinley (AL), **RF**—Frank Secory (NL). **T**—2:16. **A**—67,101.

— 9 —

Game Four
October 11

> "This is the most unpredictable sport of all. I've been trying to figure it out for years. But the more I do, the more confusing it gets."[1]
> —Pittsburgh manager Danny Murtaugh

The baseball world was still talking about the heroics of Mickey Mantle in Game Three as the fourth contest of the 1964 World Series approached. It began a lovely, sunny Sunday afternoon at Yankee Stadium, but the temperature dropped rapidly once the action began. Hot coffee rather than cold soft drinks became the beverage of choice for the fans. Nevertheless, the mood of the home crowd was greatly improved with the home team now leading the Series two games to one after Mantle's game-winning blast the previous afternoon.

Al Downing was on the Yankee Stadium mound for the home team to begin Game Four. Whitey Ford, the Game One starter, was originally slated to be the Yankee starter for this game too, but he was nursing a bruised heel—at least that was the official medical reason the team offered to the media. Accordingly, it was reported that after New York had won Game Three, Yogi Berra decided to give Ford an extra day's rest and penciled in Downing as the starting pitcher. A 23-year-old strikeout artist from Trenton, New Jersey, Downing threw harder than anyone else on the Yankee staff and whiffed 217 AL batters in 1964—a total that led his league that season. It was the most strikeouts for any Yankee pitcher since the days of Jack Chesbro at the turn of the 20th century. Chesbro had struck out 239 batters in 1904. That was the year he won the amazing total of 41 games.

Curt Flood led off Game Four for St. Louis. He was retired on a rare 1-6-3 putout as Flood's ground ball was deflected by Downing to shortstop Phil Linz. The latter fired the ball to Joe Pepitone at first base to just

9. Game Four

nip the fast-running Flood. The second Cardinal to bat was Lou Brock. He grounded out to third baseman Clete Boyer. Dick Groat did the same as Downing cruised through the first inning. The Cardinals' bats, generally, had not produced much in the first three games of the Series. That trend was continuing.

Ray Sadecki, the victorious Cardinal pitcher from Game One, was back on the mound in Game Four. His specialty was a palm ball that acted like a sinker when it was working as planned. In 1964, he became the first lefthanded St. Louis pitcher in 11 years to win 20 games in a season. However, Johnny Keane knew Sadecki, despite winning it, had struggled with the Yankees in Game One. Keane was not going to give him a lot of wiggle room if he got into trouble. Before Sadecki had thrown one pitch, the Cardinal manager warned pitcher Roger Craig to be ready to enter the game on very short notice for some very long relief work.

The first batter Sadecki faced in Game Four was shortstop Phil Linz. He hit a flare that fell into right field for a hit. Linz alertly used his speed to extend it into a double as right fielder Mike Shannon, who was playing Linz deep, had to run a long way to collect the ball. With Bobby Richardson batting, Linz attempted to steal third base. It should have been an easy out for St. Louis as Ken Boyer; the third baseman had the ball well ahead of the Yankee runner. However, Linz put on the brakes and retreated toward second base. Boyer slipped slightly and made a terrible throw towards the bag that ended up in center field. Linz quickly reversed his direction again and moved up to third base. Boyer was properly charged with an error on the play—the first one committed by a Cardinal in the 1964 World Series. Not long afterward, Yankee second baseman Bobby Richardson got his third RBI of the World Series when he smacked a double into left field. New York had quickly established a 1–0 lead—and Sadecki was in trouble early.

Things got worse for the Cardinal starter as Roger Maris' fly ball to right field dropped to the turf for a base hit as Mike Shannon, on the full run, could not get to it in time to make a catch. Richardson had to stay near second base as he thought the ball would be caught. Richardson moved to third base, however, once he saw it fall to the ground. Mickey Mantle got a huge ovation as he came to the plate for New York. Batting right-handed, he hit a line drive into right-center field. Richardson scored easily to make the score 2–0. Maris advanced to third on the hit, but Mantle was thrown out at second base trying to extend his hit into a two-bagger. Shannon's throw had been a beauty. The Associated Press labeled Mantle's baserunning as overly aggressive. Decades later, author David Halberstam called it foolish. The tag on the sliding Mantle was applied by Cardinal second baseman Dal Maxvill.

Ray Sadecki had faced four New York batters, thrown just 10 pitches, and surrendered four hits. St. Louis manager Johnny Keane had seen enough from his ineffective starter. Roger Craig, a well-traveled right-hander, took the mound to replace the battered Sadecki. The first Yankee batter the 34-year-old faced was catcher Elston Howard. He too got a base hit, a blooper hit off his fists that gently fell into right field. Maris scored easily from third base. New York's lead was now 3–0. Craig finally stopped a Yankee from reaching base. Tom Tresh struck out, ending the Yankees hitting streak at five consecutive batters. First baseman Joe Pepitone followed Tresh in the batting order. He flied out to Mike Shannon in right field for the third out of the inning, but the home team had scored three runs in their first at-bats of Game Four. The large Yankee Stadium crowd of slightly more than 66,000 patrons was greatly pleased with how things were unfolding early in the contest.

Al Downing struck out Ken Boyer, another Cardinal who was struggling at the plate, to start the top of the second inning. First baseman Bill White grounded out to New York shortstop Phil Linz for the second out. Mike Shannon struck out swinging at a Downing fastball to end another fruitless inning for St. Louis. The Yankees took their 3–0 lead into the home half of the second inning.

Roger Craig knew when he replaced Ray Sadecki with one out in the first inning that his task was to be akin to an emergency starting pitcher. Accordingly, he set out to be as effective on the mound for as long as possible. He certainly had an efficient second inning where he delivered pitches at various speeds and the movement on the ball challenged the Yankee batters. Third baseman Clete Boyer struck out. Pitcher Al Downing, who threw left but batted right, was a .176 hitter in the regular season. He struck out on three pitches. Leadoff hitter Phil Linz was retired on a strikeout as well. He was called out looking by umpire Hank Soar. Roger Craig had struck out the side, and raised his whiff total to four since replacing Sadecki. Even the partisan Yankee Stadium crowd applauded Craig's pitching feat.

Al Downing had skillfully set down the Cardinals in the first two innings without allowing a runner to reach first base. In the third inning, Tim McCarver, who was batting .444 in the World Series (4-for-9), did not get a hit, either. He flied out to Roger Maris in center field, making it seven straight Cardinals who had not gotten aboard. Dal Maxvill ended that skein; he drew a walk on a 3–2 pitch to become the first St. Louis baserunner. Pitcher Roger Craig was the next Cardinal batter. Craig made good contact, but he flied out to Maris for the second out. Curt Flood, who had just two hits in 15 at-bats in the World Series, broke his slump by dropping a Texas Leaguer into left-center field. Maxvill moved up to second

9. Game Four

base on the play. It was St. Louis' first hit of the game. The Cardinal threat died quickly, however, when Lou Brock also flied out to Maris. The Yankee center fielder had been a busy man as he made all three of the putouts in the top of the third inning—tying a World Series record by doing so, of course. New York still held its 3–0 advantage over St. Louis heading into the home half of the third.

Bobby Richardson, who already had six hits in the World Series, led off the bottom of the third for New York. He did not get his seventh. The Yankee second baseman grounded out softly to Cardinal third baseman Ken Boyer for the first out. Roger Maris followed Richardson. He hit a ground ball directly back at pitcher Roger Craig. The St. Louis hurler gloved it and made the easy throw to first base for the second out of the inning. Mickey Mantle walked on four pitches. Elston Howard, with five hits thus far in the Series, also walked on four pitches. Switch-hitter Tom Tresh, batting left-handed, drew another ball from Craig, but the inning ended when Mickey Mantle was picked off second base on a splendid timing play. Shortstop Dick Groat applied the tag. Announcer Curt Gowdy, knowledgeable in baseball history, said it was exactly the same type of pickoff play that the Cleveland Indians used so frequently and masterfully in their pennant-winning season in 1948. "Craig's throw was right on the money,"[2] NBC's Harry Caray interjected. Groat later told the press that he had helped lull Mantle into being careless by pleasantly chatting with him about his mammoth home run the previous day. Mantle was not very happy about being embarrassed that way.

By sheer luck, Dick Groat led off the fourth inning for St. Louis and struck out. Next up was Ken Boyer who flied out to Tom Tresh in left field. Tresh had to battle the sun but he made the catch without too much difficulty. Bill White then lined out to Mickey Mantle in right field. Again, the Cardinals failed to score. New York still maintained their 3–0 lead.

Tom Tresh, who was left at the plate when Mickey Mantle was picked off second base to end the home half of the third, batted for New York to start the bottom of the fourth inning. He struck out, giving Roger Craig a total of five whiffs in the game. Joe Pepitone, a pull-hitter who belted 28 home runs in 1964, batted next for New York. He drew a walk after being visibly upset at a strike call by AL plate umpire Hank Soar. Clete Boyer knocked a base hit into center field to move Pepitone to second base with one out. It was the sixth Yankee hit of the game. Pitcher Al Downing was the next New York hitter. He got a long round of applause when he stepped into the batter's box. The Cardinal defense anticipated a bunt and had White and Boyer play well in front of their respective bases. Instead, Downing swung away three times and missed the ball three times to become another Craig strikeout victim. Leadoff hitter Phil Linz, New

York's shortstop, followed Downing to the plate. Linz struck out on a deceptive, low curveball for Craig's third whiff of the inning and seventh of the game. The Yankees were finding Craig to be a tough pitcher to solve. After four innings of Game Four, New York was still ahead, 3–0, however.

"Roger Craig has done a brilliant job shutting down the Yankees. Now it's up to his teammates to get him some runs,"[3] Curt Gowdy stated to his radio audience. The Cardinal bats again did not come through, however. Mike Shannon struck out to lead off the top of the fifth frame. It was the fifth strikeout for Al Downing. Tim McCarver bounced out to Joe Pepitone who made an unassisted putout at first base for the second St. Louis out of the inning. Dal Maxvill flied out to Mickey Mantle in right field to conclude things for the visitors in the fifth.

Harry Caray took over behind the NBC play-by-play microphone from Curt Gowdy when the Yankees batted in the bottom of the fifth inning. They went down quickly. Bobby Richardson, 6-for 16 in the World Series thus far, smacked a line drive that required Cardinal third baseman Ken Boyer to making a leaping catch for the first out. Roger Maris made the second out when he flied out to Lou Brock in deep left-center field on the first pitch he saw from Roger Craig. Mickey Mantle followed. He struck out on a slow curve ball. It was the eighth strikeout for Craig who had been nothing short of superb since relieving Ray Sadecki in the first inning when the Yankees were threatening to run away with the game. In 4⅔ innings of work, Craig had allowed no runs and just two harmless hits to New York.

Roger Craig's labors for the afternoon ceased when Carl Warwick pinch hit for him in the top of the sixth inning. Batting a perfect 1.000 in the Series, the seemingly unstoppable Warwick drilled a base hit into left field. The single was his third pinch hit success of the 1964 World Series in three at-bats. (He had also walked once.) That feat tied a record for most pinch hits in one World Series, set by Bobby Brown of the 1947 New York Yankees—and this was only Game Four. Curt Flood batted next for St. Louis and lined a hard single into right field that advanced Warwick to second base. "The Cardinal fans in Yankee Stadium are making a little noise,"[4] commented Harry Caray. That was actually an understatement. Indeed, the excited din of the noisy minority of Cardinal supporters was clearly audible on NBC radio. To a listener hearing the broadcast today, it almost sounds as if Game Four were a home game for St. Louis.

The next batter, Lou Brock, flied out to Roger Maris in center field on a full count for the first out. Dick Groat then got an enormous break. Slow-footed for his position, he hit what should have been a simple double-play grounder to Bobby Richardson, but somehow it turned into an adventure: As he attempted to shovel the ball to shortstop Phil Linz who was covering second base, the Yankee second baseman could not quickly get the ball out of his glove. By the time he did, his relay to Linz was off target—and everyone was safe. After some delay, the play was ruled an error on Richardson.

It turned out to be a tremendously costly gaffe as the next batter, Ken Boyer, perfectly timed a changeup from Al Downing and drove a grand slam home run high into Yankee Stadium's left field seats. It was fair by just a few feet, perhaps because of the prevailing breeze blowing fly balls toward right field. It was the ninth bases-clearing home run in World Series history—and Boyer was only the second NL hitter to achieve the feat. (Six of the seven AL players were Yankees!) "The happiest Cardinal of all four who scored on the shot was Groat, who danced and pranced around the bases like an overjoyed schoolboy," declared Al Abrams in his column in the next day's *Pittsburgh-Post Gazette*. From his spot in the visitors' dugout, St. Louis manager Johnny Keane did not have a very good view of where the ball was headed. But he instinctually yelled, "Stay fair!" twice. Suddenly the visiting Redbirds were ahead in Game Four, 4–3. With the crowd still buzzing about the dramatic shift in the game, Bill White fouled out to catcher Elston Howard and Mike Shannon flied out to Roger Maris to end the inning, but the damage had been done. Boyer's homer would prove to be the turning point of the entire 1964 World Series.

The Yankees were now trailing for the first time in Game Four. With Roger Craig having been removed for a pinch hitter, he was replaced on the mound by Ron Taylor, a 27-year-old sinkerball pitcher from Toronto. Harry Caray said, "Craig did a magnificent job in relief,"[5] which was undeniably true. Elston Howard, the first Yankee to bat in the bottom of the sixth, bounced out easily to St. Louis first baseman Bill White. Tom Tresh struck out for the third time in a row for the second Yankee out. Joe Pepitone grounded out to second baseman Dal Maxvill for the third out.

Tim McCarver, the St. Louis catcher, led off the top of the seventh inning. He drew a four-pitch walk off Al Downing—the second base on balls he had issued in Game Four. The next Cardinal hitter, Dal Maxvill, got two balls from Downing. The pitcher then got a mound visit from both catcher Elston Howard and his manager, Yogi Berra. Downing's afternoon was over. Pete Mikkelsen came into the game to face Maxvill who had a 2–0 count. Curt Gowdy informed fans that Mikkelson was a surprise even to make the Yankee roster in 1964, but he was so impressive in spring training that he earned a spot on the MLB team. Maxvill grounded to Bobby Richardson. This time the Yankee second baseman got the ball out of his glove and threw to first base for the out. McCarver moved to second base on the fielder's choice. Ron Taylor batted next and struck out. Curt Flood hit a hot smash to Clete Boyer at third base. The Yankee Boyer brother knocked down the ball and threw out Flood at first base to retire the side. St. Louis did not add to their one-run lead. Heading into the seventh-inning stretch, the Cards still led, 4–3.

Clete Boyer led off the home half of the seventh inning for New York against Ron Taylor. On the second pitch he saw, Boyer popped out to Bill White, the Cardinal first baseman, in foul territory. Johnny Blanchard was sent in to pinch hit for New York pitcher Pete Mikkelson. Blanchard flied out to Curt Flood to quickly become the second out. Phil Linz attempted to reach base via a bunt down the third-base line. However, Ken Boyer played it well and threw out Linz at first base. St. Louis was still enjoying a 4–3 lead after seven full innings had entered the books.

Ralph Terry, the hero of a previous World Series for the Yankees, got the call to replace Pete Mikkelson who had been lifted for a pinch hitter in the previous frame. (Terry, an Oklahoman, was the winning pitcher in the seventh game of the 1962 Fall Classic versus the San Francisco Giants. He threw a 1–0 shutout that afternoon at Candlestick Park. He had a difficult 1964 season, but the World Series was Terry's fifth.) Lou Brock was the first batter that Terry faced. Brock was struggling at the plate, batting .125, with just two hits in 16 official at-bats in the World Series. His woes continued. Terry struck him out swinging. Dick Groat was the next Cardinal batter. He poked a single into right-center field. Ken Boyer got a surprisingly huge cheer when he batted after Groat. He was not at bat very long. Boyer hit into a 4–6–3 double play to end the inning.

Bobby Richardson led off the bottom of the eighth versus Ron Taylor. Harry Caray told his NBC radio listeners, "This could be the key inning of the ballgame because Richardson, Maris and Mantle come up."[6] Richardson bounced out to shortstop Dick Groat. Maris looked to have gotten a base hit off Taylor, but Groat made a terrific defensive play. He ventured well to his left behind second base to scoop up Maris' ground ball. Groat then made an accurate throw to first baseman Bill White for the putout. Many impressed Yankee fans responded with a standing ovation for the St. Louis infielder's fine effort. "That's the kind of thrill that makes baseball first in popularity!" Harry Caray would later state when doing the narration for the official 1964 World Series film for MLB. An air of hopeful expectation accompanied Mickey Mantle to the plate. After a long at-bat, in which Mantle fouled off a couple of 3–2 pitches, the great Yankee slugger drew a walk off Taylor. Mantle became the first Yankee to reach base in Game Four since the fourth inning. Taylor regained his composure and struck out Elston Howard, stranding Mantle at first base. With an inning left to play, St. Louis was still in front, 4–3.

9. Game Four

Ralph Terry began the top of the ninth inning by facing Bill White, the Cardinal first baseman, who was a miserable 1-for-14 at the plate in the World Series. White went down swinging, lowering his batting average further. He was the seventeenth man (both teams included) to go down on strikes in Game Four. Mike Shannon was next up to face Terry. He flied out to Roger Maris in center field. Tim McCarver followed Shannon, but the St. Louis catcher lined a single into center field. McCarver was stranded on base when Dal Maxvill struck out. The Cardinals were three defensive outs away from leveling the 1964 World Series at two games apiece.

Tom Tresh led off the bottom of the ninth inning. Tresh had struck out three times in Game Four already. He tried something new—a drag bunt—but it went directly to Taylor on the mound. Taylor made the easy throw to Bill White at first base for the first out of the inning. Joe Pepitone batted next. He hit a ground ball to White. The St. Louis first baseman outraced Pepitone to the bag for the second out. Clete Boyer came to the plate representing the Yankees' final hope. He too grounded out to Bill White. The Cardinals trotted off the field as the 4–3 victors of Game Four. The win evened the World Series at two games apiece and ensured it would return to Busch Stadium in St. Louis for at least Game Six, and perhaps Game Seven. Ron Taylor had hurled four hitless innings of relief. He walked just one batter—and that was when he cautiously pitched Mickey Mantle well out of the strike zone.

The Associated Press encapsulated the goings-on with the following lead, "Ken Boyer's grand slam homer, Bobby Richardson's messed up double play ball, and stout relief pitching by Roger Craig and Ron Taylor squared the World Series for the St. Louis Cardinals on Sunday with a 4–3 victory over the New York Yankees."[7]

The next day's *New York Times* summarized Game Four this way:

> One swing of the bat and eight innings of scoreless relief pitching enabled the St. Louis Cardinals yesterday to even the 1964 World Series at two games apiece.
>
> Ken Boyer's home run with the bases filled provided all the Cardinal runs in a 4–3 victory over the New York Yankees before a crowd of 66,312 at Yankee Stadium. And it turned a developing rout back into a closely contested series.

Al Abrams, covering the World Series for the *Pittsburgh Post-Gazette*, believed that Game Four was a great example of why baseball played at its highest level in a sport that captivates millions of fans. "There were the mighty Yankees pounding out five hits for a 3–0 lead in the first inning," he wrote, "and to all intents and purposes, well on their way to an easy victory, the third of the World Series over the shell-shocked St. Louis Cardinals." Abrams continued,

Suddenly, and without warning, New York's big guns stopped booming against St. Louis relief pitching. Only one puny single, this by light-hitting Clete Boyer, was produced the rest of the way. And, of course, no more runs.

There too was Al Downing, a chunky southpaw, spinning a one-hitter through the first five innings, while holding down what looked a comfortable 3–0 lead. Then came the explosion....[8]

Sports Illustrated described the game's dramatic shift in momentum this way:

As quick as you can say Linz, Richardson, Maris and Mantle—all of whom got consecutive hits—starting pitcher Ray Sadecki was out of the fourth game and the Yankees had a 2–0 lead. Keane brought in Roger Craig. Howard hit Craig's first pitch for a single ... making the score 3–0, but also driving in the last Yankee run of the game. Thereafter, except for a brief lapse in the third, Craig's curve worked beautifully.[9]

During the game, NBC's Harry Caray had labeled Cardinal pitcher Roger Craig "baseball's biggest loser"[10]—a comment that sounded far worse than the broadcaster meant—before heaping praise on him for his terrific relief job which earned him the win in Game Four. Caray was alluding to Craig's reputation as a good pitcher who did not get many wins. That certainly may have been the case because Craig had been on the roster of the horrendous 1962 and 1963 New York Mets. In both those season he led the NL in games lost. In his first season with the famously inept expansion club, Craig had 10 victories against 24 losses, which meant he had accounted for a quarter of the team's 40 wins that year. In the latter season, Craig compiled a miserable record of just five wins against 22 losses. But his ERA was a passable 3.78 in 1963, so most of those losses could be attributed to being associated with a terrible team. "I lost a lot of ballgames," he admitted, "but I had 27 complete games in those two years." He also noted, " I started the first game the New York Mets ever played."[11] Prior to his two-year stint with the Mets, Craig had been a capable pitcher with both the Brooklyn and Los Angeles Dodgers from 1955 to 1961, where he twice achieved double digits in victories. In 1959, a season when the Dodgers won the World Series, Craig was 11–5 and had a 2.06 ERA. He finished 13th in his league's MVP voting despite having spent part of the season in the minors with the Spokane Indians. The Cardinals did well to ignore Craig's misleading stats and trade for him after the 1963 season. St. Louis parted with two players, George Altman and Bill Wakefield, to acquire Craig.

Harold Kaese of the *Boston Globe* noted that the Yankees were an unhappy bunch after the game. Most of them—but not all—retreated to the sanctuary of an annex of their clubhouse once the game concluded and

9. Game Four

were unavailable for comment. Two Yankees did not hide. One of them was second baseman Bobby Richardson, the man who made a mess of the double-play ball that should have ended the top of the sixth inning before Ken Boyer had a chance to hit his grand slam home run for the visitors. Richardson, a perennial Gold Glove winner, lingered in the main area for media interviews and dutifully answered reporters' questions. The other talkative Yankee was shortstop Phil Linz. "A toast for their consideration, good manners, and understanding," wrote the impressed Kaese, "for they were the two goats of the game." With great admiration, Kaese continued,

> Richardson did not admit—he CLAIMED that he was the malefactor. Where others yell for credit, he shouted for blame. Linz, he said, was a non-accessory to the crime—practically an innocent bystander.
>
> Noted for the high quality of his playing and his moral standards, Richardson is an outstanding second baseman and a YMCA worker. Baseball could stand more YMCA workers.[12]

Indeed, when Richardson explained what had happened on the play, he took full responsibility for the mess. "It was my fault," he insisted, "not Linz's. He had nothing to do with it. I didn't field the ball cleanly. It was between bounces. It was caught in the web and I messed up his timing. I gave him the ball too late and it was behind him. I threw the ball with my glove."[13]

Linz agreed with Richardson's description of the play. "I was reaching back for [the ball] when Flood [who has sliding hard into second base] hit me. The ball hit the tip of my glove. I was trying to keep my foot on the base. Flood might have been safe. If I'd got the ball, I don't think I could have made the double play."[14]

Dick Groat was the most relieved man in a St. Louis uniform when he realized that no one was put out on the seemingly routine play. He admitted, "I thought it was a double play when the ball left my bat."[15]

Yankee Manager Yogi Berra later explained to the *New York Times* that he was on the verge of removing his starting pitcher when Groat had his fateful at-bat. Said Berra, "If Groat had gotten a hit, Downing was out. I had Ralph Terry ready to face Ken Boyer and Steve Hamilton for the lefthander [Bill White] after that."[16] But Groat had reached on an error— not a hit—so Berra figured Downing had done his job capably and left him in the game to face Ken Boyer.

The AP scribe whose game report ran in the *Montreal Gazette* the following day without a byline, emphasized that Ken Boyer had made an amateurish throwing blunder in the first inning that eventually led to three Yankee runs being scored before he made amends in a big way. He wrote, "Thus, with one sweep of his bat, the most famous of the seven ball-playing brothers from Alba, Missouri, shed the goat's horns for the hero's mantle."[17]

As for Boyer's decisive home run, journalist Keane questioned the wisdom of Al Downing throwing the powerful St. Louis third baseman a changeup in that situation, given his track record with that pitch. "Downing this season has lost a half dozen games on late-inning home runs," the scribe penned. "Felix Mantilla and Lee Thomas of the Red Sox both beat him with home runs like this one in recent weeks."[18] He noted that Downing did Boyer a huge favor by throwing him a slow pitch against a hitting background at Yankee Stadium that was notoriously difficult for batters with thousands of fans sitting in the center field bleachers. "It's the worst I've ever hit against,"[19] said Dick Groat who had to deal with it during the 1960 World Series, too. Curt Flood agreed with his teammate. Flood added, "With the sun on those seats behind him, the pitcher looks like a silhouette."[20]

St. Louis manager Johnny Keane had a different gripe—the color of the AL baseballs. He claimed those he had seen in the first two World Series games at Yankee Stadium were markedly darker than what his club was used to playing with in NL games. "We use white balls in our league," grumbled the Cardinal pilot. "What kind of mud do they use to rub up balls here? It can't be National League mud."[21]

Curt Flood was not at all surprised by the way the game unfolded. He said to the media afterward, "When the Yankees got those three runs in the first inning, it whacked our butts. We play better when we have to come from behind, because we're a team that keeps bouncing. We've been bouncing all year."[22]

With the minimum four games in the books, it was now possible to at least reasonably estimate what the winning and losing World Series shares would be for the players. It was roughly calculated that a member of the winning team would get a check for a figure close to $8,800 while a member of the losing side would receive a consolation prize of about $5,700. Those figures were based on a pool of $732,523.13. To avoid any hint of collusion or other shenanigans that might artificially extend the Fall Classic, the players' pool in the World Series is always based on the receipts from the first four games only.

The Cardinals' victory in Game Four did not impress Big Magic, the Philadelphia-based Honeywell 1400 computer that had predicted a seven-game Yankee triumph slightly less than a week earlier. After factoring in the latest result, the machine still figured the New Yorkers had a 60 percent chance to win the World Series and a 57 percent chance to take Game Five at Yankee Stadium on Monday.

Al Abrams, sports editor of the *Pittsburgh Post-Gazette,* reported that when New York was up 3–0 at the end of the fifth inning, an unnamed reporter in the Yankee Stadium press box declared, "I don't think anyone but the Cardinals are going back to St. Louis from here." Abrams wrote, "Heads [of other reporters] nodded like pigeons in agreement. A New York win would put them one game away from being champions." The fact that the Cardinals scored four runs in the top of the sixth inning for a comeback win pleased him and many vocal St. Louis supporters to no end. "It was a popular victory the Cards scored," Abrams added. "Aside from the hatred fans hold for the perennial successful Yankees, most of the crowd was rooting for Johnny Keane...."[23]

Game Four Box Score
St. Louis Cardinals 4, New York Yankees 3
Game played on Sunday, October 11, 1964, at Yankee Stadium

St. Louis Cardinals	ab	r	h	rbi	New York Yankees	ab	r	h	rbi
Flood cf	4	1	2	0	Linz ss	4	1	1	0
Brock lf	4	0	0	0	Richardson 2b	4	1	1	1
Groat ss	4	1	1	0	Maris cf	4	1	1	0
Boyer 3b	4	1	1	4	Mantle rf	2	0	1	1
White 1b	4	0	0	0	Howard c	3	0	1	1
Shannon rf	4	0	0	0	Tresh lf	4	0	0	0
McCarver c	3	0	1	0	Pepitone 1b	3	0	0	0
Maxvill 2b	3	0	0	0	Boyer 3b	4	0	1	0
Sadecki p	0	0	0	0	Downing p	2	0	0	0
Craig p	1	0	0	0	Mikkelsen p	0	0	0	0
Warwick ph	1	1	1	0	Blanchard ph	1	0	0	0
Taylor p	1	0	0	0	Terry p	0	0	0	0
Totals	33	4	6	4	**Totals**	31	3	6	3

St. Louis	0	0	0	0	0	4	0	0	0	– 4	6 1
New York	3	0	0	0	0	0	0	0	0	– 3	6 1

St. Louis Cardinals	IP	H	R	ER	BB	SO
Sadecki	0.1	4	3	2	0	0
Craig W (1–0)	4.2	2	0	0	3	8
Taylor SV (1)	4.0	0	0	0	1	2
Totals	9.0	6	3	2	4	10

New York Yankees	IP	H	R	ER	BB	SO
Downing L (0–1)	6.0	4	4	3	2	4
Mikkelsen	1.0	0	0	0	0	1
Terry	2.0	2	0	0	0	3
Totals	9.0	6	4	3	2	8

E—Boyer (1), Richardson (1). **DP**—New York 1. **2B**—New York Linz (1,off Sadecki); Richardson (2,off Sadecki). **HR**—St. Louis Boyer (1,6th inning off Downing 3 on, 1 out). **CS**—Linz (1,3rd base by Sadecki/McCarver). **U-HP**—Hank Soar (AL), **1B**—Vinnie Smith (NL), **2B**—Al Smith (AL), **3B**—Frank Secory (NL), **LF**—Ken Burkhart (NL), **RF**—Bill McKinley (AL). **T**—2:18. **A**—66,312.

— 10 —

"Let's All Play What's My Line?"

> "...Now will our mystery guest enter and sign in, please."—John Daly

On the night of October 11, 1964, the hugely popular panel/game show *What's My Line?* aired live, as usual, from CBS studios in New York City. Despite its unfavorable time slot of 10:30 on Sundays, the 30-minute television program did very well in the Nielsen ratings for more than a decade.

The object of the game was simple: With distinguished moderator John Daly running the show, four panelists, using questions that could only be answered yes or no, tried to divulge the occupation of a challenger. If the challenger managed to accrue 10 "no" answers, the game was over—and he or she would win a whopping $50. (The puny prize money never changed over the years.) At least that was how the regular portion of the game was played. At or near the end of the program, with the panelists blindfolded, a famous "mystery challenger" would enter as a contestant. The panel, using the same questioning rules, simply had to identify him or her. Sometimes it was two or more celebrities who appeared as a group, such as Lucille Ball and Desi Arnaz; the Harlem Globetrotters; or the cast from the Broadway production of *The Sound of Music*. Being a *WML* mystery guest, on some level, certified one's celebrity status as genuine and mainstream.

The program ran for a remarkable 17½ years from February 1950 to September 1967. Its success spawned a few imitators, the most enduring of which were *To Tell the Truth* and *I've Got a Secret*. Occasionally there were two mystery-guest segments on a single show. October 11, 1964 was one such instance. Comedienne Phyllis Diller appeared as the regular mystery challenger at the end of the program. Opening the show, however, were baseball's battling brothers from the ongoing World Series, Ken and Clete Boyer—who were scheduled to play Game Five in about 14 hours. Here is how things went.

Host John Daly announced there would be some surprises on the program. Blindfolds would be necessary for the first challenger's visit. The brothers walked in. The applause from the studio audience is reserved at first, perhaps because the Boyers are both wearing civilian clothing. But when the brothers write their names with chalk on the framed poster board—a peculiar custom of *WML*—the cheering grows to thunderous proportions. They jointly sign in as "Cletis and Ken Boyer." The graphic on the screen identifies them as "The Boyer Brothers." Both men sit next to John Daly's right. To TV viewers, Clete sits to the left of Ken. The graphic on the screen now says "World Series 3rd Basemen." The studio audience loudly applauds again.

Panelist Dorothy Kilgallen quickly asks if the mystery guest is part of the entertainment or sports world and gets an affirmative answer from Ken. When she narrows it down to sports, Clete says yes. Dorthy also figures out there is more than one person and they have something to do with baseball and the ongoing 1964 World Series.

The Boyers take turns answering questions, which causes some amusing confusion among both Kilgallen and Sammy Davis, Jr.

Arlene Francis, a big baseball fan, deduces that both teams are represented. Somewhat oddly, Arlene does not put the pieces together. It takes Bennett Cerf to identify the "mystery guest" as both Boyer brothers.

In the follow-up discussion the brothers say they are just two of seven Boyers who have played professional baseball at some level.

When asked if their father was athletic, Clete cheekily says his dad fathered 13 children so he was good in one particular field. The slightly risqué remark brings howls of laughter from the studio audience, the panel, and John Daly.

When Daly composes himself, he opines that the yet-to-be completed World Series has been one of the best ever. Bennett Cerf agrees and says he was pleased that a former Met, Roger Craig, was the pitching hero in the game played earlier that day. Ken concurs.

John Day wraps things up by wishing both Boyer brothers good luck … and Arlene Francis advises them to get right to bed.

Authors' note: This was not the first game show that Clete Boyer was on in 1964. On January 13 he appeared as an imposter on *To Tell the Truth*, pretending to be a sponge diver. He was a convincing liar. Three of the four panelists wrongly thought Boyer was the real thing!

— 11 —

Game Five

October 12

> "In the fifth game the Yankees saw the real Bob Gibson. The advantage of [Gibson] pitching in the shadows of the Stadium and against the background of the center-field bleachers made it all the more difficult for the hitters to pick up his ball."[1]—David Halberstam

With the 1964 World Series tied at two games apiece, Curt Gowdy welcomed his NBC radio audience to the broadcast. He reported that the temperature in New York City was back in the sixties for the Monday afternoon of Game Five and the wind was not nearly as prevalent as it had been the previous day. The big news story entering the game, said Gowdy, was that New York pitching star Whitey Ford was still sidelined with a bruised heel. He had been scheduled to start Game Four on Sunday, but the injury delayed his second start appearance to Game Five. Ford was still unable to go on Monday, too, so Mel Stottlemyre, a right-handed sinker-ball artist, was called upon to reprise his role as a starter. He had been the Yankees pitcher in Game Two at Busch Stadium in St. Louis—which he deservedly won, 8–3—to bring the Yankees back to level terms after they had dropped the opener.

Gowdy also reported what that day's morning newspapers were saying: Many of the visiting Cardinals were displeased with the hitting background they encountered in Yankee Stadium. Famous and historic as the baseball venue was, the Cards were glad that Monday afternoon's game would be the last one they had to play in New York's home ballpark in this World Series.

Harry Caray said the Series being level at two games apiece was justified by the closeness of the two teams' statistics from the first four games. The most basic of them was runs scored. The Yankees had 18 to St. Louis' 17.

Mel Stottlemyre took the mound shortly after 1 p.m. and began Game Five poorly. Center fielder Curt Flood, who was having a subpar Series at the plate, drew a walk. That marked a milestone for the visiting club: It was the first time that St. Louis' leadoff batter in any of the five games had reached base by any manner in the 1964 World Series. Lou Brock followed Flood to the plate. He was called out on strikes and angrily argued the point with NL plate umpire Vinnie Smith. Bill White, the Cardinal first baseman, struck out too. He looked bad in chasing a low curveball that was well out of the strike zone. Ken Boyer, the Game Four hero for St. Louis for his timely grand slam homer, got a respectful cheer from the New York crowd when he came to bat. He apparently bounced into a force play to shortstop Fred Linz to end the inning. The Yankees, thinking they had made the third out, understandably began to trot off the field. However, the home plate umpire put a halt to that. Harry Caray saw plate umpire gesticulating with his arms seconds before he was going to send the NBC radio broadcast to a commercial. The 48-year-old Smith had called interference on New York catcher Elston Howard, who had touched Boyer's bat during the latter's swing. The Yankees did not dispute Smith's call. By rule, Boyer was awarded first base while Flood moved to second base—and Elston Howard was charged with an error on the play. For those fans who enjoyed scoring the game at home, Harry Caray informed the NBC radio audience that Boyer was not charged with an at-bat on the baseball rarity. It certainly had the puzzled crowd buzzing once stadium announcer Bob Sheppard informed them what had happened and why the inning was continuing. Caray's broadcast partner, Curt Gowdy, who called games for both the network and the Boston Red Sox interjected, "I haven't seen that for years in the American League during the regular season, Harry."[2] Caray told Gowdy he had seen it happen three times in covering Cardinals games in 1964 alone—and all three catcher's interference calls occurred while Julián Javier had been batting. When play resumed, Cardinal shortstop Dick Groat drew a walk on a full count to load the bases. St. Louis catcher Tim McCarver did not take advantage of the opportunity to knock in a run or two. He struck out swinging, thus the atypical rules transgression by catcher Howard did not punish the hometown Yankees in the end.

The fearsome Bob Gibson was the Cardinals' starting pitcher for Game Five. He had been the losing pitcher in Game Two at Busch Stadium. According to an article published in the *St. Louis Post-Dispatch* the next day, Gibson privately complained to backup catcher Bob Uecker that he was battling the flu and had not slept well. Uecker did his best to convince Gibson he would be fine once the game was underway. Yankee shortstop Phil Linz, who was batting .250 in the World Series, struck out swinging on a curve ball for the first out. A curve ball did not fool Bobby

11. Game Five

Richardson, however. He followed Linz by solidly hitting one into center field for a line drive single. Roger Maris batted third for New York. He hit the ball into the ground to the right side of the infield, which resulted in a 4-6-3 double play being niftily turned by the Cardinals. Game Five was scoreless after one inning.

Mike Shannon led off the top of the second inning for St. Louis. He broke his bat as he bounced out to Clete Boyer at third base. Dal Maxvill came up and lined the first pitch he saw into right field. Mickey Mantle fielded the ball quickly to dissuade Maxvill from attempting to advance to second base. Next up, in the ninth spot in the Cardinal batting order, was pitcher Bob Gibson. He painfully fouled Stottlemyre's first pitch off his foot. Gibson fouled off several more pitches before whiffing on a curve ball. Stottlemyre had efficiently recorded four strikeouts already. Curt Flood, batting for the second time in the game, hit into a fielder's choice (shortstop Phil Linz to Bobby Richardson at second base) for the third out. Zeroes remained in the runs column on the Yankee Stadium scoreboard.

Mickey Mantle was the first Yankee batter to face Bob Gibson in the home half of the second inning. Gibson pitched the New York slugger very carefully—and walked Mantle on four pitches. Harry Caray told NBC's radio listeners that Mantle, despite his ailing legs, was still a threat to steal second base. Mantle did not need to do that; he trotted to the next bag as Elston Howard was hit by a Gibson pitch. Without the benefit of a hit, the Yankees now had runners at first and second with none out. First baseman Joe Pepitone came to the plate next. He hit a slow bouncer toward the mound. Having no chance to retire either Mantle or Howard, Gibson fielded the ball and ran it himself to first base to put out Pepitone. With first base empty and one out, St. Louis manager Johnny Keane opted to intentionally walk Tom Tresh to load the bases with Clete Boyer, the number-eight hitter in the Yankee order, coming to bat. With the St. Louis infield playing in, Gibson did his job and struck out Boyer on a high curveball. It was a big second out for the visitors. New York pitcher Mel Stottlemyre followed Boyer to the plate and also struck out on another Gibson curveball. The Yankee threat amounted to naught. The score was still tied, 0-0, after two complete innings had been played.

Leading off the top of the third inning for St. Louis was Lou Brock. Displaying a change of strategy, Brock tried to bunt his way on base, but his bunt went too far up the first base line. It was deftly scooped up by Yankee first baseman Joe Pepitone who applied a tag to Brock's upper arm to retire the Cardinal left fielder. Next up was first baseman Bill White. He made solid contact, but he flied out to deep right field where Mickey Mantle made the catch for the second out of the inning. (On the NBC radio broadcast, Harry Caray speculated that White's long out might have been a home run on Sunday when there was a much stronger wind pushing fly balls toward the right field seats.) The next Cardinal hitter, Ken Boyer, grounded out on a hot smash to his fellow third baseman, brother Clete. Called "a sensational play"[3] by Caray, it was a fine backhanded stop at the hot corner that earned a large cheer from the New York crowd. It was a three-up-three-down frame for St. Louis as the game remained scoreless heading to the home half of the third inning.

The start of the bottom of the third inning saw Phil Linz bat for the home team. New York's shortstop had struck out in his first at-bat. This time he made contact off Bob Gibson, but Linz merely grounded out to St. Louis shortstop Dick Groat. Bobby Richardson, the most productive batter so far in the 1964 World Series with seven hits, came to the plate after teammate Linz. He popped up to his fellow second baseman, Dal Maxvill, in shallow right field for the second out. Roger Maris flied out to deep left center field to end the third inning. Like the Cardinals in the top of the frame, the Yankees swiftly went down in order in the bottom half. "We have quite a pitchers' duel going on,"[4] commented Harry Caray as he sent the NBC radio broadcast to a commercial break before the top of the fourth inning began.

St. Louis accomplished nothing offensively off Mel Stottlemyre in the top of the fourth inning. Dick Groat grounded out to fellow shortstop Phil Linz to make the first Cardinal out. Tim McCarver wasted his at-bat. He meekly grounded back to the mound where Stottlemyre easily fielded the ball and threw to Joe Pepitone at first base for the inning's second out. Mike Shannon, the next St. Louis hitter, at least propelled the ball out of the infield, but his long fly into Yankee Stadium's vast center field was caught by Roger Maris, but not without difficulty. Maris had to make a running stab at the ball to prevent it from falling onto the turf for an extra-base hit. Again, the Cardinals went down in order. The visitors had managed just one hit and scored no runs after 3½ innings of Game Five, but the score was tied 0–0.

Mickey Mantle was the first Yankee batter Bob Gibson faced in the bottom half of the fourth inning. In his previous plate appearance, Mantle had drawn a four-pitch walk off the St. Louis starter. This time Gibson was more assertive in his hurling and struck out Mantle swinging on a 2–2 count. Gibson thus had his fourth strikeout of the game. New York catcher Elston Howard came up next. He hit the ball off the end of his bat to Bill White at first base. Gibson headed over to cover the bag, but White waved him off and ran the ball to the base himself for an unassisted putout. Joe Pepitone fouled off a few pitches against Gibson's fastball, but he eventually struck out swinging just as Mantle had. The score of Game Five was still 0–0 after four pitcher-dominated innings.

11. Game Five

In the top of the fifth Dal Maxvill was called out on strikes. Then things got interesting. With one man out, Gibson deposited a base hit into left field. Tresh, who had been playing Gibson deeper than perhaps he should have, charged at the rapidly descending baseball, lunged at it, but failed to snag it. Possessing good footspeed for a pitcher, Gibson should have made it to second base easily, but he fell rounding first and had to hastily retreat back to the bag with only his dignity injured. History repeated itself when Curt Flood hit a "made-to-order double-play ball"[5] (according to Harry Caray) in the direction of Yankee second baseman Bobby Richardson, who mishandled the fielding chance—and everyone was safe. Lou Brock came up next for St. Louis. His single to right field promptly drove in Gibson to give the visitors a 1–0 lead. Flood advanced to third base. It was Brock's fourth RBI of the World Series. Bill White followed Brock. Caray told his audience that White had underrated speed and, therefore, seldom hit into double plays. He proved Caray to be accurate when he hit a ground ball to Yankee second baseman Bobby Richardson. His throw to shortstop Phil Linz retired Brock, but Linz's throw to first baseman Joe Pepitone bounced to him—and did not arrive at the base ahead of White, according to AL umpire Al Smith. The safe call meant Flood had scored from third base to up the Cardinals' advantage to 2–0. Smith's call created a rhubarb as an animated Pepitone argued loudly that Linz's throw had beaten White to the bag and the Cardinal batter-runner should have been the third out of the inning (which would have nullified the St. Louis run). Yogi Berra left the Yankee dugout to join the fray. He did not argue for long, "Yogi had his say and walked off the field,"[6] Caray reported. Ken Boyer ended the inning by hitting a ground ball to brother Clete for the second time in the game. The New York third baseman opted for the force play at second base to end the inning. Now there were runs on the scoreboard. St. Louis was leading 2–0 after 4½ innings of Game Five.

Curt Gowdy took over the play-by-play duties on the NBC radio broadcast for the second half of the game. Tom Tresh flied out to right fielder Mike Shannon to start the bottom of the fifth. Clete Boyer became Bob Gibson's sixth strikeout of the game when he whiffed on a fastball. New York got their second hit of the game when pitcher Mel Stottlemyre, who got an extended round of applause, knocked a single into right field on the first pitch he saw. Leadoff hitter Phil Linz, batting .166 in the World Series, tried to bunt with two strikes and, embarrassingly, missed the ball completely. Thus, Linz became strikeout victim number seven for Gibson.

Leading off the top of the sixth inning, St. Louis shortstop Dick Groat hit a harmless fly ball to Roger Maris in center field. Once the out was made, Curt Gowdy mentioned it "was one of the infrequent fly balls that the Cardinals have hit off Stottlemyre, who was known as a sinkerball pitcher."[7] Catcher Tim McCarver got his sixth hit of the World Series—the highest total for any Cardinal—with a single into center field. Shannon hit a double-play ball to shortstop Phil Linz. This one the home team turned perfectly—Linz to Richardson to Pepitone—to efficiently record two outs and end the inning. St Louis failed to add to their 2–0 lead.

Bobby Richardson led off the bottom of the sixth inning for the home team. The New York shortstop, continuing his impressive work with the bat, got his eighth hit of the 1964 World Series—a single up the middle into center field. Roger Maris was the next Yankee batter. Curt Gowdy mentioned that the St. Louis defense was playing Maris as a dead pull hitter to right field, but Maris instead hit a high fly ball to straightaway center field that Curt Flood caught easily. Mickey Mantle followed Maris to the plate. He went down swinging, the eighth man to whiff against Gibson in Game Five. Elston Howard was the next Yankee batter. This time the visitors played the Yankee catcher to the opposite field. It mattered little as Howard became Gibson's ninth strikeout victim. Richardson was stranded at first base. The score stood 2–0 for the visitors from St. Louis after six complete innings.

The top of the seventh began with second baseman Dal Maxvill batting for the Cards. He had a hit earlier in the game and was now 3-for-11 for the World Series. "Bob Gibson will be up next," Curt Gowdy told his NBC radio listeners, "and he's sure to get a big hand."[8] Maxvill grounded to Richardson, who had to make a terrific backhanded play to field it. He did, and Maxvill was thrown out at first base. Gibson did get the polite round of applause when he stepped into the batter's box that Gowdy had anticipated. He struck out looking at a knee-high fastball. It was Mel Stottlemyre's sixth whiff of the afternoon. Curt Flood did not go down so easily when he batted after Gibson. He smacked a hard, two-out single into left field. Lou Brock followed Flood. He singled into center field, advancing Flood to third base. Bill White, who was just 1-for-18 in the Series, came up next. "I guess you could say he's due,"[9] opined Gowdy. His broadcast partner Harry Caray agreed. He made solid contact that forced left fielder Tom Tresh to make a long run in to deep left field, but Tresh did make the catch to retire the side. Two Cardinal runners were stranded, but the score was still 2–0 for St. Louis.

New York began well in the bottom of the seventh frame with first baseman Joe Pepitone knocking a base hit into right field to reach first base. Yankee left fielder Tom Tresh batted next. Bob Gibson promptly made him his tenth strikeout victim. With the innings being whittled away by Gibson's shutout work, Yogi Berra decided to roll the dice twice. He first sent up Johnny Blanchard, a 31-year-old to bat for the light-hitting Cletis Boyer. That moved paid no dividends as Blanchard popped up to

11. Game Five

Cardinal third baseman Ken Boyer in foul territory. Another pinch hitter entered the game, with 35-year-old Hector Lopez batting for Stottlemyre. His manager, Yogi Berra, once said of Lopez that he had the fastest bat he had ever seen. Be that as it may, Gibson blew a fastball by him for his eleventh strikeout of the game.

Neither pinch hitter stayed in the game for New York. Hal Reniff, a 26-year-old right-hander, was the new Yankee pitcher, replacing Stottlemyre who had done very well in his seven innings of work—just not as well as his mound rival Bob Gibson. Twenty-six-year-old Pedro González (whose nickname was, of course, Speedy) became the new Yankee third baseman. Ken Boyer led off the top of the eighth inning for St. Louis by grounding out to the new man at the hot corner. Shortstop Dick Groat did better; he lined a single that was fielded by Mickey Mantle in right field. Catcher Tim McCarver blooped a single into left field that just eluded the grasp of Tom Tresh who was running full speed to catch it. The base hit moved Groat to second base. It also drove Reniff out of the game after he had faced just three St. Louis batters. Reniff was replaced on the mound by Pete Mikkelsen. It was his third appearance of the 1964 World Series. During his warmup tosses, plate umpire Vinnie Smith also went into a crouch behind Elston Howard, which amused Curt Gowdy. Smith, having never worked behind the plate when Mikkelsen had pitched, wanted to gauge the new pitcher's speed. Mike Shannon was the first Cardinal he would face. He struck out on a beautiful changeup that drew loud gasps from the crowd. With two out, Dal Maxvill grounded to Pedro González at third base. He threw to second baseman Bobby Richards who was positioned on second base for an inning-ending force play. The St. Louis threat died, and the visitors' lead was still just two runs.

Yankee shortstop Phil Linz, hitless in the game, remained that way when he grounded out to Ken Boyer to start the bottom of the eighth inning. Bobby Richardson followed by lofting an easy infield popup to Dick Groat, the Cardinal shortstop. Shortly thereafter center fielder Roger Maris grounded out to Bill White at first base who made the play unassisted to end the eighth frame. Bob Gibson still looked strong as St. Louis remained ahead 2–0 with three outs to go in Game Five.

This time Bob Gibson got more than polite applause from the fair-minded Yankee Stadium crowd of in excess of 65,000 when he led off the top of the ninth inning for St. Louis. He did not have much of an at-bat, though. Mikkelsen struck him out swinging on a low fastball. Gibson was the eighth Cardinal to whiff in the game. Two other St. Louis batters went down quickly: Curt Flood lined out hard to Pedro González at third base followed by Lou Brock flying out to Roger Maris. St. Louis entered the bottom of the ninth inning holding a 2–0 lead.

During the top of the ninth inning when St. Louis was attempting to pad their two-run lead, Harry Caray cautioned the NBC radio audience that despite Bob Gibson's dominance through eight innings, the game was not yet over. One could be forgiven for thinking that Gibson would not falter. Gibson was tossing a shutout and had only surrendered four hits to New York, but he had Mickey Mantle, Elston Howard and Joe Pepitone to contend with in the Yankee ninth. Mantle caught a break when Cardinal shortstop Dick Groat mishandled what Roger Birtwell of the *Boston Globe* called "a running push bunt."[10] The charging infielder had the ball roll up his sleeve. (Some writers criticized Groat for being too aggressive with his fielding on the play. He, perhaps, could have waited for a high bounce rather than charge towards it. After all, the aging Mantle was not nearly as speedy as he once was.) Mantle was safe at first base, but he was limping. He had hurt himself straining for first base on a play where Groat had made no throw. Manager Yogi Berra did not remove Mantle for a pinch runner, however. Catcher Elston Howard helped Gibson considerably by amateurishly chasing a pitch at eye level for a strikeout for the first out.

The next New York batter, Joe Pepitone, drove a ball straight back toward the mound that struck Gibson below the belt. Curt Gowdy thought it had crashed into his hip. Other observers believed Gibson had been whacked on his derriere. (Afterwards, the St. Louis pitcher confirmed the latter was true when he joked that he would not be able to sit down for a month.) Whatever the case, Gibson grimaced in pain as the ball bounced 10 to 12 feet from him. Nevertheless, the St. Louis pitcher somehow chased the ball to the baseline between home and third base where it had stopped rolling—and made the top defensive play of the game. "It was the greatest off-balance throw in World Series history,"[11] declared Birtwell. Gibson raced to the ball, collected it, wheeled around, and flung the ball to first base. The throw did not have much on it, but was an accurate one that nipped Pepitone by an eyelash—at least in the opinion of AL umpire Al Smith. "I didn't dream Pepitone could be thrown out,"[12] catcher Tim McCarver later marveled when he spoke to reporters about Gibson's athletic assist.

Smith's call was not at all popular with the home team nor its supporters. A brief rhubarb ensued in which first-base coach Jimmy Gleeson hotly confronted the umpire. Yogi Berra marched onto the field to express his displeasure, too. Meanwhile, the Cardinals were understandably concerned about Gibson's fitness after being smacked on the rump by Pepitone's hot line drive. With only one more out needed, Johnny Keane opted not to pull Gibson—and, in hindsight, it was perhaps a costly decision. The first pitch Gibson threw to Tom Tresh was a thigh-high fastball that was hit into the right-center field bleachers. The two-run shot leveled the score, 2–2. The roar from the huge crowd was deafening as Tresh circled the bases for the second time in the Series. Mantle scored in front of him. Gibson's bid for a World Series shutout was suddenly lost, although both Yankee runs were unearned because of Groat's error. Gibson remained on the mound for St. Louis. With a chance to win the game for New York with a home run, Pedro González popped out harmlessly to Cardinal first baseman Bill White for the third out. Game Five of the excellent 1964 World Series was heading to extra innings.

It was the first time that extra innings were required to decide a World Series contest since the first game of the 1957 World Series when the Milwaukee Braves triumphed over the New York Yankees, 4–3, at County Stadium. Statistics showed that World Series extra-inning games usually were decided in the tenth inning and only rarely went beyond 12 innings. The Cardinals seemed inspired to keep that trend meaningful.

Bill White, batting just .053 in the World Series, led off the top of the tenth frame for St. Louis by drawing a base on balls on a full count from Pete Mikkelsen, the Yankee hurler who was entering his third inning of relief work for the home team. Slugging third baseman Ken Boyer batted next and surprised many people with a perfect bunt between the mound and first base. Roger Birtwell wrote that it "bisected the plate-mound-first base triangle."[13] It turned into a timely base hit as it went past Mikkelsen and neither Joe Pepitone at first base, nor second baseman Bobby Richardson—who was moving to cover first base—had a play on it. The Cardinals had runners at second and first with no one out.

St. Louis first baseman Bill White should have been put out while Dick Groat was batting. More correctly, he was bunting. However, Groat missed Mikelson's pitch entirely and White was caught off the bag when Yankee catcher Elston Howard threw to second base. There to catch the throw was New York shortstop Phil Linz. White was so far off the bag that he smartly broke for third base. It was really his only option. Linz may have unnecessarily panicked as his throw to Pedro González at third base was in the dirt. It eluded the substitute infielder's grasp. White slid into the bag headlong and was credited, perhaps very generously, with a stolen base on the play. The Cardinals now had runners at the corners with nobody out.

To cut off a ground ball to the infield, the New York infielders moved in. The defensive strategy worked to some degree as Groat hit a one-hopper to González. White held at third base, and González had to wait a moment for Richardson to get to second base before throwing the ball to him. When the throw came, there was no chance for a double play. Boyer was out at second on the force play as Groat reached first base on the fielder's choice. That brought catcher Tim McCarver to the plate with one Cardinal out.

Some writers expected Berra to pull Mikkelsen at this point in the game and send in left-handed reliever Steve Hamilton to face the left-handed McCarver. That did not happen; Berra stayed put on the Yankee bench. Mikkelsen fell behind the red-hot McCarver with a 3–1 count. McCarver looked for a signal and received the message to swing away at any pitch that was hittable. Following orders, he did swing away. McCarver fouled the pitch off.

On a full count, however, McCarver connected for a dramatic home run that dropped into the lower section of seats in right field over the small scoreboard in that section of Yankee Stadium. It was St. Louis' third homer of the World Series—and they had all been huge in their impact during each Cardinal victory. McCarver's belt gave the Cardinals a daunting 5–2 lead. Harry Caray speculated, "They must be dancing in the streets of his hometown of Memphis, Tennessee, where he is king. McCarver really put the wood to it."[14] The St. Louis catcher was now 8-for 17 in the Series, and he had gotten three hits in row in Game Five. He would later tell reporters that his primary goal in that at-bat was to make decent contact with the ball to drive home Bill White from third base with at least a sacrifice fly.

Mikkelsen still remained in the game as New York's pitcher and got the final two outs of the top of the tenth. Mike Shannon batted and struck out swinging. Dal Maxvill followed Shannon. He made the third out on a ground ball to Joe Pepitone that forced the first baseman to stray from the bag and toss the ball to an onrushing Pete Mikkelsen who had left the mound to cover the base. Pepitone's toss was a high one. It was a close play as Mikkelson had to leap for the bag. Umpire Al Smith's out call received some dissension from the visitors' bench—some players and first-base coach Joe Schultz thought Mikkelson might have completely missed the base when he landed—but their arguments were half-hearted. The Cards had to be content with a three-run lead as the Yankees prepared for another comeback attempt.

Bob Gibson returned to the pitcher's mound to try for a complete game. Harry Caray said Gibson's major task was to dispense of the Yankees quickly before their "siege guns"[15] came to bat. The putout that Pete Mikkelsen had made at first base to end the top of the tenth inning was his last action of Game Five. Because the first scheduled batter of the inning was the Yankee relief pitcher, manager Yogi Berra chose to use Mike Hegan as a pinch hitter. A 22-year-old left-handed hitter, Hegan was batting for the first time in his MLB career! He was called out on strikes. Hegan was the game's thirteenth strikeout victim of Gibson—and the first of those defeated batters to watch strike three sail by him. The next New York batter, shortstop Phil Linz, also failed to reach base. He popped out to Ken Boyer near third base on the first pitch he saw. Down to their last out of Game Five, Bobby Richardson, the Yankees' most reliable batsman in the World Series, kept the inning alive with a base hit—a ground ball that scooted through the middle of the infield. It was Richardson's third hit of the game and his ninth of the Series. An air of excitement suddenly reinvigorated the Yankee fans when Roger Maris walked to the plate. If the New York center fielder could get a hit, Mickey Mantle would come to bat representing the tying run. Caray noted, "Many of the fans who had begun to head for the exits have now stopped and are jamming up the aisles."[16] Alas, for the home team and its rooters, it was not to be. Maris hit a high foul ball that St. Louis third baseman Ken Boyer chased toward the box seats. He ran as far as he could, then lunged for the ball, sticking his glove over the heads of some fans to dramatically make the game-ending catch. One of those fans was NL president Warren Giles, who was thrilled that Boyer successfully made the difficult play. Giles applauded Boyer's defensive effort heartily.

The Cardinals left the field as 5–2 winners. Game Five had taken 2 hours and 37 minutes to complete. That portion of the 1964 World Series played at Yankee Stadium was now done. When Ken Boyer squeezed the third out in the bottom of the tenth inning, few people could imagine that the next Fall Classic game played at MLB's most famous ballpark would occur more than a dozen years later—on October 19, 1976—at nighttime.

Tim McCarver was the primary center of attention in the visitors' clubhouse after the game for his home-run heroics. He mentioned to journalists that his parents had made a special trip from Memphis to attend Game Five. (According to McCarver, the journey featured his mother's first airplane ride. It was also the first time she had ever visited New York City.) When asked by a reporter if he thought his parents would be thrilled by his game-winning home run, McCarver answered the silly inquiry by saying, "I should hope so. Their son sure was."[17] McCarver had given himself an early birthday present. He would turn 23 four days later, on October 16.

The handsome, blue-eyed Cardinal catcher relished his moment in the national spotlight, but the scrutiny did not interfere with his refreshing and endearing politeness with which he spoke to baseball writers. He always addressed them as "sir" when responding to their questions. At one point he said, "It was the biggest hit of my life sir, yes, sir. I hit it good. It was a waist-high fastball, sir. At first, I didn't think it would be a home run, sir. I did not think it would carry that far, sir."[18] McCarver was a little less staid when sitting in the dugout. He confessed to *Sports Illustrated* that after he had circled the bases he had laughed like a crazy man once he was safely among his Cardinal teammates.

Bob Gibson's comments on his catcher's batting heroics were short but to the point. "When McCarver hit that homer, I was the happiest man in the world," Gibson declared.[19]

Cardinal Manager Johnny Keane managed to inject some deadpan humor about his youthful catcher. "Steady kid, that McCarver," he said with a straight face to Harold Kaese of the *Boston Globe*. "[He's] only 23. That homer might help his career a good deal. It might help my career, too."[20]

Bob Gibson got his share of bouquets from the writers, too. The Associated Press' recap of the game, which appeared widely in North American dailies, stated, "The rangy right-hander from Omaha, hit hard in the second game, rebounded with a spectacular effort that left the Yankees hanging on the ropes." The report also acknowledged the fairness of the New York fans, noting, "The big crowd of 65,633 cheered for Gibson as he marched along, getting better the longer he pitched."[21] Gibson hated the fact that he did not complete his Game One start—or any start, for that matter. No one realized it at the time, of course, but this fifth contest of the 1964 World Series was the start of eight straight complete games in the Fall Classic for "Hoot."

Proving that fame can be very fleeting, Tom Tresh's dramatic home run for New York with two outs in the bottom of the ninth inning was largely overlooked because of the Cardinals' eventual victory. Nevertheless, when the Yankee left fielder was asked about it, he had an interesting perspective. Tresh figured the two-pronged hullaballoo following the play where Gibson was hit with Pepitone's line drive may have distracted the St. Louis pitcher when he (Tresh) came to the plate next. "Sometimes after a situation arises," he theorized, "after a controversial play or like something that happened to Gibson, that breaks a pitcher's concentration. Then I look for a chance to swing at the next pitch. It was a real good fastball, and I was lucky to be swinging in the same zone."[22] Indeed, Tresh had homered on the very first pitch Gibson threw after Pepitone was controversially called out at first base.

That ninth-inning play was continuing to bother the Yankees well after Maris' foul popup ended the game. Pepitone certainly thought he had been robbed of a hit by first-base umpire Al Smith's out call. "I want to see those pictures," the irked Yankee first baseman bitterly said to reporters. "My foot hit the base and then I heard the ball hit his [Bill White's] glove. I couldn't believe it when the umpire called me out."[23]

When the Yankees were traveling to the airport for their flight to St. Louis, general manager Ralph Houk spoke to pitcher Steve Hamilton—who was not brought in to face Tim McCarver in the tenth inning. Houk calmly asked Hamilton about his health and if he could have pitched against the St. Louis catcher. Hamilton said yes, he was perfectly fine, and yes, he could have pitched to McCarver if he had been summoned. It then dawned on Hamilton that Houk was silently very miffed at Berra for not making the pitching change that a great many baseball people expected in that situation. Hamilton had a feeling that Berra's job was now in serious jeopardy.

In his game report, Kaese noted that the 1964 World Series was exactly paralleling the exciting 1960 Pirates-Yankees World Series regarding which games of the first five were won by the home teams. As was the case four autumns before, the home team had only won the first and third games. Kaese penned, "To continue [the trend from 1960], the Yankees must win the sixth game in St. Louis, and the Cardinals the seventh."[24] Kaese noted that the Series returning to St. Louis and the Cardinals' smaller ballpark might benefit the Yankees' sluggers. "But if anything is sure today," he continued, "is that the baseball world has once again overrated the Yankees and underrated a National League opponent."[25] Kaese calculated that fully 10 of the 22 St. Louis runs scored thus far in the World Series could be directly attributed to Yankee blunders. "They have made more mistakes than the army of a banana republic,"[26] the Boston scribe amusingly wrote.

Sports Illustrated summed up the mood of the AL champs following their defeat in Game Five and the tough task they were now facing.

> The Yankees, behind three games to two, were not laughing. Their expected edge in home-run hitting in the Stadium had not materialized. They had won one game with a homer, but St. Louis had won two the same way. The Yankees headed back to St. Louis with a long hill to climb.[27]

With Tuesday being a travel day for the two pennant winners, the Yankees had plenty of time to address their perceived shortcomings, while the Cardinals looked forward to winning MLB's grandest prize before their excited hometown supporters. Game Six on Wednesday could not come fast enough for the NL champs and their fans. There were about 10,000 Cardinal rooters present at Lambert International Airport to greet the team when they returned home following Game Five. Their presence en route to the airport caused a major traffic jam.

Game Five Box Score
St. Louis Cardinals 5, New York Yankees 2 (10 innings)
Game played on Monday, October 12, 1964, at Yankee Stadium

St. Louis Cardinals	ab	r	h	rbi	New York Yankees	ab	r	h	rbi
Flood cf	4	1	1	0	Linz ss	5	0	0	0
Brock lf	5	0	2	1	Richardson 2b	5	0	3	0
White 1b	4	1	0	1	Maris cf	5	0	0	0

St. Louis Cardinals	ab	r	h	rbi	New York Yankees	ab	r	h	rbi
Boyer 3b	4	0	1	0	Mantle rf	3	1	0	0
Groat ss	4	1	1	0	Howard c	3	0	0	0
McCarver c	5	1	3	3	Pepitone 1b	4	0	1	0
Shannon rf	5	0	0	0	Tresh lf	3	1	1	2
Maxvill 2b	5	0	1	0	Boyer 3b	2	0	0	0
Gibson p	4	1	1	0	Blanchard ph	1	0	0	0
Totals	40	5	10	5	Gonzalez 3b	1	0	0	0
					Stottlemyre p	2	0	1	0
					Lopez ph	1	0	0	0
					Reniff p	0	0	0	0
					Mikkelsen p	0	0	0	0
					Hegan ph	1	0	0	0
					Totals	36	2	6	2

```
St. Louis   0 0 0   0 2 0   0 0 0   3  -  5  10  1
New York    0 0 0   0 0 0   0 0 2   0  -  2   6  1
```

St. Louis Cardinals	IP	H	R	ER	BB	SO
Gibson W (1-1)	10.0	6	2	0	2	13
Totals	10.0	6	2	0	2	13
New York Yankees	**IP**	**H**	**R**	**ER**	**BB**	**SO**
Stottlemyre	7.0	6	2	1	2	6
Reniff	0.1	2	0	0	0	0
Mikkelsen L (0-1)	2.2	2	3	3	1	3
Totals	10.0	10	5	4	3	9

E—Groat (1), Richardson (2). **DP**—St. Louis 1, New York 1. **HR**—St. Louis McCarver (1,10th inning off Mikkelsen 2 on, 1 out), New York Tresh (2,9th inning off Gibson 1 on, 2 out). **HBP**—Howard (1,by Gibson). **IBB**—Tresh (2,by Gibson). **SB**—White (1,3rd base off Mikkelsen/Howard). **HBP**—Gibson (2,Howard). **IBB**—Gibson (2,Tresh). **U-HP**—Vinnie Smith (NL), **1B**—Al Smith (AL), **2B**—Frank Secory (NL), **3B**—Bill McKinley (AL), **LF**—Hank Soar (AL), **RF**—Ken Burkhart (NL). **T**—2:37. **A**—65,633.

— 12 —

Game Six

October 14

> "If the other side played the kind of baseball the New York Yankees are putting on display in the 1964 World Series, the critics would be quick with their quips about pressure, choking, inexperience, etc. But it's the Yankees, the wondrous, all-conquering, talented pinstripe demons, who are shaking like rookies, making mistakes like tyros, and playing so un–Yankee-like most of the way."
> —Al Abrams, *Pittsburgh Post-Gazette* sports editor

On a day when the political leadership of the Soviet Union was in severe doubt because of Nikita Khrushchev's surprising resignation as that country's leader, average Americans shrugged at the news from Moscow and turned their collective attentions to Game Six of the World Series. They might not know nor care about the inner workings of the world's other superpower, but championship baseball was definitely something they could readily understand.

Many of the nation's baseball writers assigned to the Series (such as Al Abrams, the author of the quote atop this page) were now openly questioning whether the present version of the Yankees was a mere shadow of the team they had once been. Other scribes were more than happy to give full credit to the underdog crew from St. Louis for their 3–2 advantage. Still, their manager thought they were the underachievers.

"We feel we can play better than we've been playing."[1] That was the message that Johnny Keane had for the press when his team's airplane landed in St. Louis on Monday night after their victory in New York earlier that afternoon. The comment was a little bit surprising because the Cardinals were just one win away from winning their first Fall Classic title since 1946. Keane then acknowledged that his club was in "very good shape now. We're ahead 3–2 now [in games] and ready with our pitching no matter what happens."² Las Vegas bookmakers agreed. St. Louis was now listed as 13:10 favorites to wrap up the World Series in six games.

Curt Simmons, his 35-year-old left-hander, would be his starting pitcher for Game Six on Wednesday, but Keane conceded that if the Series were to be extended to Thursday, his plans for such a winner-take-all contest had not yet been devised. "I am not sure what I would do if we go to a seventh game. It might be Bob Gibson again or it might be Ray Sadecki or it might be Roger Craig. It all depends on the sixth game. I won't use Gibson on Wednesday, but Craig will be in the bullpen."³

Although Bill White had scored the winning run in Game Five, the first baseman's anemic World Series batting average of .053 was troubling to his manager. Keane remained hopeful, however. "I sort of figure White will break out here at home,"⁴ Keane told Jack Hand of the Associated Press. White himself, who had batted .303 during the 1964 regular season, seemed anything but discouraged. He maintained a sense of humor about his slump. White told Harold Kaese of the *Boston Globe*, "I don't want to hit the ball good for an out anymore. I want to hit it bad for a base hit. But I don't care if I get a hit or not, as long as we win."⁵ Kaese overheard White tell the Cardinals' clubhouse attendant to make sure the champagne was ready following Game Six.

At Busch Stadium, White and his Cardinal teammates were pleasantly surprised to find a large assortment of gifts placed at their lockers. They had been sent to them by numerous happy fans. The wide variety of unexpected presents included peanut balls, duffel bags, model automobiles, tobacco products, and ashtrays.

The Yankees did not leave for St. Louis until late in the afternoon on Tuesday. They had a workout at Yankee Stadium early on Tuesday afternoon to try to regroup after Game Five's extra-inning loss to the Cardinals. Their workout was not a solo one. The NFL's New York Giants also called Yankee Stadium home. As the Yankees wrapped up their drills, the pro footballers arrived for their practice session scheduled immediately afterward. The two Gotham teams intermingled for a while—and the Yankees briefly borrowed some of the football club's equipment for a bit of fun. Johnny Blanchard and Clete Boyer were tossing wobbly passes to each other before Yogi Berra put a stop to it, afraid that it would be bad for their baseball-throwing motions. Similarly, coach Frank Crosetti impounded a football that Mickey Mantle and Joe Pepitone were about to use to attempt a few placekicks at the enticing goalposts.

Manager Yogi Berra announced that Jim Bouton would be his starting pitcher for the sixth game. Veteran hurler Whitey Ford was still unavailable for New York as he continued to nurse what was referred to as a troublesome sore right heel. (The scuttlebutt was that Ford would be available

12. Game Six

for relief duties in Game Seven, if absolutely necessary.) Decades later Bouton recalled an odd directive the Yankee players were given by team management: They were to pack their bags and check out of their hotel before leaving for Busch Stadium for Game Six. If they happened to win that day, they would return to the hotel and check in for an additional night. To Bouton, this was a defeatist mentality, an expectation that the Cardinals would win the Series in six games. Of course, it was a way to prevent the team from having to pay for a night's worth of hotel rooms they may not need, but it rubbed the Yankees' Game Six starter the wrong way. As David Halberstam put it, "In the past the Yankees had always been arrogant and parsimonious, but this was the first time that [Bouton] could remember their parsimoniousness outweighing their arrogance."[6]

Phil Rizzuto welcomed NBC's radio audience to Busch Stadium in St. Louis for Game Six. He and Joe Garagiola returned to that medium while Curt Gowdy and Harry Caray went back to the network's television coverage. Rizzuto reported that the weather at the ballpark was terrific for October. The thermometer read 75 degrees Fahrenheit and there was a slight breeze. He noted that the grass was a little bit higher in the infield than it was for the first two games. Rizzuto and Garagiola—the latter had made a guest appearance on *The Tonight Show* the previous evening—listed four players who were overdue to get on track offensively, at least as far as their batting averages indicated: Bill White, Ken Boyer (despite his grand slam homer), Lou Brock and Roger Maris. Bill White and Dick Groat switched places in the St. Louis batting order. The pitching matchup was Curt Simmons for the home team and Jim Bouton for the Yankees. Lisa Drake, a local TV celebrity, sang the national anthem with gusto.

The Cardinals received a huge ovation from the hometown rooters when they took the field to begin Game Six. Based on Simmons' performance in Game Three, Joe Garagiola precited that he would not strike out many Yankees in Game Six. Simmons had only two whiffs in that contest—and his first one did not come until the seventh inning. New York's Phil Linz jumped on Simmons' first pitch and flied out to Lou Brock in left field. Brock had to make a running catch to record the putout. Yankee second baseman Bobby Richardson lined a single between Dick Groat and Ken Boyer into left field. With Roger Maris batting, Richardson promptly stole second base. It was only the third stolen base of the World Series; New York had two of them. "It looks as though Yogi gave his team a pep talk. They've come out flying,"[7] Garagiola said. Maris struck out, however. Shortly thereafter, Simmons struck out Mickey Mantle, too, thus making a mockery of Garagiola's prediction. The St. Louis junkball pitcher had equaled his strikeout total from Game Three in just a single inning.

Jim Bouton took the mound for the Yankees. The first Cardinal he faced was Curt Flood. ("I promise not to count how many times Bouton's cap falls off if you'll do the same," Joe Garagiola said to his radio broadcast partner Phil Rizzuto.[8]) The Cardinal center fielder singled into left field. Tom Tresh bobbled the ball momentarily, but Flood chose not to test the outfielder's arm. He happily stayed at first base. Lou Brock was up next and promptly singled into center field, driving Flood to third base with nobody out as the crowd became excited. The struggling Bill White hit into a 4–6–3 double play. Flood scored to give the home team a 1–0 lead. By scoring rule, no RBI was awarded to White. Ken Boyer then flied out to Tresh in left field to end the bottom of the first inning.

Catcher Elston Howard, 5-for-16 in the World Series thus far, led off the top of the second inning for New York. He popped out to Dal Maxvill in short center field with Curt Flood nearby. Switch-hitting Tom Tresh, batting right-handed against the left-handed Simmons, grounded out to Ken Boyer at third base for the second out. Joe Pepitone batted next. He drove a ball to right field where Mike Shannon made a running, leaping, one-handed catch to rob the Yankee first baseman of an extra-base hit and end the inning. The partisan crowd roared its approval of the fine defensive play. St. Louis maintained a 1–0 lead in Game Six heading to the home half of the second frame.

Shortstop Dick Groat led off the bottom of the second inning for the home team. He went down on strikes, looking, for out number one. Tim McCarver got a terrific round of applause from the hometown fans when he came to bat. He earned more with a base hit off Jim Bouton into center field. Upon reaching first base, McCarver's World Series batting average was exactly .500. Mike Shannon followed McCarver to the plate. He struck out on a 2–2 fastball for the second out. Dal Maxvill batted next for the Cardinals. (Joe Garagiola made a point of praising Maxvill for the fine work he had done as a replacement at second base for the injured Julián Javier.) His fly ball to shallow right field was caught with no difficulty by Mickey Mantle to end the second inning.

Third baseman Clete Boyer was first to bat for New York in the top of the third inning. His fly ball to short center field was caught by Curt Flood. Pitcher Jim Bouton, a right-handed hitter, followed Boyer. On the third pitch Bouton saw, he hit a foul ball that clipped catcher Tim McCarver's hand. The latter was briefly examined by the Cardinals' trainer and resumed his duties. Bouton struck out on a full count, making him the third Yankee to go down on strikes to Simmons in Game Six. Phil Linz struck out too to end the top of the third inning. St. Louis remained in front, 1–0.

Pitcher Curt Simmons received a hearty round of applause when he walked to the plate to lead off the home half of the third inning. He too earned more when he hit a Bouton fastball through the middle of the infield. The base hit scattered a few pigeons that had gathered there. Simmons donned a jacket as he stood on first base. New York anticipated a bunt with Curt Flood batting. He did not attempt one. On a 3–1 pitch, Flood lofted a ball into right-center field where there was nearly a collision between Mickey Mantle and Roger Maris. Center fielder Maris cut in front of Mantle to make the catch for the first out. (Phil Rizzuto commented that many times in 1964 Maris had taken balls hit to right field to save the legs of the often-hobbling Mantle.) Lou Brock followed Flood to the plate. Brock hit a sinking fly ball into center field. Maris hustled and made a fine, lunging catch. Simmons had left first base and Maris attempted to double him off. An accurate throw likely would have done it, but Maris' toss was far off the mark. Fortunately for the visitors, pitcher Jim Bouton had hustled on the play and was in great position behind Pepitone to prevent the ball from rolling into the dugout. Joe Garagiola was impressed by Bouton's heads-up defense. "How often do you see a pitcher turn into a spectator on a play like that?"[9] he asked rhetorically. Simmons remained at first base, but now there were two out. Bill White, now batting .050 in the World Series, hit a high bouncer to Joe Pepitone at first base. Pepitone fielded it and tossed the ball to the sprinting Bouton who stepped on first base for the putout. The Cardinals failed to increase their 1–0 lead in the bottom of the third. As he entered the visitors' dugout, Bouton was warmly congratulated by his teammates for his pair of outstanding defensive plays during that inning.

Between innings, the official attendance at Busch Stadium was announced for Game Six. For the third straight game, it was the permissible ballpark maximum of 30,805. Bobby Richardson batted first for New York in the top of the fourth inning. He timed a slow curveball well for a base hit to center field—his eleventh of the World Series. With Richardson running on the play, Roger Maris popped up in foul territory to first baseman Bill White. It was an easy catch, and Richardson got back to the bag in plenty of time to avoid a double play. On a check swing, Mickey Mantle tapped a ground ball to White who was positioned well off the base. He threw to Dick Groat who was covering second base for the force out on Richardson. Mantle beat the return throw and was called safe at first base by umpire Frank Secory. Elston Howard grounded out to second baseman Dal Maxvill for the third out. After 3½ innings, the Yankees, who were facing elimination, had yet to score. St. Louis led the game, 1–0.

Home plate at Busch Stadium was covered by a shadow when Ken Boyer strode to the batter's box to be the first Cardinal to face Jim Bouton in the bottom of the fourth. Boyer struck out, the third St. Louis batter to do that in Game Six. A flyball to right-center field by shortstop Dick Groat caused Roger Maris to hustle into Mickey Mantle's territory to make an excellent running catch. "Maris will be the Yankee center fielder for a long time to come,"[10] opined Phil Rizzuto when the out was made. Tim McCarver reached base again for the Cardinals when his ground ball eluded the grasp of third baseman Clete Boyer. Phil Linz fielded it behind Boyer, but McCarver's footspeed was the difference. He beat Linz's throw to first base for an infield hit. McCarver was stranded at first base, however, as Mike Shannon struck out. The Cardinals still held a one-run edge over the visitors heading to the fifth inning.

Tom Tresh led off the top of the fifth. He lined a ball that fell slightly foul of the left field line. On the following pitch, Tresh straightened it out and dropped a fair ball just inside the same line. Lou Brock sprawled for the ball but he could not catch it. Fortunately for Brock, the ball bounded into the field-level seats for a ground-rule double. (Brock momentarily questioned left-field umpire Vinnie Smith over his fair-ball call, but not too passionately.) Curt Simmons rallied to strike out Joe Pepitone for the first out of the inning. The next Yankee to bat, Clete Boyer, failed to reach base. He was retired on a ground ball to second baseman Dal Maxvill. It advanced Tresh to third base with two out. Yankee pitcher Jim Bouton helped his own cause with a solid line drive into left-center field. "There was nothing fluky about that one!"[11] Joe Garagiola declared. The base hit drove in Tresh with the tying run. Phil Linz, hitless in two at-bats in Game Six, stayed that way. He flied out to Lou Brock in left field. Halfway through Game Six, the score was tied, 1–1.

Phil Rizzuto took over the play-by-play duties for NBC radio when the bottom of the fifth inning commenced. Dal Maxvill's fly ball gave Mickey Mantle some problems momentarily in right field, but the Yankee outfielder made the catch. Rizzuto noted that the aging Mantle had trouble moving laterally for fly balls—and it nearly cost him in this instance. The next Cardinal batter, Curt Simmons, got an extended round of applause from the Busch Stadium crowd, but he popped up on a 2–1 pitch. The ball was caught for the second out by shortstop Phil Linz on the edge of the outfield grass. Curt Flood batted next and drew a walk on a full count. It was the first base on balls surrendered in Game Six by either pitcher. The Yankees fully expected Flood to try to steal second. However, Flood stayed put on a pitchout. Two pitches later, Brock knocked a base hit into deep right center field. Flood had run on the pitch. He got to third base easily but was held. Both Rizzuto and Garagiola agreed it would have been a close play at the plate had Flood tried to score. Bill White failed to drive Flood home, however. The Cardinal first baseman, mired in a horrible slump, bounced a grounder back to Jim Bouton on the mound. With Joe Pepitone playing well off the bag, Bouton ran the ball to first base himself

12. Game Six 131

to record the inning-ending putout for New York. The score stayed deadlocked at a run apiece.

Curt Simmons began the top of the sixth inning by retiring the red-hot Bobby Richardson on a popout to shortstop Dick Groat in shallow left field. Roger Maris, batting .250, stepped up to the plate for New York. Phil Rizzuto noticed that the St. Louis defense was playing Maris straight away, which was unusual, as most AL clubs shifted their outfielder towards right field when Maris batted. No shift would have thwarted Maris in this at-bat, however, as the Yankee center fielder crushed Simmons' sidearm curveball over the right-field roof at Bush Stadium to give the visitors a 2–1 lead. It was Maris' first extra-base hit of the Series. Remarkably, on the very next pitch Curt Simmons threw, Mickey Mantle did the same thing. Mantle's ball was considerably further to the left of the foul pole than Maris' had been, but the effect was the same. It sailed out of the ballpark, too. New York suddenly was in front 3–1. (Curiously, research showed there had not been back-to-back home runs struck in a World Series contest since the third game of the 1932 Fall Classic. The twosome who did it that day were Babe Ruth and Lou Gehrig.) It was Mantle's 17th World Series home run, extending his MLB record in that category. The Cardinal bullpen became a busy place in a hurry. Still, Simmons remained in the game. He regrouped and got Elston Howard to fly out to Mike Shannon. Tom Tresh batted next. On one pitch, Tresh swung and lost control of his bat which traveled about 60 feet toward third base. Tresh retrieved his bat and liberally applied some pine tar to it for an improved grip. Tresh was caught looking for strike three, however. The St. Louis Cardinals now found themselves trailing by a pair of runs to the AL champions.

Ken Boyer batted for the home team to begin the bottom of the sixth inning. He grounded out to Bobby Richardson at second base on the second pitch he saw from Jim Bouton. Next up, Dick Groat lined a ball to Mickey Mantle who juggled it considerably with his bare hand and his glove before catching it as the crowd gasped. "If you're scoring," joked Joe Garagiola, "I think you ought to give Mantle a putout and three assists."[12] Bouton completed the quick inning by retiring Cardinal catcher Tim McCarver on a fly ball to Roger Maris in center field. New York still led, 3–1, heading into the seventh inning.

The bottom third of the New York order was scheduled to face Curt Simmons in the top of the seventh inning. Joe Pepitone was the first Yankee batter of the frame. Phil Rizzuto noted that the floodlights had been turned on at Busch Stadium despite the shining sun in the sky. On a full count, Pepitone popped out to Cardinal first baseman Bill White in foul territory. Clete Boyer lined a base hit to left field. The bouncing ball took a wicked hop and got by Lou Brock allowing Boyer to advance to second base. The play was officially scored as a single and an error to Brock. The misplay heralded Simmons' exit. Ron Taylor replaced him on the mound. New York hurler Jim Bouton was the first Yankee to face the Canadian-born Taylor. He lined out to second baseman Maxvill, who made a terrific catch. Boyer was doubled up at second base for a spectacular twin killing to conclude the inning. New York still led 3–1.

Mike Shannon led off the home half of the seventh inning for St. Louis. He had struck out in his first two at-bats of Game Six. Shannon hit a long foul ball to left field on a high pitch from Jim Bouton. The pitch was a mistake, but Bouton was not punished for it. Catcher Elston Howard briefly chatted with Bouton to settle him down. The pep talk worked as Shannon eventually struck out for the third time in the game. Carl Warwick was summoned by Cardinal manager Johnny Keane to bat for Dal Maxvill. Warwick was 3-for-3 with a walk so far in the 1964 World Series as a pinch hitter, giving him a 1.000 batting average. He could not maintain his perfect batting record, though. Warwick failed to get a hit this time, fouling out to Clete Boyer near the box seats along the third-base line for the second out of the inning. Charlie James, who batted in place of Cardinal pitcher Ron Taylor, hit a high bouncer to Clete Boyer. The Yankee third baseman had to leap to snag the ball, after which he threw out James at first base.

The Cardinals made two defensive substitutions after the failed pair of pinch-hitting attempts in the home half of the seventh. In the top of the eighth, knuckleball artist Barney Schultz took over on the mound for St. Louis while reserve infielder Jerry Buchek replaced Dal Maxvill at second base.

The first batter for New York was Phil Linz who literally threw his bat at Schultz' pitch and connected for a single to left field. Bobby Richardson squared to bunt. There was a bit of confusion when the bunt bounced straight up after hitting home plate. Plate umpire Al Smith signaled fair ball when catcher Tim McCarver touched it directly over the plate. McCarver applied the tag on Richardson who was still in the batter's box. Linz, who was running on contact, advanced to second base on the sacrifice. (For a few moments, the Cards argued that the ball had hit Richardson in fair territory after his bunt, but their complaints—which were dismissed by Smith—were not too strenuous.) Roger Maris batted after Richardson. On a full count, Maris hit a ground ball to Jerry Buchek who made the throw to first base while Linz moved to third base with two out. Mickey Mantle was intentionally waked—the first base on balls the Yankees had gotten in the game. The strategy did not pay off as Elston Howard singled home Linz to pad New York's advantage to 4–1. The hit moved Mantle to second base. Tom Tresh drew a walk—and manager Johnny Keane had seen enough of Schultz. Keane brought in a new pitcher, left-hander Gordie

12. Game Six

Richardson—no relation to New York's Bobby Richardson. Joe Pepitone, the Yankee first baseman, was the first batter he faced. He drilled a no-doubt home run into the right-field seats that quieted the home crowd considerably. The grand-slam homer gave New York a huge 8–1 lead. Richardson got the next batter, Yankee third baseman Clete Boyer, to fly out to Mike Shannon in right field, but the damage had been done. The five-run inning had given the Yankees a comfortable cushion going into the bottom of the eighth frame.

The top of the Cardinal batting order faced Jim Bouton in the St. Louis half of the eighth. Curt Flood led off with his second walk of the game. The free pass caused the Yankee bullpen to get busy. Lou Brock quickly followed with a stand-up double that got by Mickey Mantle in right field. Mantle, however, upon collecting the ball, made a terrific throw into the infield to hold Flood at third base. Yogi Berra entered the field to chat with Bouton, but he did not choose to make a pitching change. Bill White batted next. He grounded out, with Pepitone tossing the ball to Bouton covering the play at first base. It was another hitless at-bat for the snake-bitten White, but he did get an RBI on the play as Flood scored the second St. Louis run of the game. (Flood had also scored his team's first run back in the first inning.) Brock moved to third base on the fielder's choice. Ken Boyer was the next Cardinal batter. He popped up to first baseman Pepitone. Dick Groat grounded out to fellow shortstop Phil Linz to end the eighth inning. The Cards had whittled away some of the Yankees' lead, but the visitors were still ahead, 8–2.

Bob Humphreys, a 29-year-old right-handed pitcher, became the fourth St. Louis hurler of Game Six. Both Joe Garagiola and Phil Rizzuto noted to their radio audience that Humphreys had a deceptive delivery in which he "hid" the ball momentarily from the batter. He set down the New Yorkers in order. Jim Bouton led off for the Yankees. He watched a third strike sail past him into catcher Tim McCarver's mitt. Phil Linz grounded out to Ken Boyer for the second out. The Cardinal third baseman Boyer made another throw to first baseman Bill White when Bobby Richardson hit a high chopper to him. It was a fruitless inning for the visitors, but New York carried a secure 8–2 lead into the bottom of the ninth.

Jim Bouton started the bottom of the ninth on the mound for New York. Tim McCarver, batting .500 in the World Series with ten hits thus far, was the first Cardinal whom Bouton confronted. The St. Louis catcher popped up to Bobby Richardson in shallow center field for the first out. Mike Shannon slugged a ball over Mickey Mantle's head in right field. The ball struck the wall and rebounded nicely to the right fielder. Shannon ran the bases very conservatively and stayed at first. Jerry Buchek batted next. He launched another hit, this one to left field, off the tiring Bouton.

Shannon surprised everyone in the ballpark—especially Tom Tresh by trying to advance to third base. He arrived safely, putting Cardinal runners at the corners with one out. Buchek's hit finished Bouton's successful day on the mound for the Yankees. Left-hander Steve Hamilton, who was 6'7", was summoned by manager Yogi Berra to replace Bouton. Pinch hitter Bob Skinner bounced a hit up the middle to score Shannon, making the score of Game Six a tad closer at 8–3. The Busch Stadium crowd became a little bit livelier as Curt Flood came to the plate. It was misplaced confidence, however, as Flood grounded into a 6–4–3 double play to end the contest. Now that Game Seven was a certainty, the Yankees returned to their hotel to check in one more time.

Game Six—which finished with exactly same score as Game Two—had taken 2 hours and 37 minutes to complete. Both clubs had gotten exactly 10 hits, but the Yankees obviously made the most of theirs. Game Seven was now a necessity. It would be played the following afternoon at Busch Stadium. One-game, winner-takes-all clashes were becoming the norm in October. It was the seventh time in a decade that the World Series needed a seventh game to decide MLB's championship club.

"The slumbering New York Yankee power awoke with a grand slam home run by Joe Pepitone and back-to-back blasts by Roger Maris and Mickey Mantle in an 8–3 victory behind Jim Bouton on Wednesday that squared the World Series with St. Louis at three games apiece,"[13] declared the Associated Press report on Game Six.

Despite the Yankees belting three spectacular home runs, in his brief postgame summary on NBC radio, Joe Garagiola classified pitcher Jim Bouton as the game's biggest hero for New York. Garagiola pointed out that not only did Bouton give the victorious visitors 8⅓ innings of standout pitching, he also drove in the tying run when New York was trailing St. Louis 1–0 in the top of the fifth inning.

"Bouton, a strong youngster who throws himself at the plate with every pitch, finally needed some relief help from lefty Steve Hamilton to put out a last-gasp Card rally in the ninth,"[14] the AP report continued. It was Bouton's second win of the 1964 World Series.

Even though it did not happen until the fourth inning in Game Six, baseball reporters were still fascinated by the number of times Bouton would lose his cap during the course of a typical game. According to the *Boston Globe*, Bouton's unofficial record high for 1964 was 26 times, which occurred in a start versus Cleveland. (*Sports Illustrated* disagreed. It reported that Bouton's cap fell off 47 times in Game Three.) "I hope they don't make a rule about my losing my cap next year,"[15] commented Bouton with apparent seriousness. One rumor said the AL poohbahs were going to force Bouton to wear a cap with a chin strap in 1965.

When asked about more substantial matters, Bouton confessed that his shaky start in the first inning was somewhat worrying to him. "After [the Cardinals] got the two hits, I got a little shaky," he admitted. "I had to kick myself to get myself to concentrate." Overall, Bouton rated his outing as not quite as good as the one he pitched earlier in the World Series. "I think I did a better job in Saturday's game, but I had better stuff and control today. But I'm happy about both games."[16]

Joe Pepitone was quick to thank Yankee hitting coach Wally Moses and teammate Tom Tresh for helping him connect for the grand slam home run that put Game Six out of reach of the NL champions. The Yankee first baseman told reporters, "I hadn't been hitting well in the Series. Moses noticed that I was over-striding, getting my body ahead of my swing. He told me about it before the game and had Tommy remind me every time I came to bat. He (Tresh) just wouldn't let me forget."[17] Pepitone also claimed the constant booing he had been receiving from the St. Louis crowd did not unnerve him. He instead insisted it made him try a little bit harder.

Harold Kaese of the *Boston Globe* used his Game Six report to needle Yankee second baseman Bobby Richardson. Kaese wrote,

> Transients started to think of cancelling plane reservations as soon as Bobby Richardson fielded Bill White's double-play grounder [in the first inning] without making an error. If the little second baseman had made a couple of these plays earlier, the Series would have been over some time ago—but think of all the excitement we would have missed.[18]

Al Abrams of the *Pittsburgh Post-Gazette* showed that there were occasionally strong allegiances about which major league an individual sports writer often favored when reporting on the World Series. The biases were generally based on the circuit in which the scribe's local team competed. In concluding his coverage of Game Six, Abrams unabashedly penned, "It's anyone's Series now. We're still rooting for the Cards."[19]

Game Six Box Score
New York Yankees 8, St. Louis Cardinals 3
Game played on Wednesday, October 14, 1964, at Busch Stadium I

New York Yankees	ab	r	h	rbi	St. Louis Cardinals	ab	r	h	rbi
Linz ss	5	1	1	0	Flood cf	3	2	1	0
Richardson 2b	4	0	2	0	Brock lf	4	0	3	0
Maris cf	4	1	1	1	White 1b	4	0	0	1
Mantle rf	3	2	1	1	Boyer 3b	4	0	0	0
Howard c	4	1	1	1	Groat ss	4	0	0	0
Tresh lf	3	2	1	0	McCarver c	4	0	2	0

World Series '64

New York Yankees	ab	r	h	rbi	St. Louis Cardinals	ab	r	h	rbi
Pepitone 1b	4	1	1	4	Shannon rf	4	1	1	0
Boyer 3b	4	0	1	0	Maxvill 2b	2	0	0	0
Bouton p	4	0	1	1	Warwick ph	1	0	0	0
Hamilton p	0	0	0	0	Buchek 2b	1	0	1	0
Totals	35	8	10	8	Simmons p	2	0	1	0
					Taylor p	0	0	0	0
					James ph	1	0	0	0
					Schultz p	0	0	0	0
					Richardson p	0	0	0	0
					Humphreys p	0	0	0	0
					Skinner ph	1	0	1	1
					Totals	35	3	10	2

New York	0	0	0	0	1	2	0	5	0	-	8	10	0
St. Louis	1	0	0	0	0	0	0	1	1	-	3	10	1

New York Yankees	IP	H	R	ER	BB	SO
Bouton W (2-0)	8.1	9	3	3	2	5
Hamilton SV (1)	0.2	1	0	0	0	0
Totals	9.0	10	3	3	2	5

St. Louis Cardinals	IP	H	R	ER	BB	SO
Simmons L (0-1)	6.1	7	3	3	0	6
Taylor	0.2	0	0	0	0	0
Schultz	0.2	2	4	4	2	0
Richardson	0.1	1	1	1	0	0
Humphreys	1.0	0	0	0	0	1
Totals	9.0	10	8	8	2	7

E—Brock (1). DP—New York 2, St. Louis 1. 2B—New York Tresh (2,off Simmons), St. Louis Brock (2,off Bouton). HR—New York Maris (1,6th inning off Simmons 0 on, 1 out); Mantle (2,6th inning off Simmons 0 on, 1 out); Pepitone (1,8th inning off Richardson 3 on, 2 out). SH—Richardson (1,off Schultz). IBB—Mantle (1,by Schultz). SB—Richardson (1,2nd base off Simmons/McCarver). IBB—Schultz (1,Mantle). U-HP—Al Smith (AL), 1B—Frank Secory (NL), 2B—Bill McKinley (AL), 3B—Ken Burkhart (NL), LF—Vinnie Smith (NL), RF—Hank Soar (AL). T—2:37. A—30,805.

— 13 —

Game Seven

October 15

"You never feel bad when you're in the World Series. You've got all winter to rest."[1]
—Don Larsen, pitching hero of the 1956 World Series

"It's a beautiful day for baseball here in St. Louis—a perfect afternoon,"[2] stated Joe Garagiola in his pregame comments on NBC radio before the climactic game of the 1964 World Series. He got to the big news at once: Whitey Ford's troubles now extended beyond a painful heel; he also had a sore pitching arm and, therefore, would not be starting decisive Game Seven for the New York Yankees. The visitors' pitching duties were handed to young Mel Stottlemyre instead. Bob Gibson got the call for the Cardinals. Both starters would be pitching on just two days' rest.

The wind at Busch Stadium was blowing in, Garagiola reported, and only the pitchers would be pleased about it. He also said the ballpark's infield grass was a little taller than he expected to see it. There were also some uneven patches throughout the outfield which could cause bad hops on bouncing balls to the outfielders. Garagiola noted that the players on both teams seemed remarkably relaxed during batting and infield practice. Contrary to his quiet nature, Lou Brock even dared to chirp at the Yankees. The Cardinal left fielder asked Joe Pepitone if his team's starting pitcher had heard the weather forecast. Pepitone took the bait. "No, what is it?" he asked. "An early shower," replied Brock.

Perhaps the Cardinals thought history was on their side. Four previous times in World Series play they had gone to a decisive seventh game— and they had won all four, in 1926, 1931, 1934 and 1946. All four had come against different AL opponents. The New York Yankees of Babe Ruth and Lou Gehrig were the first of them.

As an ex-player who understood the enormity of the Fall Classic,

Garagiola also uttered a few words of sympathy for two players whose respective injuries had kept them out of the World Series: Julián Javier of the Cardinals and Tony Kubek for the Yankees. Garagiola noted that Kubek had been sitting in the New York dugout in his street clothes and had endured some good-natured ribbing about his civilian brown suit being his road uniform.

The six-man umpiring crew, having completed one full positional rotation over the first six games of the Series, were now back at the same spots they had been in for Game One eight days earlier. Generally, speaking, they had been an anonymous bunch thus far in the Fall Classic. A couple of debatable calls at first base and Joe Pepitone's controversial hit-by-pitch incident were the only times they had drawn attention to themselves. Frank Secory was the plate umpire for Game Seven.

The national anthem was sung by Mary Ellen Schoendienst, the wife of former baseball star Red Schoendienst who had skillfully played in the majors from 1945 to 1963, most of those years with the Cardinals. She was the head of the Pinch Hitters Club, a group that did a considerable amount of charitable work in the St. Louis area. According to Garagiola, she was representing all the ballplayers' wives. Both Garagiola and his broadcast partner Phil Rizzuto agreed she had done an admirable job with her rendition of "The Star-Spangled Banner."

Bob Gibson threw nothing but strikes to the Yankees in the top of the first inning. Phil Linz was surprised, as was most of the crowd at Busch Stadium, to see Gibson uncharacteristically toss a curveball as his first offering of Game Seven. Linz eventually grounded out to Ken Boyer at third base. Bobby Richardson struck out on three pitches. Roger Maris followed Richardson in the Yankee batting order and grounded out to second baseman Dal Maxvill. The side had been retired without any of Gibson's pitches being called a ball by plate umpire Frank Secory.

Mel Stottlemyre was making his third appearance on the mound for the Yankees in the 1964 World Series. The first man he faced from the home team was Curt Flood. The Cardinal center fielder missed an extra-base hit down the right-field line as he smacked a Stottlemyre delivery that touched down a few inches wide of the foul line. Flood eventually grounded out on a high chopper to third baseman Clete Boyer. The next Cardinal hitter, left fielder Lou Brock, tried to bunt his way on base, but the ball came to rest in an area in front of the mound. Stottlemyre retrieved the ball and just nipped the speedy Brock with his toss to first baseman Joe Pepitone. Broadcaster Phil Rizzuto opined, "Any place but back to the pitcher and that would have been a base hit."[3] First baseman Bill White, batting an anemic .043 in the World Series with just one hit in 23 at-bats, got an encouraging round of applause from the

13. Game Seven

hometown supporters when he strode to the plate. It must have helped. He drove a Stottlemyre pitch well over Roger Maris' head in center field. It smacked against the outfield wall, 420 feet from home plate, on just one hop. Maris played the carom well, however. With a strong throw he held White to a double. Rizzuto thought it might have been the hardest hit ball he had seen in any of the seven games. In the end, though, it counted for naught. White was stranded on base when the Cardinal cleanup hitter, Ken Boyer, struck out chasing an effective Stottlemyre curveball. Busch Stadium's scoreboard showed zeroes at the end of one full inning of Game Seven.

The top of the second inning began with Mickey Mantle batting for the visitors. Bob Gibson struck him out. Elston Howard, the next Yankee batter, fared much better. He knocked a base hit into left field. When Joe Pepitone was announced as the third Yankee batter, a loud chorus of boos cascaded down from the stands. Pepitone laughed at the negative reception he was getting. He popped out to third baseman Ken Boyer in foul territory for the second out of the inning. Tom Tresh successfully battled Gibson and, like Elston Howard, got himself a single into left field. Howard moved to second base. Clete Boyer, batting .200 in the World Series, came to the plate with two outs and two Yankee runners on base. His ground ball to Dick Groat was misplayed by the Cardinal shortstop. Groat was distracted when he looked up to see if second base was being covered by Dal Maxvill. Groat was charged with an error. The bases were now loaded, but the batter was pitcher Mel Stottlemyre. Gibson threw three quick strikes past his mound rival. The third one was dropped by catcher Tim McCarver, but the St. Louis catcher had the wherewithal to simply step on home plate to force out Howard without having to make a throw. On NBC radio, Phil Rizzuto remarkably said he had never seen that play end an inning in all his years in organized baseball.

Dick Groat grounded out to start the bottom of the second inning. Groat's ground ball was fielded by Yankee first baseman Joe Pepitone who relayed it to Mel Stottlemyre who was smartly covering the bag. Tim McCarver was cheered loudly as he came to the plate. McCarver drew a walk on a 3–2 count. Ball four was considerably wide of the strike zone. Mike Shannon, batting just .208, followed McCarver to the plate. Mel Stottlemyre struck out Shannon who was way ahead of a changeup. Dal Maxvill made the third out of the home half of the second inning by flying out to Tom Tresh in left field. The score remained 0–0.

New York shortstop Phil Linz led off the top of the third inning for the visitors. On a strange play, a 1–2 pitch was hit toward third baseman Ken Boyer. Linz shattered his bat. A large chuck of lumber headed toward Boyer ahead of the ball. Boyer had to get out of the way of the jagged wood before he could field Linz's ground ball. When he did field it, Boyer threw across the diamond to first baseman Bill White. Umpire Bill McKinley called Linz safe at first base, but somehow White thought an out had been made. Catcher Tim McCarver was backing up the play—and White casually flipped the ball in a high arc towards him. Given the safe call by McKinley, McCarver was not expecting this to happen. He had to react quickly to stop the ball from rolling into the Yankee dugout. The end result was that Linz, the leadoff hitter, was safe at first base on what was ruled a base hit.

Second baseman Bobby Richardson was the next Yankee batter to confront Bob Gibson in the top of the third inning. His at-bat was far more routine than teammate Linz's had been. He hit into a 6–4–3 double play. Second baseman Dal Maxvill knew he was going to be upended by Linz's hard slide, but Maxvill stood his ground to make an accurate relay throw to first base. That act of courage won praise from the old Yankee shortstop in the NBC broadcast booth, Phil Rizzuto. "Maxvill showed me something there because Linz was coming at him!"[4] he told both Joe Garagiola and the listening audience. (Garagiola agreed that the St. Louis second baseman had displayed noticeable grit beyond his years. Maxvill was not exactly a green rookie; he was 25 years old when Game Seven was played.) Next to bat was Roger Maris. He grounded out to Ken Boyer at third base to conclude the visitors' third time at bat in Game Seven. It was still a 0–0 affair after 2½ innings.

Bob Gibson led off the bottom of the third inning for the Cardinals. He got a huge hand from the sellout crowd. Gibson was batting .400 in the Series (2-for-5). His average dropped to .333 after he flied out to Roger Maris in center field. Maris had to battle the wind a little bit before he safely secured the ball. Curt Flood followed Gibson to the plate. Flood grounded out to Clete Boyer at third base, but not without controversy. Flood's bouncing ball drove Boyer into foul territory, but both the third base and home plate umpires ruled that the ball had been played by Boyer in fair territory. Flood assumed a call of foul was forthcoming—but it did not happen. He was only a few feet from the batter's box when Boyer's throw to Joe Pepitone at first base beat Flood by 80 feet. St. Louis manager Johnny Keane entered the field to calmly discuss the play with both plate umpire Frank Secory and third-base umpire Hank Soar. The argument was a short one. The out call on Flood stood. Lou Brock batted next and singled. Brock was nearly picked off by Mel Stottlemyre. (Joe Pepitone briefly argued the safe called by first-base umpire Bill McKinley as suddenly the umpires were playing a prominent role in Game Seven.) Brock's presence on first base was causing some concern to the Yankee hurler, but it amounted to nothing. Bill White grounded out to second baseman

13. Game Seven

Bobby Richardson for an easy third out. One-third of the season-deciding game had been played without a run being scored by either team.

Bob Gibson would face the heart of the New York order in the top of the fourth inning. Mickey Mantle, who struck out in his first at-bat, led off the frame. He at least made contact this time, but his check swing sent the ball gently bouncing back to Gibson in front of the mound. Mantle was retired easily, Gibson to first baseman White. Elston Howard sent a bounding ball just past the reach of Gibson, but second baseman Dal Maxvill was well positioned to field it and throw out the Yankee catcher by a large Margin. Joe Pepitone received his usual share of loud boos when his name was announced as the next Yankee batter. (Phil Rizzuto humorously labeled it "the Pepitone chorus."[5]) He hit a ball off his fists to the busy Maxvill too as the Yankees went down in order. "There are nothing but goose eggs up on the scoreboard,"[6] reported Rizzuto.

The bottom of the fourth inning was replete with excitement. Cardinal third baseman Ken Boyer was the first batter. He rapped Mel Stottlemyre's first pitch back over the mound. Stottlemyre could not react in time to field the ball. It bounced into the outfield for a single. Dick Groat batted next for the home team. He drew a walk. (Catcher Elston Howard turned around to argue umpire Frank Secory's ball three call as tempers were beginning to flare.) Tim McCarver came to bat with runners at second and first bases with nobody out. He drove in a run, but not officially. He hit a hard ground ball to Pepitone, who fielded it cleanly. The Yankee first baseman threw accurately to shortstop Linz, who was covering second base, to force out Howard. Pepitone was in no position to accept a return throw for a double play, but Stottlemyre realized the situation. He was running towards first base as Linz threw in that direction. The ball went by the New York pitcher's moving target and struck the wall beside the Yankee dugout. Stottlemyre made a diving lunge at the ball. (It was later revealed that Stottlemyre's landing had hurt his shoulder slightly.) Bobby Richardson alertly collected the ball to keep McCarver from advancing beyond first base, but Boyer scored on Linz's offline throw. Linz was charged with an error on the play. By MLB's scoring rules, no RBI was awarded to McCarver. With one out in the bottom of the fourth inning, the home team took a 1–0 lead in Game Seven.

The Cardinals were not yet done with their fourth-inning scoring. Mike Shannon contributed to the home side's rally with a base hit into right field that sent McCarver scurrying from first base to third base. With Dal Maxvill batting with one strike on him, the Cardinals executed one of the highlights of the World Series: a daring double steal. On the next pitch, which Maxvill swung at and missed, Shannon broke for second base. He seemed to hesitate slightly when he was about two-thirds of the way there, perhaps to draw a throw. For a moment, Catcher Elston Howard looked at McCarver, who had taken a slight lead off third base, before firing the ball toward second baseman Bobby Richardson. It was not a great throw as it was high and it pulled Richardson off the bag and toward first base. Shannon tumbled awkwardly into second base in front of Richardson and was called safe. Meanwhile, McCarver, who had broken for home on Howard's throw, was signaled safe there as Richardson's return toss was too late to nab him. Richardson's throw was never cleanly caught by Howard. He lost control of the ball while trying to make a frantic sweep tag on the sliding runner, so there was no doubt McCarver was safe. Batter Maxvill began waving at Shannon to go to third base, but he was content to remain at second base for the moment. "I want to tell you that was beautifully executed!"[7] said Phil Rizzuto in an excited manner. It was the first steal of home in a World Series game since Jackie Robinson did it in 1955 against the Yankees. (Of course, Robinson's had famously been a straight steal. Yogi Berra was the New York catcher that afternoon.)

St. Louis now had a two-run lead over the Yankees, but it was soon upped to three. Maxvill, still batting, drove a base hit into right field off the rattled New York pitcher. Shannon aggressively tried to score on the play—and did. His slide beat Mickey Mantle's throw to the plate because it was slightly offline. Maxvill took second base on the play. The Cardinals were now ahead, 3–0. "Holy cow! These Cardinals are red-hot right now!"[8] exclaimed Rizzuto with his catch phrase. It had taken seven games before the superior speed of the Cardinal lineup paid big dividends, but it was surely on display now. The St. Louis crowd roared its approval. The attack petered out, however. Bob Gibson popped up to Joe Pepitone at first base for the second out of the inning. Curt Flood made the third out shortly thereafter by grounding to Bobby Richardson at second base. Another huge round of applause came from the crowd as the Cardinals took their defensive positions for the top of the fifth inning.

Tom Tresh batted first for New York and drew a walk. It was the first base on balls issued by Bob Gibson in the game. Clete Boyer popped out to Curt Flood in shallow center field for the first out. The number-nine spot was next to bat, so Yankee manager Yogi Berra sent youthful Mike Hegan to the plate to bat for pitcher Mel Stottlemyre. Hegan too drew a walk on a full count, pushing Tresh to second base. There was now action in the St. Louis bullpen. Phil Linz, the next New York batter, hit a sinking line drive into right field. Mike Shannon, running at full speed, snared the ball with a basket catch, an outcome that surprised many observers. One person who definitely did not expect Linz's ball to be snagged was lead runner Tom Tresh. He had confidently headed toward third base and now had to make a hasty retreat back to second base. He was not fast enough to get

13. Game Seven

back on time. Shannon's accurate one-hop throw to Cardinal shortstop Dick Groat at the bag successfully doubled off Tresh. (The official MLB World Series film shows St. Louis second baseman Dal Maxvill amusingly signaling the out at the same time as second-base umpire Ken Burkhart.) The potential Yankee rally was quickly quashed. St. Louis still held a 3–0 lead after the top of the fifth inning.

With Mel Stottlemyre removed from the game for a pinch hitter, Al Downing took over the pitching duties for New York in the home half of the fifth inning. Lou Brock was the first Cardinal batter the left-hander faced. On the first pitch, Brock smacked a tremendous home run onto the pavilion roof in right field. With St. Louis now sporting a 4–0 advantage, the din from the home crowd was deafening. It increased when Bill White singled on the next pitch. Ken Boyer then doubled to right field, sending White to third base. Yogi Berra marched with great purpose to the pitcher's mound. Downing's brief and awful stint was done, having surrendered a homer, a single and a double to the three Cardinal batters he faced.

Rollie Sheldon, a right-hander, replaced Downing to face Dick Groat. The St. Louis shortstop fouled off several pitches before bouncing out to Bobby Richardson at second base for the first out of the inning. White scored on the fielder's choice while Boyer moved to third base to stand next to his big brother, Clete. They had a brief chat. Ken was the happier of the two siblings as his club was ahead, 5–0. Tim McCarver hit a sacrifice fly to Mickey Mantle in right field that scored the younger Boyer. The home team was now enjoying a sizable 6–0 lead. Sheldon struck out Mike Shannon to finally put an end to the Cardinal fifth inning.

The lights were turned on at Busch Stadium just before the top of the sixth inning began. Bobby Richardson was the first New York batter to face Bob Gibson. He hit a slow dribbler to third base. Ken Boyer's throw to Bill White was not in time for an out. It was not a thing of beauty, but it was Richardson's twelfth hit of the World Series, a new record for a seven-game Fall Classic. Roger Maris singled into right field to give the local fans some cause for worry. Richardson stopped at second base. Up came Mickey Mantle, who would celebrate his 33rd birthday five days after Game Seven was played. He was 0-for-2 in the game so far. Mantle atoned for his poor first two at-bats by blasting a home run over the 379-foot sign in left center field. It was his 18th—and final—World Series homer. The Cardinals' lead had suddenly been halved to a threatening 6–3. Johnny Keane came to the mound to speak to Bob Gibson, but the St. Louis manager opted to leave his starter in the game. Applause greeted that decision. Gibson responded by striking out Elston Howard looking on a fastball that nipped the outside corner of the plate. Joe Pepitone, booed once again by the ticketholders, was the next hitter. Pepitone hit a Gibson pitch near his fists. The result was an easy, soft liner to Dal Maxvill at second base. Tom Tresh drew a base on balls to keep the inning alive, but Clete Boyer struck out on a Gibson fastball to end the frame. The Yankees, down just 6–3, were still in Game Seven.

The bottom of the sixth inning began with Dal Maxvill leading off for the Cardinals. As Maxvill made his way to the plate, Joe Garagiola, now doing play-by-play duties, noted something odd: The scoreboard operator at Busch Stadium had lost track of the inning, having given the Yankees a zero in the top of the seventh inning even though it was the bottom of the sixth. Earlier, during the fourth inning, he had credited St. Louis with an extra run. "He's a little excited out there. I wonder who he's rooting for?" Garagiola joked. "It's been a long time since they've had a World Series here in St. Louis, and that scoreboard operator is on fast time!"[9] Maxvill did not reach base. Rollie Sheldon whiffed him. Bob Gibson, the second Cardinal batter of the inning, flied out to Tom Tresh, who nearly collided with Roger Maris in center field as Tresh drifted into Maris' territory. Curt Flood lined out hard to Mickey Mantle in right field. The score was 6–3 after six innings—regardless of what the ballpark's scoreboard said.

Bob Gibson was still pitching in the seventh inning. Relievers were occasionally warming up in the Cardinal bullpen in case Gibson faltered. Gibson got his sixth strikeout as pinch hitter Hector Lopez, batting for Rollie Sheldon, swung and missed badly with two strikes. Lopez lost the handle of his bat and it skittered toward Gibson who was standing on the pitcher's mound. Gibson had to jump to avoid being hit by it. (A terrific photo of Gibson's high leap was on the front page of the *Boston Globe*'s sports section the following day.) Shortstop Phil Linz, 1-for-3 in the game, flied out to Mike Shannon in right field. Bobby Richardson got his thirteenth hit of the Series, a single into center field. The base hit extended Richardson's own World Series record. (In the six decades since the 1964 World Series was contested, Richardson's mark for hits has been equaled twice but never surpassed. Lou Brock got his baker's dozen in 1968. Marty Barrett did it in 1986 for Boston. Oddly, the three men all played on losing teams.) Yankee third-base coach Jim Gleeson made sure Richardson collected the ball as a souvenir. Roger Maris was the final batter in the seventh for New York. He hit the ball hard off Gibson, but his line drive ended up in Mike Shannon's glove. Going into the seventh-inning stretch, St. Louis maintained a 6–3 lead over the AL champions from New York.

The bottom of the seventh inning began with the Cardinals having to cope with a new Yankee pitcher. This one was Steve Hamilton. Lou Brock faced him. Hamilton struck him out on a sidearm toss. Bill White, who had broken out of his batting slump with two well-struck hits in Game Seven, did not get a third one. He struck out looking. Ken Boyer, who had

13. Game Seven

already recorded two hits and two runs for the Cardinals, increased those stats by hitting a ball into the left field stands over the 351-foot marker. By doing so, Boyer became the first Cardinal to ever connect for two home runs in the same World Series. On the NBC television broadcast, Harry Caray thought he had spotted the unusual sight of Clete Boyer giving his bother a congratulatory pat on the back as he circled the bases. Curt Gowdy was not sure about that. The lead was now 7–3 for the home team. Dick Groat grounded out to Clete Boyer at third base to end the frame.

Mickey Mantle led off the top of the eighth inning for New York. He flied out to Curt Flood in center field for the first out. Elston Howard followed Mantle to the plate. He struck out swinging. It was Gibson's seventh strikeout of the game. The home crowd roared. They were starting to count outs. Tradition dictated that Joe Pepitone be booed as he strode to the plate, and he was. The Yankee first baseman was retired by second baseman Dal Maxvill who caught a popup in shallow center field in front of his onrushing teammate Curt Flood. The Yankees had been retired in order in the eighth inning—and had just three outs left to pull out a comeback.

It was sincerely hoped by the Cardinal fans and players that the bottom of the eighth inning would be the final time the team batted in 1964. "I'm sure you can feel the electricity in the ballpark,"[10] stated Joe Garagiola above the din of the full house at Busch Stadium. First up for the home team was catcher Tim McCarver. The climax of his long at-bat was an infield hit that was stopped by Joe Pepitone wide of first base, but he could not make a play on McCarver who was credited with a single. A second Cardinal reached base when Mike Shannon's ground ball to Clete Boyer at third base was mishandled. A fine bunt by Dal Maxvill moved each of his two Cardinal teammates up a base. At this point in the game, Yogi Berra decided to replace pitcher Steve Hamilton with Pete Mikkelsen.

Bob Gibson was the first man he faced. Gibson was accorded a huge ovation when he came to bat with one out. His plate appearance resulted in the craziest sequence of the whole World Series: a rundown in which four of the six Yankee infielders participated. Gibson hit a ground ball to Clete Boyer. This resulted in McCarver being caught in a rundown between third base and home. However, it was briefly botched as a throw hit the runner—which allowed McCarver to return to third base. Unfortunately for him, Mike Shannon was only a few feet away from the bag, and Shannon was quickly put into a rundown between second and third base. McCarver figured he ought to try for the plate again while the Yankees were fixated on Shannon. Seeing McCarver on the move again, the Yankees' focus changed as the ball was abruptly thrown to Elston Howard begetting yet another rundown featuring the Cardinal catcher as prey.

Eventually McCarver was tagged out. Shannon was back at second base, and Gibson occupied first base. Two Cardinals were now out. Joe Garagiola tried to walk his radio audience through what exactly had happened. After conferring with his nearby NBC stats man, Garagiola said the play went from Boyer to Howard to Boyer to Linz to Mikkelsen who finally made the tag at third base. Curt Flood ended the inning by flying out. The Cardinals did not score despite the promising start to the bottom of the eighth, but the home side still led Game Seven, 7–3.

Tom Tresh was the first batter in the top of the ninth for New York. He was batting left-handed versus the right-handed Gibson. The Cardinal starter was tired. Gibson gave himself a brief pep talk to stay focused and get three more outs. Remarkably, Tresh was retired on an 0–2 pitch that was fouled back to McCarver in which his catcher's mitt was knocked off, but McCarver managed to hang onto the ball in his bare hand! Now it was the turn of Garagiola—a former catcher himself—to say he had never seen such an occurrence before. Clete Boyer was up next for New York. He ran the count to 3–2 before hitting a home run over Lou Brock's head into the left-field stands. (It marked the first time in World Series history that two brothers had homered in the same game. Moreover, it was only the fourth time in MLB history that brothers on opposing teams had performed the feat.) The score was now 7–4 in favor of St. Louis.

With a glimmer of life still present for the visitors, Yogi Berra sent Johnny Blanchard up to pinch hit for Pete Mikkelsen. He fared poorly, going down on strikes for the second out in the top of the ninth. Blanchard was Gibson's ninth strikeout of the game and the 31st man to whiff against him during the World Series. The umpires busily had to chase several fans, who were straddling the outfield fence, back into the stands before play could resume. Shortstop Phil Linz came up representing the Yankees' final hope—and he did his best. Like Clete Boyer, he hit a home run into the left field seats to make the score 7–5. "The Yankees keep battling, just like they've battled all season,"[11] said an impressed Joe Garagiola.

The excited crowd was now more slightly subdued as Bobby Richardson, the most consistent batter in the 1964 World Series, came up. Slugger Roger Maris was on deck. On the second pitch he saw from Gibson, Richardson hit a high infield popup. Dal Maxvill positioned himself under it. (While waiting for the ball to descend, shortstop Dick Groat amusingly yelled at Maxvill not to let the ball hit him on the head! It did not.) Maxvill made the simple catch for the series-ending out. Eighteen years to the day from when they won their last World Series, the St. Louis Cardinals had defeated the favored New York Yankees in the seventh game of the 1964 Fall Classic, 7–5. Jack Hernon of the *Pittsburgh Post-Gazette* reported that when Maxvill squeezed the final out in his glove, "Gibson's legs gave out on him [and he] folded up into captain Ken Boyer's arms on the mound." The once invincible-in-October Yankees had lost World Series in consecutive autumns for the first time since 1921 and 1922 when they fell to the crosstown New York Giants.

"This ballpark is really bedlam,"[12] declared Joe Garagiola, as hundreds of fans invaded the playing field to celebrate. The Associated Press story in the next day's *Montreal Gazette* noted, "Gibson needed help from a burly cop and two special park attendants to escape from the well-wishers, finally scooting under the rail in front of the dugout."[13]

In contrast, a news photographer captured Mickey Mantle sitting by himself in the visitors' dugout well after his teammates had headed to the sanctuary of their clubhouse. Mantle had a distant and forlorn look about him. On October 20 he would have his 33rd birthday. Given his health, the age of his Yankee teammates, and how competitive the rest of the AL was becoming, he was probably wondering if he had just played his final World Series game. Mantle had no intention of retiring, though. When the subject came up, Mantle firmly quashed the idea, saying he would not know what do with himself if he quit playing baseball.

Warren Giles, the 68-year-old president of the National League, made a special trip to the chaotic St. Louis clubhouse to personally congratulate the new champions. He seemed as excited as any of the Cardinals whom NBC's Harry Caray was attempting to interview for both the radio and television broadcasts. Giles praised the Cardinals tenacity in both coming from far back to win the NL pennant and rallying to defeat the Yankees after trailing in the World Series.

Bob Gibson was the first player Caray cornered for a brief chat. Gibson told Caray his World Series strikeout record of 31 did not mean anything to him—the only thing that mattered to him was his team's victory. He would later tell the press that baseball records are nice to possess—but having money is far better. (Authors' note: The previous record of 28 strikeouts in a single World Series, set by Bill Dinneen way back in 1903, probably required an asterisk, but it was still impressive. It occurred in the first modern World Series, which was a best-of-nine affair won by the Boston Red Stockings, five games to three, over the Pittsburgh Pirates. Dinneen pitched four complete games, compiling a 3–1 record over the space of 12 days, in which he tossed 35 innings. Dinneen joined the AL umpiring staff in 1909 at age 33—just 17 days after pitching his last MLB game! He would eventually work in eight World Series as an arbiter.)

Giddy Tim McCarver said he did not think anything could possibly feel better than when the Cardinals won the NL pennant less than two weeks earlier—but this day's joy had proven him wrong. He made a point of saying what a pro Gibson was. (Caray wrongly stated that McCarver had batted .500 in the Series. That was slightly off the mark. McCarver's 11-for-23 total gave him a .478 average.)

MLB Commissioner Ford Frick, a former sports writer, noted that this had been the 42nd consecutive World Series he had witnessed and they had never become tiresome to him. Dick Groat said this victory surpassed the one he experienced four years earlier as a member of the 1960 Pittsburgh Pirates—which was quite a statement. Caray also spoke with Ken Boyer. The two men were quite cordial despite their history. Caray asked Boyer if his brother had subtly patted him of the back when he was rounding third base after his home run. Boyer could not confirm that, but he did acknowledge that his brother had verbally congratulated him on his way around the bases. MLB's official World Series film shows that it was Ken who took the liberty of playfully nudging Clete as he passed by him.

"Iron Man Bob Gibson, working with only two days' rest," the Associated Press report said, "pitched the scrappy St. Louis Cardinals to their first World Series championship since 1946 with a 7–5 victory over the favored New York Yankees in Thursday's crucial seventh Series game."[14]

"You've got to have heart, the song says. Bob Gibson had it," Roger Birtwell of the *Boston Globe* admiringly wrote of the winning pitcher, who was named World Series MVP. The scribe continued,

> The 28-year-old son of an Omaha laundress pitched the Cardinals to the championship of the world.
> There was a bump on his hip and a lump on his foot. The other instep was swollen and hurting where he broke it two seasons ago. But Bob Gibson had heart. He forced his weary arm and body to strike out nine Yankees.[15]

In summarizing the Cardinals' victory to conclude his narration of the official MLB highlight film, Harry Caray said of the winning team, "It was a stirring triumph by a Cardinal team reminiscent of the Gashouse Gang. It had some of the speed of that colorful team from the Thirties, some of the pitching, and all of its great heart and courage. That, in the end, carried them through to baseball's highest honor … the world championship."[16]

Winning manager Johnny Keane was too busy fielding reporters' questions and accepting congratulations to be interviewed on NBC radio. He was a thoroughly happy man, though. An Associated Press story poetically described Keane as "standing in the middle of the victorious St. Louis Cardinals' dressing room, champagne dripping from his matted grey-thatched head and mingling with the tears of joy escaping from his blue-grey eyes."[17]

"I've waited 35 years for this," Keane told a scrum of baseball scribes

13. Game Seven

half an hour after Dal Maxvill's catch locked up the World Series for his team. "That's a long wait, but it's worth it." In a tremulous voice, he said, "I never dreamed a human being could be this happy. Now I know why every other manager would give his right arm to be in this spot." Keane, clearly emotionally overwhelmed by the triumph of his team, hesitated for a moment before adding, "So would I."

Almost voiceless from answering dozens upon dozens of questions from the media, Keane continued to express what it all meant to him, "I'm not going to sleep tonight, I'm going to stay up and enjoy it. This entire day has been so wonderful I want to relive it."[18]

At one point, Keane was interrupted by team owner Gussie Busch, who had quietly walked into the Cardinal clubhouse and somehow pushed his way through a swarm of journalists. Busch excitedly grabbed Keane with both arms and loudly exclaimed, "Johnny, a million congratulations and a million thanks! You did a helluva job!"[19] With a slight smile, Keane redirected the praise to his players. "Those boys out there did it," he stated. "They're the greatest bunch I've ever managed. They're a treat to watch. I'd pay to see them any day, even in [my] uniform."[20]

Bob Gibson was in a rare, chatty mood in the Cardinal clubhouse. As the outstanding player of the 1964 World Series, Gibson's prize was a new Chevrolet Corvette donated by *Sport* magazine, which pleased him. Gibson admitted that with the luxury of having a four-run lead in the ninth inning, he had simply challenged the Yankee batters to hit his best fastballs. "After all," he rhetorically asked, "how often are these guys going to lean back and hit the ball into the stands like they did in the ninth?" Gibson grinned and added, "Kenny Boyer sort of made up for his brother's homer. He cracked it pretty good."[21]

While Yogi Berra assumed if Bobby Richardson had gotten on base instead of popping out to end the game, Gibson would have been yanked from the mound, Johnny Keane said that would not have been the case, even with Roger Maris and Mickey Mantle coming up next in the Yankee batting order. "I left [Gibson] in when I saw how strong he was going and how courageously he was throwing. When the Yankees were hitting him, they were hitting his good stuff."[22]

In his comments to the reporters surrounding him, Gibson praised Mickey Mantle. "That man has power," he strongly said. When the Yankees were trailing 6–0 in the top of the sixth inning, Mantle had tagged Gibson for a massive three-run homer. The winning pitcher recalled, "He hit a fastball away from the plate and rode it to left [field]. We still had a 6–3 lead and it didn't worry me too much, although I was a little concerned."[23]

Gibson showed a smidgen of the well-hidden, sensitive side of his personality when he stated, "You know, the one thing I've now got on my mind is getting home to Omaha and seeing my two little girls. My wife is here, but I've probably been pretty tough on her lately. I think all the tension has made me a bit snappy."[24]

While Game Seven showcased plenty of home run power, Yankee manager Yogi Berra believed the key point of the game occurred in the bottom of the fourth inning when St. Louis scored three time to take a lead they would not relinquish. Berra pointed to Phil Linz's throwing error aimed at first base when he tried to complete a double play. The wild toss hurt the visitors in many areas: It allowed Ken Boyer to score on the play; it allowed the inning to continue in which the Cardinals scored two more runs; and starting pitcher Mel Stottlemyre was never the same after crashing to the infield trying to reach Linz's off-the-mark throw. "He just made a bad throw," Berra said of Linz. "It could happen to anybody."[25] When asked if Dick Groat's slide to hinder the double play had caused his poor throw to first base, Linz shook his head. "No," the New York shortstop told reporters. "The runner coming from first base didn't bother me. It was just a bad throw."[26]

Indeed, one important aspect of the Yankee dynasty from 1947 to 1964 that was well known within the ranks of the club but lesser known and often overlooked by baseball fans and media is the team's solid defense season after season—especially by its infielders. Strong glove men with weak bats, such as Clete Boyer, were often reassured by Yankee managers and general managers that their batting averages were secondary to their fielding percentages. Therefore, it is telling that Game Seven was lost by the Yankees on a series of bad throws: Linz to first base, Howard to Richardson on the first part of the Shannon–McCarver double steal; Richardson's return thrown to Howard on the same play; and, to a lesser extent, Mantle's off-the-mark throws from right field. Over the course of the 1964 World Series, New York, made nine errors to the Cardinals' four.

The quietly ailing Mel Stottlemyre did not pitch after the fourth inning. The young Yankee starter told reporters his arm and shoulder got stiff after his fall, which affected his performance for the brief time he stayed on the mound after the botched double play. "I probably would have been able to stay in otherwise," he ruefully stated. "I felt as strong as in any other game, but my control was not as sharp."[27] Stottlemyre would enjoy a terrific, 11-year MLB career, all of it spent with the New York Yankees. He would win 164 regular-season games, ranking him seventh on the all-time victories list for his club at the end of the 2023 season. But most of it was spent with substandard Yankee outfits. Stottlemyre pitched mostly with mediocre or worse Yankee clubs. By the time he hung up his glove after the 1974 season, it was clearly no longer the era of Ruth or Gehrig,

13. Game Seven

or DiMaggio, or Berra, or Mantle. Stottlemyre never appeared in another World Series game after his four innings of work on October 15, 1964.

The Cardinals held a private victory party at Stan Musial's restaurant after the game. It occurred to some of them to telephone Ernie Broglio, whom they had traded to Chicago in June for Lou Brock. Broglio was both surprised and appreciative of the call. He spoke to several of his ex-teammates. He recalled, "I popped open my own bottle of champagne and drank along with them. They had won the pennant by one game. I won three games for the Cardinals before I was traded, so I thought I helped them win it." Under MLB World Series rules in 1964, Broglio received neither a championship ring nor a share of the postseason money. "It would have been nice to have a ring," Broglio said, "but I didn't get one, so I didn't worry about it." Sometime after Broglio stepped away from baseball, he acquired an autographed photo of Brock that was displayed proudly in his home until his 2019 death at age 83. Broglio had kiddingly advised Brock not to die first because "as long as people remember him, I know they also are going to remember me."[28]

William Leggett of *Sports Illustrated* thought the entire World Series had been a thoroughly compelling affair regardless of one's rooting interests. He glowingly wrote, "Seldom has there been a Series quite like this one. It sustained to the very last inning of the last game those tensions and frustrations of the league pennant races that had thrilled Americans. The Cardinals and Yankees were almost perfectly matched and they gave baseball fans everything they could have hoped for."[29]

Three days after the last out of the 1964 MLB season was made, Tim McCarver and Bob Gibson jointly appeared live onstage in New York City on *The Ed Sullivan Show* to take bows and presumably be interviewed. The segment lasted 84 seconds with Sullivan doing almost all of the talking. McCarver said two words when asked to confirm his World Series batting average (".478, Ed."). Gibson said nothing at all.

Game Seven Box Score
New York Yankees 5, St. Louis Cardinals 7
Game played on Thursday, October 15, 1964, at Busch Stadium I

New York Yankees	ab	r	h	rbi	St. Louis Cardinals	ab	r	h	rbi
Linz ss	5	1	2	1	Flood cf	5	0	0	0
Richardson 2b	5	1	2	0	Brock lf	4	1	2	1
Maris cf	4	1	1	0	White 1b	4	1	2	0
Mantle rf	4	1	1	3	Boyer 3b	4	3	3	1
Howard c	4	0	1	0	Groat ss	3	0	0	1
Pepitone 1b	4	0	0	0	McCarver c	2	1	1	1
Tresh lf	2	0	1	0	Shannon rf	4	1	1	0

New York Yankees	ab	r	h	rbi
Boyer 3b	4	1	1	1
Stottlemyre p	1	0	0	0
Hegan ph	0	0	0	0
Downing p	0	0	0	0
Sheldon p	0	0	0	0
Lopez ph	1	0	0	0
Hamilton p	0	0	0	0
Mikkelsen p	0	0	0	0
Blanchard ph	1	0	0	0
Totals	35	5	9	5

St. Louis Cardinals	ab	r	h	rbi
Maxvill 2b	3	0	1	1
Gibson p	4	0	0	0
Totals	33	7	10	5

New York	0	0	0	0	0	3	0	0	2	–	5	9	2
St. Louis	0	0	0	3	3	0	1	0	x	–	7	10	1

New York Yankees	IP	H	R	ER	BB	SO
Stottlemyre L (1–1)	4.0	5	3	3	2	2
Downing	0.0	3	3	3	0	0
Sheldon	2.0	0	0	0	0	2
Hamilton	1.1	2	1	1	0	2
Mikkelsen	0.2	0	0	0	0	0
Totals	8.0	10	7	7	2	6

St. Louis Cardinals	IP	H	R	ER	BB	SO
Gibson W (2–1)	9.0	9	5	5	3	9
Totals	9.0	9	5	5	3	9

E—Linz (2), Boyer (2), Groat (2). **DP**—St. Louis 2. **2B**—St. Louis White (1,off Stottlemyre); Boyer (1,off Downing). **HR**—New York Mantle (3,6th inning off Gibson 2 on, 0 out); Boyer (1,9th inning off Gibson 0 on, 1 out); Linz (2,9th inning off Gibson 0 on, 2 out), St. Louis Brock (1,5th inning off Downing 0 on, 0 out); Boyer (2,7th inning off Hamilton 0 on, 2 out). **SH**—Maxvill (1,off Hamilton). **SF**—McCarver (1,off Sheldon). **SB**—McCarver (1,Home off Stottlemyre/Howard); Shannon (1,2nd base off Stottlemyre/Howard). **U-HP**—Frank Secory (NL), **1B**—Bill McKinley (AL), **2B**—Ken Burkhart (NL), **3B**—Hank Soar (AL), **LF**—Al Smith (AL), **RF**—Vinnie Smith (NL). **T**—2:40. **A**—30,346.

— 14 —

The Yankees Get Old ... Then They Get Sold

> "The Yankees, the dominant power in baseball for more than 40 years, are a valuable property."[1]
> —*New York Times*

Less than 24 hours after the glamorous New York Yankees lost the seventh game of the 1964 World Series, they were already being written off as a championship outfit for 1965—at least by some writers. Journalist Milton Gross penned, "The blow that struck the Yankees as they lost the World Series to the Cardinals is only the first which may fall on Yogi Berra's shaky crew before they play baseball again next spring."[2]

Gross continued, "Many are thinking this is the beginning of the end for the Yankee dynasty as we've known it. That is not necessarily true. There is too much solid talent here for it to finish this way."[3] Gross thought that the immediate denials by general manager Ralph Houk were unbelievable. The writer figured that the five-time defending AL champions "will be severely broken up," during the upcoming fall and winter.

"We really haven't thought about it," insisted Houk. "This is still a pretty good club."[4]

Gross begged to differ with Houk. The writer thought the Yankees had gotten into first place largely because of the steady relief work of Pedro Ramos, who was ineligible for the World Series because of the lateness of his being added to the club's roster. Gross also noted that Whitey Ford was now a huge question mark for the AL champions. The scribe penned, "He may have to face surgery and the end of his pitching career because of a circulatory blockage in his left shoulder."[5] Gross reminded everyone that despite his three World Series home runs, "Mickey Mantle has defied legs that no longer obey."[6]

However, Gross thought the problems were deeper than the breakdown of the two Yankee superstars' bodies. "There is too much baggage being carried on the [New York] roster," he opined. "There isn't much down on the farm for the Yankees to replace the parts that can't contribute, and all of it means that Houk may be forced to enter the trading market in earnest for the greater glory of CBS."[7]

Gross also reported that Yankee second baseman Bobby Richardson had made up his mind to retire after the 1965 season ended. This came as a big surprise to many baseball followers as Richardson was just 29 years old. "Something has come up within the past week that made me decide to play only one more year," Richardson told the media. "Betsy [Mrs. Richardson] and I talked it over and made the decision. I've four little children and I've been away from my family too much. I told the front office long ago that I was getting out."[8]

Third baseman Clete Boyer told Gross that he believed he was being measured for "trade bait" because of his weak hitting throughout much of the 1964 season. It was suggested by several writers on the Yankee beat that Phil Linz could easily move into that position once Tony Kubek grew healthy enough to return to the Yankee lineup as the team's regular shortstop.

There was also the uncertainty of who would be making the decisions at the very top of the New York Yankees hierarchy in the near future. Despite controlling the most famous and successful sports franchise in the United States, Del Webb and Dan Topping, the dual owners of the Yankees, were looking to get out of the baseball business—at least they wanted to rid themselves of having majority ownership of the perennial AL champions. The two construction moguls had held at least partial control of the club and Yankee Stadium since 1945. In the 20 seasons the twosome had run its business operations, the Yankees had won 15 AL pennants, a fantastic achievement far beyond the wildest dreams of any other MLB franchise.

Only the formalities remained to be settled—but within three weeks after the 1964 World Series concluded, the Columbia Broadcasting System (CBS), the wealthy radio and television company, purchased 80 percent control of the famous baseball empire from Topping and Webb for $11.2 million. (That is the equivalent of about $111.2 million in 2023.) Topping and Webb each retained 10 percent ownership. The papers were duly signed on November 2.

The deal had been rumored and discussed throughout the 1964 AL season. It was finally announced on August 14. The *New York Times* reported the network's acquisition of the baseball team was confirmed by AL president Joe Cronin. Its report noted,

14. The Yankees Get Old ... Then They Get Sold

He said the league had been "advised that if approval was granted, the Yankees will be a separate entity ... independent of CBS, with Dan Topping as president and other members of the organization continuing to formulate policy."

League approval was not unanimous. [Kansas City and Chicago both disapproved.] But the eight other [AL] franchises, including the Yankees, gave the necessary three-quarters approval in a vote by telegram and mail conducted by Mr. Cronin.[9]

The Yankees' acquisition by CBS amounted to only a small fraction of the company's enormous holdings, so it was feared by many baseball people not within New York City that the Yankees could, more than ever, buy the AL pennant every year by purchasing the best players from clubs that had nowhere near the financial resources the longtime MLB powerhouse had. Remarkably, the exact opposite occurred. In 1965, just a year after being one win short of capturing yet another World Series, the Yankees won just 77 games—marking the first time the club had a sub-.500 season since 1925. The next year, the team completely nosedived, finishing dead last in the AL for the first time in 54 years. In the eight years that CBS owned the team, the Yankees' best finish was second place in the AL East in 1970, but they were still 15 games behind the front-running Baltimore Orioles when the season ended. No other time in the CBS era did New York ascend to a higher spot than fourth. AL pennants and World Series championships were now revered nostalgia at Yankee Stadium.

The New York Yankees had become just another MLB franchise when they allowed their farm system to atrophy as a cost-cutting measure. Capable newcomers were no longer in plentiful supply to replace the pinstriped veterans who had hung up their spikes or had been traded away. Furthermore, starting in 1965, the institution of MLB's amateur draft, which the Yankees opposed strongly and voted against, spread the talent around every team more equitably. Only one prospect, a catcher named Thurman Munson, panned out as an excellent draft choice from the CBS years.

Topping and Webb died within two months of each other in 1974. By that time, George Steinbrenner had been the owner of the Yankees for more than a year, having purchased the floundering AL franchise in January 1973 for the bargain-basement price of $8.7 million—an amount $2.5 million cheaper than the selling price in 1964. Thus, CBS had bought the Yankee logo but none of its excellence. Within a decade, the network seemed to be anxious to rid themselves of MLB's most decorated franchise.

— 15 —

Managerial Musical Chairs

> "I don't believe a manager ever won a pennant. Casey Stengel won all those pennants with the Yankees. How many did he win with the Boston Braves and Mets?"[1]
> —Sparky Anderson

When the World Series began, no one could have foreseen that both Johnny Keane and Yogi Berra would not return to the teams they had successfully managed to pennants during the 1964 Fall Classic. But that is precisely how things panned out for both men. There was an oddball twist to the proceedings, too.

Keane suddenly resigned as St. Louis' manager in mid–October. Actually, it was more of a slow-motion resignation than something done on a rash impulse. Keane, with the assistance of his daughter (Pat), had dictated a letter of resignation to his wife (Lela), which the latter had dutifully typed out for future use. It was dated September 28, 1964, at a time when the Cardinals were still deep in the battle to win their ninth NL pennant and a berth in the World Series was far from certain. Keane kept the missive nearby him for the rest of the season. When the suddenly grateful Cardinals management attempted to offer Keane a new contract shortly after the World Series ended, he gave them the surprise of their lives by dramatically producing the letter saying he had decided to leave the only franchise he had ever been associated with in his professional baseball career. It was a stunning development. When asked about the September date atop the letter, Keane calmly said his mind "was made up"[2] by that point in the season. He had no intention of returning to the Cardinals in 1965 regardless of how the 1964 campaign turned out for his club. Winning the World Series did not alter his decision one iota. The latter stated that his resignation was effective following the Cardinals' last game of 1964, be it a regular-season tilt or a World Series encounter.

15. Managerial Musical Chairs

What had caused Keane to leave so abruptly? In mid–August, the Cardinals had fired general manager Bing Devine, a close friend of Keane's, a move which irked him. Devine had been the Cards' GM since 1957. Apparently, Keane figured he was next to go. Rumor had it that his job was in serious jeopardy. Moreover, Keane had gotten wind of a plan to replace him with bombastic Leo Durocher, formerly of the Giants and Dodgers. Newspaper writers in St. Louis and further afield openly speculated about such a move. Durocher would later recall that in the middle of August—with the Cardinals nine games behind the front-running Phillies—he had been invited to a secret meeting with team owner Gussie Busch. At this get-together, Durocher verbally agreed to take over the Cardinals beginning in 1965. Busch always denied such a meeting had ever taken place, but Durocher absolutely insisted it had. He said, "When a man says to me 'Do we have a deal?' and I answer, 'We have a deal,' and we shake hands on it, what does that mean?"[3]

In a retrospective article published online in 2022, baseball historian Gary Livicari penned,

> Loyalty was sacrosanct to a man of principle like Johnny Keane. He felt betrayed and thought he deserved better treatment. He put the blame squarely on the Cardinals' owner. Busch had broken one of Johnny's cardinal rules, and he just couldn't forgive him. Johnny's personal code of ethics required that he take action: He decided to quit.[4]

Therefore, on Friday, October 16, a day that was intended to feature a routine, feel-good, post–Series news conference in St. Louis, Keane showed up, grim-faced, and stated he had politely refused the hefty new contract offered to him by Gussie Busch to continue his role as manager of the champion St. Louis Cardinals—and officially resigned by presenting the Cardinals owner with the letter Lela Keane had typed three weeks earlier. Keane had been in the Cardinals' vast system in one capacity or another for 35 years. He had been St. Louis' manager since the middle of the 1961 season when he replaced the ineffective and wholly unpopular Solly Hemus.

Busch admitted he was completely astonished by Keane's announcement. "I tried to find the main reason why John is resigning," he told the *St. Louis Globe-Democrat*. "I don't know what caused him to make this decision. This came as a complete bombshell this morning."[5]

It was a day of surprises in MLB. That shocking development in St. Louis occurred on the very same day the Yankees fired their manager, Yogi Berra, after just one season at the helm of MLB's most decorated and famous club—a season where the club won its fifth straight AL championship and came within a single game of capturing MLB's top prize. Berra had entered the meeting with the idea of asking the club for a two-year deal. He was shocked that he was instead given a pink slip. Four days later, the New York Yankees hired the newly unemployed Keane to fill their managerial vacancy. Many writers found the merry-go-round of managers to be rather amusing, penning that the Yankees had modified the adage of "if you can't beat them join them" to "if you can't beat *him*, have him join you." A manager switching allegiances to the team he had just defeated in a World Series was something completely unprecedented. Research by MLB scholars found that only two other managers had resigned or had been fired after winning a World Series: The most recent was another Cardinal pilot: Rogers Hornsby in 1926. The other was Bill Carrigan of the Boston Red Sox a decade earlier in 1916.

Berra was fired after receiving a message that general manager Ralph Houk wanted to meet with him. Although Berra was axed, he would still remain employed by the AL champs in 1965 as an aide to Houk who was returning to his familiar place in the Yankee dugout. Berra's official new title would be "special field consultant." The old Yankee catcher took the news of his ouster in stride—at least he did so publicly—and played his regular golf game in a foursome that day in Haworth, New Jersey. "I don't mind," Berra told a skeptical reporter between holes, trying to remain cheerful about the odd goings-on. "I'll be spending the year at home. Where can you get a job like this? I don't have to sign in or punch a clock. And the pay is good."[6]

Those plans did not last long, however. When Berra was offered a coaching job with the New York Mets in 1965, he accepted it. So much for taking a year off from the daily grind and pressures of professional baseball. Berra would eventually manage in the majors again—but not until April 1972 when he was offered the position with the Mets upon the sudden death of Gil Hodges just before the season was about to begin.

Berra and Keane were not the only MLB managers whose jobs in 1964 were not waiting for them to resume their duties in 1965. There were managerial changes afoot in two NL cities. Herman Franks took over for Alvin Dark in San Francisco, while Danny Murtaugh was replaced by Harry Walker in Pittsburgh. Dark's firing was a messy affair. He became embroiled in controversy in 1964 after a newspaper article accused him of making racist comments about the club's black players. Many baseball insiders thought the accusations were ridiculous, including Dark's SABR biographer, who penned,

> Midway through the season, Stan Isaacs of *Long Island Newsday* asked Dark about the Giants' performance. The manager responded by accusing his players of making recent "dumb" plays. Although he later insisted that his comments were specific to baserunning mistakes by Orlando Cepeda and Jesus

15. Managerial Musical Chairs

Alou, it was already too late; because his team was made up primarily of African-American, Puerto Rican, and Dominican players, Dark was unfairly painted as a racist.[7]

Dark was fired by owner Horace Stoneham, following the final weekend of 1964's regular season. It had a been a season in which the Giants, who were in first place as late as July 20, eventually finished in fourth place, three games behind St. Louis. They had lost two of three games at home to the Chicago Cubs on the final weekend of the 1964 campaign—negative and disappointing results that terminated their pennant hopes.

Among those who thought Dark had been unfairly maligned were MLB Commissioner Ford Frick and Jackie Robinson. The ex–Dodger great firmly and unequivocally stood behind Dark. In an interview with the *New York Times*, Robinson stated that he had "known Dark for many years, and my relationships with him have always been exceptional. I have found him to be a gentleman, and above all, unbiased. Our relationship has not only been on the baseball field, but off it. We played golf together."[8]

In contrast, there was zero controversy regarding the vacancy created by Danny Murtaugh in Pittsburgh. He had voluntarily relinquished his managerial duties with the Pirates for health reasons—a surprise since he was only 46 years old in 1964. "Few [people in baseball] knew the extent and nature of his health issues," his SABR biographer Andy Sturgill wrote, "and he usually blamed his illnesses on the flu and stomach ailments."[9] Murtaugh would remain with the Pirates as a scout and special adviser to general manager Joe Brown.

However, neither Dark's controversial dismissal nor Murtaugh's surprising resignation measured up to the chatter regarding Keane taking over for Berra in 1965. In an article published decades later on NBCsports.com, Craig Calcaterra stated,

> It would later come to light that Keane and the Yankees had been in communication with one another since August. Keane was understandably feeling disrespected and knew he was on the hot seat. He also knew that Berra was coming under fire in New York. Keane figured he'd need a new job for 1965, the Yankees figured they'd need a new manager, and they put things in motion to make that happen.

Calcaterra added that Keane's opportunity to publicly embarrass Busch at the press conference the day after winning the World Series "was just icing on the cake."[10]

— 16 —

The Short Life of Johnny Keane

"If you live life right, then dying young is not a problem."
—Joe Lewis, American businessman and philanthropist

The winning manager of the 1964 World Series, the man who basically unleashed Lou Brock's speed onto the baseball world, did not live very long after his great Fall Classic triumph. Before the first week of 1967 had concluded, Johnny Keane was dead, the victim of a sudden and fatal heart attack. Born in 1911, he was just 55 when he died, but photos of Keane taken in 1964 and later in his short life show him looking like a man at least in his sixties.

He was stricken at his house in Houston late on the evening of January 6. After eating dinner, Keane told Lela, his wife of 29 years, that he was feeling slightly out of sorts. A few hours later he collapsed and could not be revived. Although he was a four-pack-a-day smoker, Keane's death came totally out of the blue. In fact, it was so unexpected that, according to a story about Keane's passing in the *New York Times*, the ex-manager had purchased a new automobile earlier that same day from a local dealership.

Twenty-seven months before his death, Keane had surprised baseball fans everywhere by voluntarily leaving the Cardinals almost immediately following their seven-game victory over the Yankees in the 1964 World Series—and then joining the outfit his triumphant Cards had just beaten. When Keane took over the 1965 Yankees, he quickly proclaimed the club as "the greatest team I've ever managed."[1] However, the fabulous Yankee dynasty was starting to crumble as its greatest stars began to age and high-quality replacements simply were not there. The once vast Yankee farm system had been significantly reduced as operating minor league baseball teams became more and more costly.

Jim Bouton, Yankee pitcher and maverick author, claimed that Keane was in awe of the Yankees when he first arrived in 1965 and managed accordingly, not wanting to ruffle the feathers of the household names on the club's roster. Then, when the team struggled and he tried to reverse the negative tide, he pushed the veterans too hard. Bouton said Keane was perceived by many Yankee players to be an outsider—a Johnny-come-lately who had not worked his way up through the vast Yankee system. It was not a good fit for the likeable Keane.

Moreover, Keane was better suited to work with young players, not the aging veterans occupying the key roles in the 1965 Yankee lineup. Keane was also a bit of a martinet—perhaps more than a bit—which did not go over well with the veterans who liked to have a good time away from the ballpark. As a religious man, Keane also had issues with his players consuming alcoholic beverages. He clashed with Clete Boyer, who was a moderate imbiber.

Things got markedly worse the following year. Twenty games into the Yankees' 1966 AL season, with New York struggling badly with a 4–16 record and sitting in last place, Keane was fired while the Yankees were in Anaheim to play the Los Angeles Angels. "We simply must make a change,"[2] was the club's official explanation for giving Keane the boot. It marked the first time since 1910 that a Yankee manager had suffered the indignity of getting the ax in mid-season.

"Keane, like so many others, failed to realize that the key Yankees' players were mere shells of themselves," wrote Harold Friend in a 2010 Bleacher Report article. "He never got to know them, and they never knew the real Johnny Keane."

"It had been difficult for Yogi Berra to take over for Ralph Houk, and it now was difficult for Keane to take over for Yogi. Keane was supposed to lead the Yankees back to the World Championship, but his new team's key players were past their peaks, and Johnny was blamed for their demise."[3]

Keane, who had once briefly studied for the priesthood, was a man of honor and tried to live his life with maximum personal integrity. When the Yankees decided Keane no longer should be the club's field manager, they offered to make a deal to prevent his termination from being publicly announced as "a firing." Keane wanted no part of such a dishonest charade.

"Yes, that's what happened," Keane told reporter Chuck Fierson of the *Oneonta (N.Y.) Star* later that same baseball season. "The Yanks told me that if I said I was retiring because of my 'health' they would give me a job in the front office. But my health is okay and I don't want a front office job. Besides that, I didn't like the idea of making up excuses."[4]

At least Keane was able to come up with a funny line about his brief but trying experience piloting the Yankees: "I managed good, but they played lousy."[5]

Ralph Houk returned to manage the floundering pinstripe outfit in hopes of turning their fortunes around, but it made little difference. New York finished the 1966 schedule mired in last place for the first time since 1912 when the team was still called the Highlanders.

For the rest of the 1966 MLB season, Keane was out of baseball, but he was happily spending time at home with his family. He was quite content to be paid by the Yankees for doing nothing. Keane was apparently under consideration for the managing vacancy with the Atlanta Braves which suddenly opened up midway through the 1966 season. Keane said he would take the job in 1967, starting with a new season, but he was not at all enthusiastic about jumping into it as a mid-season replacement. At the end of 1966, the Braves opted to make interim manager Billy Hitchcock the team's full-time pilot. That decision scuttled any plans Keane might have had about managing in Atlanta.

Shortly before his demise, and needing employment, Keane had been hired by the California Angels as a scout. Keane's car purchase on the last day he lived was connected to his requiring reliable transportation for his new job.

Keane's death, shocking as it was, brought forth plentiful compliments from the respectful men he had managed on both the Cardinals and Yankees. Ken Boyer told the press, "There isn't a bad thing I know that you can say about him. As a manager, he demanded respect and he got it. He expected a lot from his ballplayers, and rightly so. He was not an easy man on players, but he was a good manager."[6] In his autobiography, *From Ghetto to Glory*, Cardinals pitcher Bob Gibson called Keane "one of the nicest people I ever met in my life" and said Keane's death "probably affected me as much as anybody's I've ever known."[7] When Gibson was inducted into the Baseball Hall of Fame in 1981, in his speech he graciously noted that Keane was the first "real manager" he had played for.

Whitey Ford, whom Keane had managed for a little over a season while the latter was with the Yankees, called him "a true gentleman and a fine baseball man."[8] Ford noted that Keane was the first baseball person to visit him in the hospital after he underwent surgery. That visit occurred when Keane had no ties to the Yankees. It was five months after Keane had been fired. Elston Howard concurred with Ford's assessment. "[Keane] was a fine gentleman. He will be missed by people in all fields of sports."[9] His widow, Lela, whom Keane had married in 1937, told reporters that "baseball was the only true interest"[10] her late husband genuinely had.

About three months after Keane's well-attended funeral in Houston, the California Angels magnanimously announced that despite Keane being on the club's payroll for only about a month, his promised full salary for 1967 would be paid to his estate.

— 17 —

The Rapid Descent of the New York Yankees

> "The gentle downward slope gets steeper and imperceptibly becomes an abyss."
> —Swedish poet Tomas Tranströmer

Between the years 1921 and 1964 the New York Yankees had a virtual monopoly on the AL pennant. In the decade that followed their defeat in the 1964 World Series, they did not win a single one. It was scarcely imaginable that such a rapid and total collapse could happen to the team of Miller Huggins, Babe Ruth, Lou Gehrig, Joe DiMaggio, Mickey Mantle and numerous other Hall of Famers who wore the Yankee pinstripes proudly. But it did. From 1965 to 1975 the Yankees fell into a tailspin that plunged them into depths not seen since the days when they played their home games at tiny Hilltop Park. However, by 1964, the signs of decay were there to be seen if one looked closely enough at the big picture.

Nobody in the club's upper management wanted to admit it, but when spring training was held the following year, the dominant Yankees were a thing of the past. "By 1965 the Yankees were an aging team and the farm system was pretty bare," wrote Craig Calcaterra in a piece for the NBC Sports website in 2020. "Mantle's knees were a mess, Elston Howard was an old 36, Whitey Ford, also 36, had a lot of miles on the odometer too. The kids coming up behind them either weren't good enough or weren't yet ready."[1] New York compiled a mediocre 77–85 record in 1965 in finishing in sixth place in the AL—a very un–Yankee-like result. Tom Tresh was likely the best player on the club that season. He won a Gold Glove for his fine play in left field and batted .279 with 26 home runs and 74 RBIs. Attendance at Yankee Stadium predictably dipped too—but only slightly, about seven percent—from a little over 1.3 million in 1964 to 1.2 million.

In 1966, the Yankees hit rock bottom—an unthinkable last-place finish. The headline in a May 1966 *Sports Illustrated* feature article about the club's stunning downfall proclaimed, "A Dying Team Screams for Help." The *SI* article, written by William Leggett, declared that the Yankees

> have been guilty of many things in the past. They have been cold, arrogant and ruthless. They have been correctly accused of forcing their advantages by muscling little people around. But last week they were guilty of the one thing nobody ever imagined them capable of: panic. Once upon a time the Yankees looked down upon a world in which the words "simply must" were always spoken by others in baseball but never by themselves.[2]

In fairness, they did win 70 games and lose just 89 in 1966, and they were just 3½ games out of seventh spot, so it could be argued that the Yankees were a "strong tenth," as the *New York Times* charitably described the situation in an October 3 article. Still, the complete collapse of MLB's most glamorous club was staggering in its swiftness. It had been just two years since they had played St. Louis in the seventh game of the 1964 World Series.

There were ample reasons for the Yankees' dismal showing in 1966. Mickey Mantle played just 108 games (but he did bat .288 and hit 23 home runs, proving he was almost superhuman in how he coped with injuries). In 119 games, Roger Maris hit just 13 home runs and batted only .233; he had the good fortune to be traded to St. Louis before the 1967 season began and to conclude his MLB career with two pennant winners. Tom Tresh hit a career high 23 home runs, but his batting average shrank to a miserable .233. Catcher Elston Howard batted just .256. Shortstop Tony Kubek had retired, on doctors' orders, after the 1965 season, just before his thirtieth birthday. He was told he risked permanent paralysis form his back injury if he continued to play baseball. (Phil Linz, Kubek's World Series replacement in 1964, had been traded after batting just .207 in 99 games for New York in 1965.)

The Yankee pitching, always top-notch during the club's glory years, generally was a problem. Twelve different men started games in 1966. Only three of them had at least 10 victories: Al Downing, Mel Stottlemyre, and a newcomer from Chicago named Fritz Peterson. (Perhaps the most underrated pitcher in Yankee history, Peterson won 109 games in his 11 seasons with New York for teams that he described in a *New York Times* interview as "mediocre at best, pathetic at worst."[3]) Whitey Ford, an obvious shell of the great pitcher he once had been, appeared in just 22 games for New York, starting just nine of them, in compiling a 2–5 mark. Jim Bouton, who never came close to replicating his terrific 1964 season, suffered with arm trouble from throwing too many fastballs. He won a mere three games. Pedro Ramos was a dismal 3–9. Bob Friend, the onetime Pittsburgh star, was 1–4.

There was not much to cheer about in 1966 for fans of the once-mighty Yankees. Optimistic supporters grasping at straws could point to a few bright spots, though: Clete Boyer still played a strong third base for New York, but he only batted .240. (Boyer played shortstop occasionally, along with Horace Clarke, a 27-year-old from the Virgin Islands. By 1967, Clarke would emerge as the regular Yankee shortstop through 1973. The term "Horace Clarke Era" is sometimes used by Yankee fans, often in an unflattering manner, to describe the period between 1964 and 1976 when the club was perennially out of the running for the AL pennant.) Joe Pepitone won a Gold Glove for his work at first base and finished 27th in AL MVP voting. Second baseman Bobby Richardson was still on the Yankee roster in 1966, playing one season longer than he had promised his wife he would in 1964—only because the Yankees said they could not afford to lose both Kubek and Richardson at once. His offensive numbers, never his strong suit, were still about the same that year. His fielding percentage remained high at .980. Richardson was named to the AL All-Star team. It must have been a joyless season for Richardson however, who would soon hang up his spikes and glove and take up coaching and working with Christian groups.

The absolute nadir for the Yankees occurred on September 22, 1966. Record rainfall had saturated New York City over the previous few days. It was still raining slightly, and many people—including television announcer Red Barber—were expecting the Yankees-White Sox game scheduled for that Thursday afternoon to be postponed. It was not. The home team opted to play—and just 413 people were present at huge Yankee Stadium on that drizzly day to watch the struggling home team contest a meaningless game versus Chicago. The White Sox won, 4–1, but the major story was what occurred during that evening's broadcast.

By order of the Yankees' public-relations department, the stadium's television cameramen were forbidden to show the vast sections of empty seats, even for a moment. Announcer Red Barber felt he had a duty to report the story and filled in the void by describing the emptiness of the ballpark with words. Barber told his audience, "I don't know what the paid attendance is today, but whatever it is, it is the smallest crowd in the history of Yankee Stadium, and this crowd is the story, not the game."[4] (Remarkably, the minuscule crowd that afternoon was an aberration. Attendance at Yankee Stadium in 1966 only declined by about 89,000 fans from 1965.) Mike Burke, a CBS executive who was now the team's president, did not appreciate Barber's candor and chose to blame the bearer of bad news. A few days later, Barber, who was just 58 years old, was at a breakfast meeting with Burke. Before Barber had consumed his coffee, Burke told him his contract would not be renewed for 1967. Barber always maintained he was axed for being an honest reporter, but some sources say growing friction between Barber and the other three regular Yankee announcers—all ex-players—had grown that season. Years later, Joe Garagiola recalled that he had made wisecracks about the pitiful attendance during that same September 22 broadcast, but no one from the Yankee brass had chastised him. Whatever the case, Barber, who lived to be 84 years old and was described by David Halberstam as "the progenitor for baseball on the radio,"[5] never regularly called MLB play-by-play again.

In 1967, the Yankees improved to ninth place as the Kansas City Athletics slid into the AL basement. Their 72 victories put them 20 games behind the pennant-winning Boston Red Sox. The following year, 1968, was the last MLB campaign with just the two leagues and no divisions. New York finished two games above .500 and came in fourth place. It was the end of an era in another way: Mickey Mantle never played again. In the 1968 expansion draft for the four new teams that would enter MLB in 1969, the Yankees had not protected him. Thus, one of the most iconic names in Yankee history could have been selected by either one of the two new AL expansion teams: the Kansas City Royals or the Seattle Pilots. That would have been a travesty. Mantle made it publicly known he was not going to suit up for an expansion outfit, so neither team wasted a draft pick on him. In March 1969 Mantle arrived for spring training. After a brief time going through the motions, he decided his body could no longer take the strain of being a professional athlete. He formally announced he was through with baseball. As Kunj Shah wrote in a retrospective piece, "[Mantle] ended his eventual Hall of Fame career having only played for the Yankees, the way it was meant to be."[6] A promising outfielder named Bobby Murcer eventually replaced Mantle in center field.

In 1972, the Yankees embarrassingly did not draw a million fans to their home games for the first time since the Second World War as only 966,328 ticketholders passed through Yankee Stadium's turnstiles. That was an average of about 12,500 spectators per game. The previous year the club barely surpassed the seven-figure mark with 1,070,771 fans entering their huge and historic ballpark. Clearly some of the luster had faded from the club that was once the most stately in American sports.

In 1973, the club played its 51st and final season at Yankee Stadium with its old design. A two-year renovation project would force the Yankees to share Shea Stadium with the New York Mets in both 1974 and 1975. After the conclusion of the final game, on September 30, 1973, the Yankees were totally shocked when fans began ripping seats out of the moorings to take home as souvenirs of the good old days. Nobody dreamed of stopping them. "Souvenir-hunting wasn't in vogue—[but some] players and fans took some keepsakes," penned journalist Anthony McCarron in the *New York Daily News*. "Some [fans] came prepared ... bringing screwdrivers and hammers to make sure they got mementos."[7] (The 296-foot marker from right field was one such prize. Years later it sold at auction for more than $46,000.) At least one toilet was taken, too. Photos that appeared in the newspaper the following day showed families happily walking out of Yankee Stadium with the benches they had just sat on to watch the Detroit Tigers defeat New York. Scavengers did not get everything. Home plate and first base were saved. They were later presented to the widows of Babe Ruth and Lou Gehrig respectively.

Apart from the farewell to the original configuration of the ballpark, the big news coming from the club in 1973 was one that occurred away from the diamond. It was the crazy story involving pitchers Mike Kekich and Fritz Peterson who decided to swap their wives, their children, their cars, and even their pet dogs. The deal was done in July 1972, went through various stages around the time of the World Series, but it was not known to the public until March 6, 1973.

Incredibly, the two men did not figure their families' bizarre realignment would be particularly interesting to anyone beyond the people directly involved, but they were horribly wrong. The story received unfavorable national attention. It merited front-page coverage on the *Boston Globe*. (In that newspaper's sports section, Leigh Montville wrote a parody article about two baseball wives actually being traded by their husbands' teams!) Moralists were outraged, of course, perceiving the arrangement to be a prime example of societal rot. Newspaper columnists across the continent—not necessarily sports writers—were denouncing the "wife-swapping Yankees" with great gusto. Kekich did not seem to be bothered at all by the volume of criticism. He told the press, "Unless people know the full details, it could turn out to be a nasty type of thing. Don't say this was wife-swapping, because it wasn't. We didn't swap wives, we swapped lives."[8] By early 1974, both pitchers were no longer with the team. New Yankee owner George Steinbrenner, a staunch conservative, saw to that.

The club returned to a refurbished Yankee Stadium in 1976—and promptly drew more than two million spectators for the first time since 1950. The novelty of the modernized ballpark, plus the chance to root for a winning team spurred the huge renewal in interest. That season, the Yankees easily won the AL East by 10½ games and the pennant, but they were beaten soundly in a four-game sweep by the star-studded Cincinnati Reds in the World Series. Nevertheless, it had taken a dozen years, but the New York Yankees were once again a perennial threat to win it all.

— 18 —

The Cardinal Juggernaut

> "The St. Louis Cardinals are the champions of the world. What is there to be bitter about?"
> —Harold Kaese's coverage of Game Seven
> of the 1967 World Series for the *Boston Globe*

Between 1964 and 1969, the St. Louis Cardinals won 541 regular-season games, an average of slightly more than 90 victories per season. Over that six-year span, the Cards accrued two more NL pennants and one World Series. The Los Angeles Dodgers, often perceived to be the dominant NL squad of the 1960s, won just 506 games over that same stretch.

The 1965 version of the Cardinals, however, was an aberration. With Johnny Keane now employed by the New York Yankees, Red Schoendienst, the club's longtime second baseman who had last played in 1963, was installed as the new manager. It was the beginning of a successful post-playing career for the 42-year-old. Schoendienst would pilot St. Louis through the 1976 season and become the winningest manager in Cardinal history. His 1,041 wins stood until Tony LaRussa came along. As defending World Series champions, the Cards struggled throughout 1965, however, winning just 80 games and finishing a surprisingly poor seventh in the 10-team NL, 10½ games in arrears of Los Angeles. St. Louis did not post a win until their fifth game of the season, never got higher than third place in the standings, and was stuck in seventh place from August 1 onward. The Cardinals were surprisingly mediocre in their own ballpark, posting only a 42–39 mark in 81 games played at Busch Stadium. "The Birds have traditionally lived high at home," wrote Neil Russo in a seasonal recap article for *The Sporting News*. "They were the best home team in '64 en route to a flag … and they were tops at home in '63."[1] The 1965 season was the last one in which the Cardinals played at old Busch Stadium—formerly called Sportsman's Park—at the northwest corner of Grand Boulevard and Dodier Street on the city's north side. It had not aged well, nor had the

18. The Cardinal Juggernaut

neighborhood. (A Cardinal fan was killed in an armed robbery near the venue on Opening Day 1964.) A newer, more modern ballpark bearing the same name would open in 1966.

Bob Gibson was a 20-game winner, but no other Cardinal hurler won more than 11 times in 1965. Ray Sadecki had an especially poor year on the mound, posting a dismal 6–15 record with a 5.21 ERA. Curt Simmons fared not a whole lot better than Sadecki. He lost 15 games too, but he won nine. His ERA was a less-than-stellar 4.08. Tim McCarver, Bill White and Lou Brock all had good seasons offensively, but all of them experienced statistical declines from 1964. (Brock stole 63 bases, but he was caught stealing 27 times too.) McCarver broke a finger early in spring training and did well to post the numbers he did. All these downturns and setbacks were ample enough to make the Cardinals a non-threat to repeat as pennant and World Series winners in 1965.

Thoroughly dissatisfied with the season's outcome, new Cardinal general manager Bob Howsam traded Bill White, Dick Groat and backup catcher Bob Uecker to the Philadelphia Phillies prior to the 1966 campaign. (Uecker's comedic remarks would be missed. Once when Lou Brock was receiving an award for his base-stealing feats, Uecker, a man with zero stolen bases on his MLB résumé, heckled him by yelling, "If I had been in the lineup every day, that could be me out there!"[2]) Ken Boyer, the 1964 NL MVP, was traded to the New York Mets. The moves did not pay immediate dividends as the 1966 Dodgers again won the NL pennant. Pitching was their strong suit. It was the last Los Angeles squad to feature both Don Drysdale and Sandy Koufax—even though Drysdale lost more games than he won that season. The Dodgers quickly fell on challenging times after the sore-armed Koufax retired at the end of the 1966 season a short time before his thirty-first birthday. Los Angeles plummeted in the standings, finishing in eighth place in 1967 with just 73 wins.

Filling the vacuum left by the declining Dodgers, the Cardinals became the best team in the NL in both 1967 and 1968. They were a quietly dominant bunch that efficiently crushed the rest of the Senior Circuit. The pitching staff now included Nelson Briles and Steve Carlton. In penning Bob Gibson's SABR biography, Terry Sloope wrote, "The development of the young pitchers was critical to the Cardinals' drive to the pennant when Gibson was forced onto the disabled list on July 15 after suffering a broken leg. In that day's game against the Pirates, a liner off the bat of Roberto Clemente caromed off Gibson's right shin. Gibson pitched to three more batters before his leg finally snapped just above the ankle." Sloope added, quite unnecessarily, "The episode cemented Gibson's reputation as a competitive, gutsy player."[3]

Thirty-year-old first baseman Orlando Cepeda won the NL MVP

Award. (He had been acquired from San Francisco during the 1966 season in a trade for pitcher Ray Sadecki.) St. Louis won 101 games to capture the NL laurels, continuing their strong, aggressive play even after the flag had been clinched. In his preview column for the 1967 World Series, Al Abrams of the *Pittsburgh Post-Gazette* noted, "Apathy in the Red Birds is understandable. Red Schoendienst and his team did such a professional job of running away with the National League pennant [that] no one else came close. They were 10½ lengths in front of the second-place San Francisco Giants."[4]

By 1967, Stan Musial was now the St. Louis general manager, having replaced Bob Howsam. Al Abrams wrote of the Cardinals' Musial-Schoendienst combination, "Leo Durocher's blaring to the contrary, nice guys do win at times. You could look all around baseball, or any other sport for that matter, and not find two nicer gentlemen."[5] The Cardinals beat the sentimental favorites, the Boston Red Sox, who had been 100:1 underdogs to win the AL title when the 1967 season began, in a tough, seven-game World Series tussle. St. Louis had won three of the first four games, but Boston rallied to level the Series at three games apiece.

Bob Gibson, fully recovered from his serious leg injury, decisively put an end to Boston's "impossible dream" season by winning the first, fourth, and seventh games for the Cardinals. He went the full nine innings in all three of his victories, extending his postseason winning streak to five games. In his 27 innings of work, Gibson struck out 26 Red Sox while issuing just five walks. Gibson allowed Boston just three hits in the climactic seventh game. For good measure, he also hit a home run in the fifth inning off Boston's overworked and tired ace, Jim Lonborg, to put the Cardinals up 3–0. Joe Gergen, covering the World Series for United Press International, wrote, "The Red Sox … never had a chance against the burly St. Louis hurler who went the distance to record his third trumph."[6] Gibson, who became the sixth pitcher in the history of the Fall Classic to post a 3–0 record in one World Series, was the obvious MVP choice.

Lowell Reidenbaugh of *The Sporting News* applauded Gibson's excellence by penning, "With a cold calculating efficiency that is his alone, the Cardinal right-hander had locked the door and thrown away the key on the American League champions, climaxing a dramatic World Series that produced the Cards' eighth world championship and second in four years."[7]

The following season, 1968, was even more dominant for Gibson. In what has been dubbed by baseball historians as "The Year of the Pitcher," no hurler outshone the star right-hander of the Cardinals. Gibson put up numbers that had not been seen in MLB since the 1910s. He won 22 games and lost nine. He threw 13 shutouts. ("I'm still mad about losing those nine games,"[8] Gibson joked half a century later during a Cardinals telecast in 2018.) Of the 34 games Gibson started for St. Louis, he completed

28 of them. Not once in the entire season was Gibson removed from the mound during an inning; he only was replaced for pinch-hitters. The most eye-catching of Gibson's stats from 1968, however, is his 1.12 earned run average—the lowest seasonal ERA in the NL since Mordecai Brown's 1.04 in 1906. He won the NL Cy Young Award and was named the Senior Circuit's MVP. Because of Gibson's dominance (along with similar overwhelming stats put up by Don Drysdale of the Dodgers and Denny McLain of the Tigers in 1968), MLB responded by lowering the height of the pitcher's mound from 15 to 10 inches for 1969 in hopes of reinvigorating declining offensive production.

The 1968 World Series began with Gibson showcasing his skills to a huge NBC television audience. Gibson defeated the Tigers and Denny McLain in Game One, striking out 17 Detroit batters in a single game to set a new World Series record that still stands. (Sandy Koufax held the old one-game mark, with 15 whiffs in a 1963 game.) Gibson tossed a complete game, of course. He followed that outing with another victory in Game Four in which he went the distance. (Proving his 1967 homer versus Boston was no fluke, Gibson hit another round-tripper versus Detroit, too.) Gibson defeated McLain again, 10–1. It was, remarkably, his seventh consecutive complete game victory in World Series competition. That triumph gave the Cardinals a daunting 3–1 lead in the World Series, exactly what they had in 1967 after four contests were in the books. But just as the Red Sox had rallied the previous October when Gibson was not pitching, so did the Tigers. Detroit won Games Five and Six, setting up a seventh-game showdown. McLain had started Game Six, and won easily, 13–1. Thus, Game Seven would be a battle between Gibson and Tigers left-hander Mickey Lolich at new Busch Stadium.

Neither team scored during the first six innings. But in the top of the seventh, with two men out and two Tigers on base, Detroit capitalized on Jim Northrup's fly ball that was misplayed by center fielder Curt Flood, whose costly misjudgment turned it into a two–RBI triple. It was a catastrophic blunder as the Tigers eventually scored three runs in the frame. Flood was quickly added to the list of infamous World Series goats by newspapermen. However, Northrup voluntarily came to the defense of Flood, who was widely regarded as one of the best defensive outfielders in MLB—if not the very best. "He slipped a little, but it still went 40 feet over his head," insisted Northrup. "He never had a chance to catch it."[9] Mike Shannon hit a solo home run for St. Louis in the ninth inning, but it merely broke Lolich's shutout. Detroit won the game, 4–1, to complete their three-game comeback and win the World Series for the first time since 1945. It was only the third time in World Series history a team had rallied from a 3–1 deficit to win a Fall Classic in seven games. It was the first time in club history that St. Louis lost the seventh game of the World Series. Had they won, the Cardinals would have been the first NL team to repeat as Series kingpins since the 1922 New York Giants. Gibson was saddled with a hard-luck, complete-game loss. Gibson played well in the Series, as did Lou Brock, who stole seven bases. On the reverse side of the coin, Julián Javier went 0-for-22 at the plate to set a wholly undesirable record. When Tim McCarver popped up to Detroit catcher Bill Freehan to conclude the game, it was also the end of the Cardinals' era of NL dominance.

The following season, 1969, saw four new expansion teams enter MLB—two in each league—and to the dismay of traditionalists, the beginning of divisional play. Professional baseball at its highest level ceased to move directly from the regular season to the World Series. Now a best-of-five playoff between each league's divisional champions would dictate which team advanced to the Fall Classic. This meant that it was no longer guaranteed that the team with the most wins in each circuit would play in MLB's showcase event, as had been the case since 1903. The new era did not treat the dynastic Cardinals kindly. The defending NL titlists finished a poor fourth in 1969 in the newly formed NL East. Their 87 wins were 13 in arrears of the New York Mets who suddenly went from jokes to champions. At the news conference where manager Red Schoendienst signed his new contract for 1970, he was asked what the greatest need of the Cardinals was going into the next season. Schoendienst quickly offered a one-word answer: "Runs." He then added, "We need someone who can pop the ball."[10] Indeed, the Cardinals were ninth in the 12-team NL in scoring in 1969. Their 595 runs were only 13 more than the total scored by the expansion Montreal Expos. Only the fact that St. Louis allowed the fewest runs in the NL (540) kept them as competitive as they were. Still, on the day the Mets clinched the AL East, New York's Art Shamsky told the press, "I still think St. Louis has the best team in the league and will bounce back next year."[11]

With Astroturf installed at Busch Stadium for the 1970 season, St. Louis finished fourth again in the NL East, but this time the club managed only 76 wins. (Bob Gibson, a rare bright spot on the Cardinals that year, won the NL Cy Young Award with his 23–7 record.) In 1971, the Cardinals accrued 90 wins and a second-place finish, but Pittsburgh won the division, the NL pennant, and the World Series. For the rest of the 1970s, the Pirates, Phillies and Mets would all be East Division champions—but not St. Louis. The Cardinals' fabulous pennant years of the 1960s were now merely the stuff of nostalgia. St. Louis did not make another appearance in the World Series until 1982 when they topped the Milwaukee Brewers—then an AL club—in seven games.

— 19 —

Fiftieth Anniversary Championship Reunion

"Every parting is a form of death, as every reunion is a type of heaven."—American theologian Tryon Edwards

On Memorial Day 2014, the St. Louis Cardinals honored their World Series-championship team from 1964. Nearly 50 years had passed since the Cardinals upset the Yankees in seven games in that terrific Fall Classic. Fittingly, their opponents that day at Busch Stadium were the New York Yankees. Interleague play, adopted in 1997, had made such a visit in the regular season by the American League club seem normal. It was simply out of the realm of possibility, however, back in 1964. Except for the annual All-Star Game and World Series, the two major leagues operated as separate entities.

A writer for the Redbirdrants.com website who used the mononym "Danielle" wrote,

> The Cardinals used the New York Yankees' first trip to Busch Stadium this season as the perfect way to honor the 50th anniversary of the 1964 squad winning the Fall Classic. After all, it was the Yankees [whom] the Cardinals defeated during the 1964 postseason. It's unfortunate, though, that the Cardinals lost [today's] game in extra innings after giving up three runs in the top of the twelfth inning.[1]

Former battery-mates Hall of Fame pitcher Bob Gibson and analyst Tim McCarver joined Fox Sports Midwest broadcaster Dan McLaughlin as guests in Busch Stadium's broadcast booth during the game played that Monday.

Following a special dinner held the previous night at Mike Shannon's restaurant, the 14 members of the 1964 team—a solid turnout, which included one coach—were honored in an on-field ceremony before the game. Those fourteen ex–Cardinals were Shannon, Gibson, McCarver,

Red Schoendienst, Lou Brock, Dick Groat, Jerry Buchek, Phil Gagliano, Ron Taylor, Gordie Richardson, Bob Humphreys, Charlie James, Carl Warwick, and Julián Javier. McCarver dared to make the poignant comment that everyone in the room fully realized that, due to advancing age, it could be the last time that they might see each other.

The veterans from 1964 all gathered twice in 2014 for a doubleheader of sorts. The official Memorial Day event was the second such reunion for the team in 2014. In January, the champions from yesteryear were also honored at the St. Louis Baseball Writers of America Association (BBWAA) chapter's annual dinner. The same 14 players, plus Bob Uecker, came to that get-together. Uecker did not make the trip to St. Louis for this occasion to be saluted at Busch Stadium by the club.

Lou Brock took a mercenary view of the Cardinals' exciting run toward the NL pennant. He remembered September 1964 as a time when the team began what he referred to as a "salary drive." Brock noted, "You could be in last place, but you would see some of the greatest baseball plays in September because you're all looking for a raise," Brock said. "It was all business: I needed to keep those scissors, a 20 percent cut, off my contract." As for the Cardinals' hot streak to win the flag, Brock added, "We just caught fire. The momentum never stopped."[2]

Fittingly, Bob Gibson threw the ceremonial first pitch, but not from the regulation 60'6" distance. Instead, the 78-year-old former fireballer gently lobbed a toss from halfway between the plate and the mound. His longtime catcher, 72-year-old Tim McCarver, was on the receiving end. When he was asked to recall his best memory from 1964, Gibson simply replied, "Beating the Yankees, that was the best part. How we did it didn't matter."[3]

McCarver said the team's unexpected late-season charge past the fading Philadelphia Phillies—and the fact the 1964 National League pennant was still up for grabs on the final day of the regular season—helped keep the Cardinal players loose but focused. As for playing the mighty New York Yankees in the subsequent World Series, McCarver opined,

> If a little team from the Midwest has a lot of time to think about it, I think any team would be intimidated by playing them. Obviously, we knew who we were playing against—Maris and Mantle and Pepitone and Ford and all the rich tradition of New York. But we weren't intimidated ... and I think that helped us.[4]

The grim prediction made by Tim McCarver that celebratory weekend in late May 2014 would be an accurate one. Over the next decade, a large percentage of the 14 men honored that day at Busch Stadium would indeed pass away, including McCarver himself.

— 20 —

Where Have You Gone, Chet Trail?

> "I think one of the greatest educations I had was being in the South. I wouldn't want to do it over again, what I had to go through, but it certainly opened my eyes up to things."[1]—Chet Trail

The 1964 World Series famously featured the batting heroics of Bobby Richardson, Tim McCarver, Ken Boyer and Mickey Mantle. Bob Gibson and Mel Stottlemyre both excelled on the mound. That same Fall Classic is also the source for an obscure baseball trivia question: Who is the only player to appear on a World Series roster without ever playing in a single MLB game? The answer is, of course, the famous Chet Trail.

If you wonder who in the world Chet Trail is, you would not be alone. One can be easily excused for not recognizing this name. In fact, you would be in the vast majority of baseball fans who consider themselves knowledgeable about the game's rich and colorful history. Trail is what baseball historians and statisticians call a "phantom player." Here is his story…

During the 1964 season, Chester Borner Trail was a 20-year-old infielder from Toledo, Ohio. He was in the New York Yankees' farm system for a good chunk of the 1960s. His father had played in the Negro Leagues. "I don't have any stats [for him]," Chester said. "But…. I could remember, [my dad] could hit the ball pretty good."[2]

In 1964, Trail was under contract to the New York Yankees. Late in the season, Yankee shortstop Tony Kubek was playing injured. As a precaution, manager Yogi Berra elevated Chet Trail from their Double-A affiliate in Greensboro, North Carolina. He would suit up for the famous New York Yankees in the midst of an exciting pennant race. This heady promotion undoubtedly pleased the young man as Trail had never appeared in a single Major League game before that call-up.

Berra never used Trail during the remainder of the regular season. The Yankees were in such a fierce battle with the Chicago White Sox for the pennant that Berra was not going to insert an untested rookie into the fray. Nevertheless, once the Yankees had captured the AL pennant, Berra opted to retain Trail on New York's roster for the 1964 World Series. During MLB's grandest stage, Trail remained firmly affixed to New York's bench, seeing no action at all in the seven games versus the St. Louis Cardinals.

Trail was returned by the Yankees to Greensboro in 1965—and he never got back to the big time. Trail later ended up in the Baltimore Orioles minor-league system. Years later he admitted, "I wasn't going to move Bobby Richardson or Dave Johnson off second base."[3] Trail retired from professional baseball in 1969. He later became a pastor and then a bishop.

Thus, Chet Trail is the only non–Major League player to ever appear on a 25-man World Series roster in the long history of the Fall Classic.

— 21 —

Whatever Happened To...

Although a few of them sadly had short lives, many of the participants in the 1964 Fall Classic made significant contributions to baseball long after that compelling seven-game series had passed into memory. Here are some brief post–1964 biographies—by no means complete ones—of the major figures from that year's World Series.

Yogi Berra remained with the New York Mets, eventually replacing Gil Hodges as manager when the latter died suddenly during spring training in 1972. Berra led the Mets to a surprise pennant in 1973 by upsetting the heavily favored Cincinnati Reds in the NLCS. In the World Series, they lost to the Oakland Athletics in seven games. Berra was dismissed by the

Yogi Berra (second from left) and Yankee team owner George Steinbrenner (right) converse in 1980, in cordial times (Library of Congress).

Mets in August 1975. He returned as a coach for the 1976 New York Yankees, the season when they advanced to the World Series for the first time since he had managed the club in 1964. Berra became manager of the team in 1984 but was dismissed early in the 1985 season. Feeling deeply betrayed, the embittered Berra vowed to never return to Yankee Stadium as long as George Steinbrenner was the team's owner—even to the point of boycotting the unveiling of his own plaque in Yankee Stadium's Monument Park. He kept that promise until he and Steinbrenner publicly patched up their differences in 1999. One of the most beloved figures in MLB history, Berra, a three-time AL MVP, died at age 90 in 2015.

Jim Bouton's ascending pitching career peaked in 1964. In 1965, however, an arm injury slowed his fastball significantly and effectively ended his status as a young mound phenomenon. Moved out of the Yankees' starting rotation, Bouton was relegated mostly to bullpen duty from that point onward. Bouton began experimenting with a knuckleball in an effort to lengthen his career. His contract was sold, on June 15, 1968, by the Yankees to the Seattle Pilots ten months before the 1969 expansion franchise played its first game. The Pilots assigned him to the minor-league Seattle Angels for the remainder of the 1968 campaign. Bouton had a so-so year with the Pilots, which ended with a trade to Houston in late August. At the suggestion of a New York sportswriter, Leonard Schecter, Bouton began keeping a diary during the 1969 season for possible publication. It became the foundation for *Ball Four*—a groundbreaking baseball book that exposed some of the sport's warts, such as drug abuse, petty jealousies, and rampant tomcatting. MLB Commissioner Bowie Kuhn described *Ball Four* as detrimental to baseball and tried to get Bouton to state that everything in the tome was pure fiction. To his credit, he refused. The book alienated him from many of his ex-teammates who felt betrayed by Bouton's exposing of the sport's bawdy locker-room culture. He was persona non grata in baseball for many years because of *Ball Four*. (Ex-teammate Mickey Mantle was said to be especially offended by the book's openness.) Among other things, Bouton was not invited to Yankee alumni events, including old-timers' games. Bouton eventually penned a sequel, cheekily titled, *I'm Glad You Didn't Take It Personally*. In 1976, Bouton starred in the forgettable CBS sitcom version of *Ball Four* which died a quick death after just five episodes. A 1975 comeback in the minor leagues eventually led to Bouton pitching a handful of games for the Atlanta Braves in 1978. Bouton suffered a stroke in 2012 that affected his memory and his ability to speak. He died in 2019, at the age of 80, from cerebral amyloid angioplasty.

Clete Boyer played three more seasons with the New York Yankees, appearing in at least 144 games each year. Boyer's teammates always recognized his defensive ability. "When I think of Clete, I think of the outstanding defensive third basemen in baseball," Bobby Richardson once said. "I know Brooks Robinson got all the Gold Gloves, and he's every bit deserving of the Hall of Fame, but Clete was as good as anyone who ever played the game."[1] Despite his excellent fielding, Boyer was traded to Atlanta after the 1967 season for Bill Robinson, a promising youngster. He played with the Braves until late May 1971, when he was released following a bitter dispute with general manager Paul Richards. Boyer then played in Japan for a time with the Taiyo Whales—where he had famous slugger Sadaharu Oh as a roommate. He coached for a while and then opened a hamburger restaurant near Cooperstown, New York. The eatery definitely had a New York Yankees flavor. Patrons could purchase such fare as the Mickey Mantle Cheeseburger Deluxe and Yogi's Special Meatball Sub. Boyer died at age 70 of a brain hemorrhage. According to news reports, his cremains were placed in an urn bearing a Yankee logo.

Ken Boyer enjoyed his best season in 1964. (By an odd quirk, it was the fourth season in succession where he hit exactly 24 home runs.) After the Cardinals' disappointing 1965 season, Boyer was traded to the New York Mets. He achieved several career milestones while playing with the dismal team, including scoring his 1,000th run and notching his 2,000th hit. Partway through the 1967 season, Boyer, who was slumping at the plate, was traded to the Chicago White Sox where his batting stats somewhat improved. However, by May 1968, his offensive numbers plummeted. He was traded to the Los Angeles Dodgers where his career concluded in 1969. Beginning in 1970, Boyer managed in the Cardinals minor league system, with one call-up to coach with the MLB team. Boyer ended up replacing the fired Vern Rapp as the St. Louis manager early in the 1978 season. It was a position he held until partway through the 1980 campaign when he was replaced by Whitey Herzog. His MLB managerial record was a mediocre 166 wins against 190 losses. The Cardinals had intended to put Boyer in charge of their AAA team in Rochester in 1981, but Boyer's fading health prevented that from occurring. He died of lung cancer at the young age of 51 on September 7, 1982. He was survived by 12 siblings.

Lou Brock continued to elevate the stolen base to a new level in MLB after 1964. He proceeded to win eight NL stolen base crowns in a span of nine years. Brock eventually broke Ty Cobb's career MLB mark of 892 in 1977, a record that many baseball fans and scribes once considered untouchable. (Brock would eventually pilfer 938 bases.) Brock would also remind people that he had underappreciated power at the plate. He clouted five home runs in the first four games of the 1967 season. Brock also got 13 hits in the 1968 World Series to equal the mark Bobby Richardson set while playing against him in 1964. Overall, Brock batted .391 in World Series competition—a record high for any player with at least 20

WS games under his belt. He also exceeded the 3,000-hit plateau, achieving that milestone in 1979, the year he retired. Both Brock and his wife, Jackie, became ordained ministers. Late in his life, Brock experienced serious health issues. His left leg had to be amputated below the knee in October 2015 due to complications from diabetes—a cruel fate for the man who was once the swiftest MLB player. In April 2017, Brock grimly announced he had been diagnosed with multiple myeloma, but surprisingly, three months later he informed the media that doctors had happily pronounced him cancer-free. Undoubtedly one of MLB's true greats, Brock died on September 6, 2020, at the age of 81 in St. Charles, Missouri.

Harry Caray, the much-beloved St. Louis broadcaster, called Cardinals games for 25 seasons. In November 1968 he was nearly killed by a car while crossing a street in St. Louis. Caray suffered two broken legs in the mishap, but he recuperated in time for Opening Day 1969. To the shock of his many fans, Caray was abruptly dismissed by the Cards after that campaign. "I was expecting a gold watch, but I got a pink slip,"[2] Caray told David Letterman many years afterward. The reason for Caray's dismissal was never revealed, but a rumored affair with Susan Busch, Gussie's daughter-in-law, persisted. Caray publicly addressed the matter only after Susan and August Busch III divorced, but he insisted he and Susan were merely longtime friends. Seeking new employment, he moved westward to call a single season of Oakland A's games alongside Monte Moore. (Typical of that era of the Athletics, Caray clashed with owner Charlie Finley. He also did not get along with Moore who resented being demoted to a secondary role behind Caray.) Seeking employment elsewhere, beginning in 1971, Caray began calling Chicago White Sox games. That gig lasted through the 1981 season. Caray switched employers and became the Chicago Cubs broadcaster in 1982. There he gained fame by singing "Take Me Out to the Ballgame" over the ballpark's P.A. system during the seventh-inning stretch at Wrigley Field. The musical tradition actually began during his tenure with the White Sox. Team owner Bill Veeck explained to Caray, "Anybody in the ballpark hearing you sing … knows he can sing as well as you can—probably better than you can. So he or she sings along. Hell, if you had a good singing voice, you'd intimidate them, and nobody would join in."[3] Despite declining health, Caray was still employed by the Cubs when he died in 1998, about a month shy of his 84th birthday.

After the 1964 World Series ended, **Roger Craig**—who did a tremendous job relieving Ray Sadecki for 4⅔ innings in Game Four—had just two seasons left as an active player, but he still had many years of service to contribute to baseball. He famously became the pitching coach who taught his hurlers the split-finger fastball which made the careers of Jack Morris and Mike Scott so successful. "People think I invented that [pitch],"

Craig said. "I did not. Bruce Sutter did. I just found a way to teach it and it worked out."[4] The 1964 Cardinals were the third World Series championship club he had pitched for, the other two being the 1955 Brooklyn Dodgers and the 1959 Los Angeles Dodgers. As well as being a renowned MLB pitching coach, Craig managed the San Francisco Giants for seven seasons from 1986 to 1992, after which he retired. (He had also managed the San Diego Padres in 1978 and 1979.) Craig proudly liked to point out he attained a special Fall Classic triple crown. "I played, coached and managed in the World Series. That's quite a feat. Not many guys have done that."[5] Craig died at age 93 on June 4, 2023.

Al Downing will forever be known to trivia buffs as the pitcher who, on April 8, 1974, famously surrendered Hank Aaron's 715th home run—the blow that put Aaron atop the all-time MLB home run list ahead of Babe Ruth. However, Downing had a substantial 17-year MLB career. It began in 1961 with the Yankees and ended in 1977 with the Los Angeles Dodgers. Certainly, it did not appear Downing would ever survive that long in MLB, given that his workload was reduced by the Yankees severely in 1968 and 1969. He was traded to Oakland in 1970, staying there only briefly before being dealt to Milwaukee. A subsequent trade to the Dodgers in 1971 seemed to completely revitalize the left-hander, however. He won 20 games that season, tossed five shutouts, and won the NL Comeback Player of the Year Award. Downing also finished third in the 1971 NL Cy Young Award balloting behind Ferguson Jenkins and Tom Seaver. Released in 1977, Downing eventually embarked on a broadcasting career with the Dodgers from 1980 through 1987. He also worked on CBS radio for a time during the 1990s, and for the Atlanta Braves in 2000. As of February 2024, the 82-year-old Downing was still listed on the Dodgers' roster of public speakers.

Curt Flood became such an important person in the history of professional sports that it is often overlooked how good an outfielder he was in his heyday. Indeed, one biographer penned, "Curt Flood was a vital cog in the 1964 Cardinals' world championship run, but that achievement may have been all but forgotten in light of Flood's subsequent role in the arrival of free agency for baseball players."[6] In the seven MLB seasons from 1962 through 1968, Flood enjoyed sustained offensive excellence. He batted a cumulative .302 during that time—including five seasons over .300 with a career high of .335 in 1967. Flood had exactly 200 hits in 1963. He bettered that total in 1964 when he tied Roberto Clemente for the NL lead with 211. Defensively he was both solid and spectacular. He was featured on the cover of the August 13, 1968, cover of *Sports Illustrated* next to a caption proclaiming him to be "baseball's best center fielder." However, a misplayed fly ball—in which Flood lost his balance when he tried to change directions—a blunder that likely cost the Cardinals the seventh game of the 1968 World Series—was the beginning of the end for him as a big-leaguer. Following a difficult 1969 season, Flood received a call on October 8 informing him that he had been traded to Philadelphia. In Flood's estimation, the Phillies were a second-class baseball outfit whose management and fans were hostile toward black players. Flood had two options: He could retire or he could report to the Phillies. He did neither. Flood refused to report. Instead, he consulted a lawyer who suggested Flood challenge Organized Baseball's reserve clause—a convenient section inserted into most every player's contract that, in effect, bound him to his club for life. Flood asked Commissioner Bowie Kuhn to declare him a free agent. When Kuhn said no, Flood began his legal case against MLB arguing that the reserve clause violated the country's antitrust laws and the provisions of the U.S. Constitution outlawing involuntary servitude and slavery. Flood's case went all the way to the U.S. Supreme Court—but Flood lost at each step along the way. However, his case against the reserve clause was so compelling that it opened the door for future victories by others. Flood himself reaped no benefits, however. George Will wrote of Flood, "He lost the 1970 season and lost in the Supreme Court, but he had lit a fuse. Six years later—too late to benefit him—his cause prevailed."[7] Flood, out of shape and in dire financial straits, played in a handful games for the 1971 Washington Senators. Manager Ted Williams had faith that Flood would get himself into shape both physically and mentally. He did not. After just 13 games, Flood bolted from the team, only leaving a brief resignation message to team owner Bob Short. He fled America for Spain in a clumsy attempt to avoid alimony and child support payments. His life generally spiraled downward thereafter. Curt Flood died from throat cancer two days after his 59th birthday in 1997.

Whitey Ford was more seriously injured after Game One than the public truly knew in the fall of 1964. The Yankees deliberately continued to mislead the Cardinals and baseball fans everywhere by saying that Ford had merely injured his heel. In truth, he had major damage to his pitching shoulder. Teammates who saw Ford try to eat were shocked to see he was having great difficulty manipulating a knife and fork because of his ailing left arm. He never appeared in another World Series, but his lifetime record of 10 wins in the Fall Classic is probably untouchable. (In fairness, so is Ford's career mark of eight losses.) Ford was 16–13 in the 1965 season, but he only won two more games after that point. As Ford's career wound down, his lifetime loss total surpassed 100. He never played for any MLB team but the Yankees. Ford's 236 wins for the pinstripe crew, five more than Red Ruffing attained between 1930 and 1946, is still the club record more than 55 years after he retired. Ford died less than a month before his

92nd birthday in 2020, outliving his two main carousing buddies—Billy Martin and Mickey Mantle—by a considerable margin.

Joe Garagiola literally grew up across the street from Yogi Berra's childhood home in the Dago Hill section of St. Louis. Garagiola once mused that anyone who makes it to the big leagues is quite often the best ballplayer in his school, his town, or even his county. However, in his case, "I wasn't even the best player on my block!"[8] Garagiola was a promising catcher who never quite lived up to his billing—a shoulder injury in 1950 may have affected him greatly—although he did have four hits for the St. Louis Cardinals during a 1946 World Series game. After playing for four NL teams from 1946 to 1954, Garagiola retired from the game but embarked on a hugely successful career behind the microphone at age 30, beginning with the Cardinals in 1955. He had always been an amusing, self-deprecating after-dinner speaker, so delving into calling baseball games was something Garagiola transitioned to with ease. From 1961 through 1988 he was under contract with NBC for Game of the Week telecasts and postseason games. He also hosted a popular pregame show called *The Baseball World of Joe Garagiola* for several seasons. Along the way he got to work with Curt Gowdy, Tony Kubek, Vin Scully and Bob Costas, becoming one of the familiar voices of summer for millions of MLB fans. Garagiola also busied himself by hosting the *Today* show and emceeing a game show, *Sale of the Century*. Things turned sour in 1988, however, when NBC did not immediately approach Garagiola about renewing his $800,000 annual contract when it expired on November 1. (Rumor had it that Tom Seaver would replace Garagiola in 1989.) Shortly after that year's World Series ended, Garagiola sent an unsolicited letter of resignation to the network. "The way things were going, I just thought it was the right time to leave,"[9] Garagiola sadly explained. As it turned out, NBC only had one more season of its MLB coverage that had begun in 1947. Garagiola did some local baseball announcing for a time for the California Angels. In 1991, Garagiola was presented with the Ford Frick Award during the Hall of Fame Induction ceremony—often inaccurately referred to as the Hall's "broadcasters' wing." He died on March 23, 2016, at the age of 90.

After 1964, **Bob Gibson** pitched in two further World Series, in 1967 and 1968. He pitched three complete games in each of them. In 1969, although Gibson went 20–13 with a 2.18 ERA, the Cardinals dropped to fourth place in the National League's newly created Eastern Division. A year later, in 1970, Gibson was still a force on the mound for St. Louis. He won 23 games and picked up his second NL Cy Young Award, although the Cardinals again struggled as a team, finishing 10 games below .500. It was the last time Gibson won 20 games in a season. Despite tossing his only career no-hitter in 1971 (against the Pirates at Three Rivers Stadium),

Gibson's record slipped to 16–13 in 1971. Gibson rebounded to enjoy a 19-win season in 1972, but an injury to his knee cartilage in 1973 reduced his playing time—and his effectiveness. Gibson finished with a 12–10 mark that year. An 11–13 record followed in 1974. By 1975, Gibson's talents had diminished to the point where he was removed from the Cardinals' rotation of starting pitchers. As a reliever he picked up his 251st and final MLB win on July 27. Upon his retirement, Gibson's 3,117 career strikeouts put him in the top spot for NL pitchers and second behind Walter Johnson in all-time MLB whiffs. (As of the end of the 2023 MLB season, Gibson had been knocked down to 16th spot on the list.) Gibson was a first-ballot Hall of Famer in 1981. He died at age 84 on October 2, 2020, not long after his friend and teammate from the 1964 Cardinals, Lou Brock, had passed away. Savvy fans realized his death occurred 52 years to the day after he struck out 17 Detroit Tigers in Game One of the 1968 World Series.

Curt Gowdy's pleasant and slightly gravelly voice, according to author John Updike, made the versatile broadcaster sound like "everybody's brother-in-law."[10] The remark was intended as a compliment for the Green River, Wyoming resident. "My flat voice sounds just the way a cowboy hat looks,"[11] Gowdy modestly penned in his autobiography. Red Barber thought very highly of Gowdy, writing in 1970, "In my measured opinion, the greatest television sports announcer of today is Curt Gowdy. He is the best man on football, baseball, basketball, track, winter or summer Olympics, or fishing. He has amazing versatility and authority."[12] His voice was familiar to fans of baseball, basketball and football for decades. (Gowdy was even loaned to ABC in July 1976 so he could cover swimming events at the Montreal Olympics.) Gowdy continued to call baseball games for NBC's *Game of the Week* and the MLB postseason through 1975. However, his strong criticism of umpire Larry Barnett's controversial no-interference call during the 1975 World Series prompted accusations that Gowdy was biased towards the Boston Red Sox—the team whose games he had called for 15 seasons before being employed full-time by NBC. Gowdy's baseball work at NBC was reduced significantly thereafter, although he continued working pro football and Rose Bowl games for the network through Super Bowl XIII in 1979. Shortly afterward, Gowdy was part of an unusual broadcaster "trade" in which CBS acquired his services in exchange for the much-younger Don Criqui moving to NBC. A man who always enjoyed the outdoors, Gowdy hosted *The American Sportsman*, a weekend staple on ABC from 1965 until its cancellation in 1984. Gowdy also narrated many of the official World Series highlight films for MLB. Gowdy died of leukemia in Florida at age 86 on February 20, 2006. His funeral procession circled Fenway Park.

Shortstop **Dick Groat** played one more season in St. Louis, where his batting average dropped to a disappointing .254 in 1965. Groat was traded to Philadelphia in 1966 where his offensive numbers remained about the same. (One highlight that season saw Groat collect his 2,000th lifetime hit against ex-teammate Bob Gibson!) During the following season, 1967, Groat was hobbled with cellulitis in his right ankle. This condition severely limited Groat's playing time. The Phillies dealt the aging Groat away to San Francisco in a cash-only deal after just 10 appearances for them. He only played in 34 games for the Giants before his excellent 14-year MLB career ended at age 36. Afterward, Groat, a former hoops star at Duke University, spent more than three decades doing radio broadcasts of University of Pittsburgh basketball games. He died on April 27, 2023, at the age of 92.

Elston Howard was old beyond his years by 1964. The 35-year-old catcher had certainly been busy on the field during that season. He set MLB seasonal records for putouts (939) and total chances (1,008) for a backstop. Almost flawless with his defense that year, Howard had a fielding percentage of .998. Struggling with the Yankees in 1967, Howard got a huge break when he was traded to the pennant-contending Boston Red Sox in early August. The Red Sox won the AL championship by a single game and advanced to play St. Louis in the 1967 World Series. Howard smacked a key two-run single in Game Five, which Boston needed to win to stay alive in the series. The Cardinals won the Series in seven games, however, making it the sixth World Series that Howard had played in and lost—equaling a dubious record held by Pee Wee Reese of the Brooklyn Dodgers. Howard was released by the Red Sox after the 1968 season, which ended the playing portion of his career. Howard rejoined the Yankees the following year as the team's first-base coach—making him the first black coach in the AL. He held that job from 1969 to 1979. After his coaching career concluded, Howard became an administrative assistant with the Yankees. That position was sadly a brief one due to the ex-catcher's declining health. Howard was diagnosed with myocarditis, a disease that causes rapid heart failure. Howard died of the ailment at the young age of 51 on December 14, 1980. On hearing of Howard's passing, newspaper columnist Red Smith penned, "The Yankees' organization lost more class on the weekend than George Steinbrenner could buy in 10 years."[13]

Phil Linz, the world's most famous harmonica enthusiast, played one more year in New York for new Yankees manager Johnny Keane. Immediately following the 1965 season, Linz was traded to the Philadelphia Phillies. In exchange, the Yankees acquired Ruben Amaro, a fellow utility player. Linz did not play much while he was with the Phillies, appearing in only 63 games in his season-and-a-half with the club. On July 11, 1967, Linz was traded to the New York Mets where he continued to struggle.

Oddly, Linz's finest game as a Met came on May 25, 1968, when he was at the lowest point in his MLB career. Entering that game, Linz was hitless (0-for-25) for the season, but he went three-for-four with two runs scored in New York's easy 9–1 triumph over the Atlanta Braves. In January 2013, Linz attended a fundraising dinner honoring Yogi Berra—where he serenaded his ex-manager with the famous harmonica. "If people remember me at all," Linz modestly told *USA Today* prior to the event, "they remember me as a harmonica player, because I sure wasn't too good of a baseball player."[14] Linz died at a Virginia nursing home on December 9, 2020, at age 81. His obituary in the *New York Times* accurately labeled the .235 career hitter "an unlikely baseball celebrity."[15]

Mickey Mantle wound down his career with substandard Yankee clubs through 1968. He did some broadcasting work for NBC during their 1969 and 1970 World Series coverage, but he was not especially good at it. Despite being one of the best paid athletes of his era, Mantle was notoriously poor in handling his finances. Mantle suffered several setbacks from business failures as well. Personal setbacks were plentiful, too. His Wikipedia page states,

> [Mantle's] private life was plagued by tumult and tragedy. His marriage fell apart due to alcoholism and [his] infidelity. Three sons became alcoholics, two of them dying from it. Towards the end of his life, Mantle came to regret his lifestyle and the damage he had inflicted on his family. In his final year, Mantle was treated for alcoholism, later warning others of the dangers of hard drinking and telling fans: "Don't be like me."

As Mantle was a 1950s cultural icon, his death was the lead news story across much of North America when he succumbed to liver cancer at age 63 on August 13, 1995. At his funeral in Dallas, broadcaster Bob Costas, an unabashed Mantle fan, delivered a touching eulogy. Costas noted, "In the last year of his life, Mickey Mantle, always so hard on himself, finally came to accept and appreciate the distinction between a role model and a hero. The first, he often was not. The second, he always will be. And, in the end, people got it."[16]

Roger Maris was never fully appreciated in New York during his lifetime. Biographer Bill Pruden wrote of the man who walloped 61 home runs in 1961, "With one extraordinary season, Roger Maris secured his place in baseball history. And yet his establishment of the major league home run record … proved to be more of a personal curse than a professional triumph." The 1965 season was disastrous for Maris—and for the Yankees as a team. In May, Maris was hit by a pitch on his right hand. The team had him x-rayed in Washington, again in Minnesota, and a third time in New York. The team told Maris—and then informed the Gotham media—the x-rays showed nothing. Maris was urged to play. He played when he could. Still, Maris missed quite a few games and was summarily labeled a malingerer, all the while continuing to take pregame fielding and batting practice. It wasn't until September that Maris found out his injury had been misdiagnosed: He had in fact broken a bone in his hand and played with bone chips and suffered a detached ligament. Maris, played in only 46 games, the fewest in his career. Things only marginally improved for Maris in 1966. He batted .233 and hit just 13 home runs as the Yankeed ingloriously dropped into the AL basement for the first time in more than half a century. As Maris pondered retirement, the Yankees dealt him to St. Louis. The move turned out to be a tonic for the sensitive Maris and a boon to the team as well. Pruden penned, "Cardinal fans were known throughout baseball as supportive and knowledgeable. Returning to his Midwestern roots, Maris's quiet, but important contributions were recognized and valued by fans and media alike."[17] Maris batted .261 in the 1967 regular season and .385 in that autumn's World Series versus

Roger Maris (left) and Mickey Mantle, the Yankees' fearsome slugging duo of the early 1960s, are photographed at Boston's Fenway Park before the second All-Star Game of 1961 (courtesy Boston Public Library, Leslie Jones Collection).

Boston. The following season, injuries reduced Maris' playing time to just 100 games for the Cardinals. He batted a miserable .158 versus Detroit in the 1968 World Series with just a single RBI—after which he retired. Maris was a beer distributor in his short post-baseball life. He shied away from any connection with the Yankees until he surprised just about everyone by showing up with no fanfare at Yankee Stadium for Opening Day 1978 to help hoist the team's 1977 World Series championship banner. He received a huge, affectionate roar from the enthusiastic full house. Sadly, Maris was diagnosed with lymphoma in 1984. He died from the disease on December 14, 1985, at the young age of 51.

Dal Maxvill, despite having a notoriously weak bat, managed to stay in MLB through the 1975 season with stops in St. Louis, Oakland and Pittsburgh. Popular with his teammates, he appeared in 1,423 regular-season games, playing on five pennant winners and four World Series champions. Maxvill obviously was not in the big leagues for his offensive prowess. His best season swinging the bat was in 1968 while he was still with the St. Louis Cardinals. He set career highs in batting average (.253), on-base percentage (.329), and slugging percentage (.298). That season Maxvill also received his only MVP Award votes—he finished in 20th place—and won the only Gold Glove in his career. In the 1968 World Series, he went a dismal 0-for-22 at the plate. That performance broke all World Series records for offensive ineptness. (Even with the expansion of the postseason baseball at the MLB level in 1969, that mark remained as the worst hitless streak to start any postseason until 2022.) Moreover, Maxvill also holds the NL record for fewest hits for a batter playing in at least 150 games: He had just 80 hits in 1970 in 399 at-bats in 152 games, for a measly .201 batting average. In 1975, Maxvill was released by the Oakland A's shortly after the team lost in the ALCS to Boston. He retired as a player a month later. Maxvill later coached the Cardinals and eventually became the club's general manager from 1985 to 1994. He briefly scouted for the Yankees, but he drifted away from baseball in his later years. Maxvill celebrated his 85th birthday on February 18, 2024.

"For those who saw **Tim McCarver** break in with the St. Louis Cardinals," wrote biographer Dave Williams, "it was probably a surprise that he became better known for his broadcasting career than for his days as a catcher. Not that he wasn't always articulate and glib, and that his finding a home in the broadcast booth was a shock; it's just that he was a pretty good ballplayer who was a major contributor on championship teams."[18] McCarver once commented, "By the time I was 26 I had played in three World Series and I thought, 'Man this is great, almost a World Series every year.' Uh-uh. The game has a way of keeping you honest. I never played in another World Series."[19] McCarver remained the Cardinals' first-string catcher until 1969—often tutoring his obvious heir apparent, Ted Simmons—when he was traded to Philadelphia in the deal involving Curt Flood. McCarver, who eventually played for Montreal and Boston too, is one of a small group of players in MLB history who appeared in four different decades. (In McCarver's case it was the 1950s, 1960s, 1970s and 1980s.) As a Phillie, McCarver was a key figure in one of MLB's most egregious baserunning blunders. On July 4, 1976, McCarver hit an apparent grand slam homer off Pittsburgh's Larry Demery. However, Garry Maddox, the runner at first base, became confused. He thought the ball had been caught and headed back towards first base. Oblivious to Maddox's actions, McCarver, who was applauding himself as he touched first base, passed him on the basepath and was properly called out. (McCarver was credited with a single and three RBIs.) After his retirement, he became an excellent baseball broadcaster. Before gaining a national platform, McCarver worked local broadcasts for four clubs: the Phillies, Mets, Yankees and Giants. He also gained a national following by covering MLB's postseason events, working games with Jack Buck. McCarver called 13 World Series, the last one in 2013. He won three Emmy Awards for his work behind the microphone. McCarver died of heart failure at age 81 on February 16, 2023. His obituary in Associated Press stories described McCarver as "one of the country's most recognized, incisive and talkative television commentators."[20]

Umpire **Bill McKinley**, by far the most conspicuous of the six men in blue during the 1964 World Series, officiated just one more year in the majors. That Fall Classic was the last of four he worked. Born in 1910, McKinley was only permitted to officiate American League games until the year of his 55th birthday—which was 1965—at which point a mandatory retirement rule forced him out of the big leagues forever. Overall, he worked 2,977 MLB games over 20 seasons. McKinley died on August 1, 1980, at the age of 70 in Mount Pleasant, Pennsylvania.

Rookie hurler **Pete Mikkelsen** enjoyed a nine-year pitching career in MLB with five different clubs. The New York Yankees were the only AL team he ever pitched for—and he was only a member of that team through 1965. His most productive season occurred in 1966 with the Pittsburgh Pirates. That year he posted a 3.07 ERA and set career highs with nine wins, 14 saves, 76 strikeouts, 126 innings pitched and 71 appearances. He finished his MLB days as a member of the Los Angeles Dodgers, spending four seasons with the club from 1969 through 1972. He recorded 24 wins and 20 saves in 155 appearances. Over his nine seasons in MLB, Mikkelsen posted a passable 45–40 record with a 3.38 ERA and 49 saves in 364 games. He died of cancer at age 67 on November 29, 2006, in Mabton, Washington—the same small town where Yankee teammate Mel Stottlemyre had grown up.

First baseman **Joe Pepitone** had passable numbers for the Yankees for the remainder of his controversial tenure with the club. For example, in 1966, he clouted 31 home runs for a last-place team. He also won three AL Gold Gloves before 1970. However, his sordid, away-from-the-park adventures always seemed to get Pepitone more attention than anything he did on the field—most of it negative. A psychiatrist eventually diagnosed Pepitone as bipolar, which might account for many of his issues. Misadventures included drug possession, DUI charges, shattered marriages, and numerous other transgressions that led to fines and suspensions wherever he played. The Yankees parted ways with him after 1969, dealing him to the Chicago Cubs. Perhaps Pepitone's best year came with the Cubs in 1971 when he batted .307 in 115 games. Overall, Pepitone had a lifetime .258 batting average and hit 219 home runs. Largely considered someone who did not live up to his potential—he was on the radar of scouts at the age of 14—Pepitone died on March 13, 2023, at the age of 82. Pepitone's 1975 autobiography exposed his numerous prurient faults in great detail. Fittingly, its rueful title is *Joe, You Coulda Made Us Proud.*

Bobby Richardson, wrote one biographer, "was by all accounts a slick, rangy glove man and a steady stick man. He won the Gold Glove Award five times. He batted over .300 in two different seasons. He was selected to the American League All-Star team eight times. [When] the October spotlight was turned on, Richardson excelled."[21] Indeed, he did. His lifetime regular season statistics show a .266 batting average, a .299 on-base percentage, and a .335 slugging percentage. In World Series play, those numbers rose sharply: Richardson batted .305 with a .331 OBP and .405 SLG. He retired, at age 31, at the end of the 1966 season to spend more time with his wife, Betsy, and his five young children. (In the last MLB game Richardson played, he drove in the only two runs the Yankees scored that day.) Throughout his playing career, Richardson kept extremely active within Christian organizations and events. He was a YMCA general secretary and was actively involved in the Fellowship of Christian Athletes and the American Tract Society. Upon Mickey Mantle's death in 1995, his widow, Merlyn, asked Richardson to deliver a eulogy and officiate at her husband's funeral service. Richardson celebrated his 88th birthday on August 19, 2023.

Phil Rizzuto spent 60 years in the employment of the New York Yankees, first as a terrific shortstop—he was the AL MVP in 1950—and then as a popular broadcaster. (His forced retirement as a player was awkwardly handled, to say the least. In August 1956, the Yankees had reacquired Enos Slaughter to bolster the team's run for the AL pennant. Rizzuto was summoned to the club's offices where he was asked to give his opinion about which player ought to be left off the potential World Series roster to make room for Slaughter. After making a few suggestions that were all quickly rejected, it suddenly dawned on the 38-year-old Rizzuto that the club wanted him to remove himself from the roster! He never played another MLB game.) Rizzuto was strongly cautioned by former Yankee teammate George (Snuffy) Stirnweiss not to openly criticize the Yankees for the shabby ouster in order to keep the door open to future employment with the club, which indeed came shortly thereafter. After receiving positive reviews for his work on New York Giants radio broadcasts for the rest of the 1956 season, Rizzuto was hired as a Yankee broadcaster beginning in 1957. Enthusiastically shouting "Holy cow!" whenever something exciting or unusual happened during a game, Rizzuto held that job for 40 years, surpassing Mel Allen's tenure with the team by 15 years. Much like his playing career, Rizzuto's broadcasting career was poised to end on a sour note in 1995 when the team refused to give him the day off to attend Mickey Mantle's funeral in Dallas because he was needed to provide color commentary for that night's Yankees-Red Sox game. Unable to focus on the game, Rizzuto left the broadcast booth in the fifth inning and did not return for the rest of the season. He was persuaded to come back in 1996 for one last season, where he got to call Derek Jeter's rookie campaign. After suffering from poor health during the last two years of his life, Rizzuto died on August 13, 2007, about a month before his 90th birthday. His death in a long-term care facility occurred exactly 12 years after Mickey Mantle had died.

Ray Sadecki had a dismal 1965 on the mound for St. Louis. Things went poorly from the outset for the palmball specialist. Sadecki began the season 0–4 with an 8.20 ERA, and ended it with a 6–15 mark. His ERA dropped by the end of the campaign, but it was still an unacceptable 5.21. Sadecki began the 1966 season in the Cardinal bullpen, a move that revitalized Sadecki for a time. He pitched one inning of the second game of the 1966 season, and struck out the side. Another successful relief appearance followed, after which Sadecki regained a position in the starting rotation. He enjoyed two successful starts. His record stood at 2–0 with a 0.98 ERA before he faced the Mets on May 4. Sadecki had a poor day and was knocked out of the box by the seventh inning. Just four days later, Sadecki was traded to the San Francisco Giants for Orlando Cepeda. (Cepeda would win the NL MVP award in 1967, frequently making Sadecki the object of Bay Area fans' displeasure.) Sadecki did not do well in 1966, but he rebounded in 1967 to post a 12–6 record and a career-best ERA of 2.78. Sadecki experienced mixed results over the rest of his career which lasted until April 1977. It saw him traded to the New York Mets, Atlanta Braves, Kansas City Royals and the Milwaukee Brewers. Overall, Sadecki posted a lifetime MLB won-lost record of 135–131. Sadecki died of blood cancer on November 17, 2014, at age 73.

Outfielder **Mike Shannon** spent 64 years on the payroll of the St. Louis Cardinals in some capacity. Half a century of it was as the club's popular broadcaster. In 1965, Shannon had a disappointing season at the plate, batting just .221. However, Red Schoendienst realized Shannon had value due to his versatility. At one point in his career, Shannon served as the team's third-string catcher. In 1966, he raised his batting average to .288 despite starting the season on the bench. A good team player, Shannon moved to third base when the Cards acquired Roger Maris in 1967 so the newcomer would have an outfield position to play. He and Maris became close friends. Nephritis, a potentially fatal kidney disease, forced Shannon's retirement from baseball as a player in 1970. The following year Shannon was hired by the club to be part of the Cards' promotional staff. By the next season he was sharing the broadcast booth with Jack Buck. That well-matched pairing lasted for nearly 30 seasons. Shannon was known for sharing his endearing baseball stories with his audience. His webpage from the Missouri Sports Hall of Fame states,

> He's the old big-leaguer with the most enjoyable stories, the kind that you could listen to all day. And Mike Shannon doesn't mind at all. Baseball stories? They're the best. Ask him about the 1967 season when he graciously moved from right field to third base to make room for Roger Maris, and he jokes, "There was a bit of selfishness in that, too. I knew if I could play third base, I'd have job security for a long time."

Buck died in 2002, after which Shannon spent most of the next 20 years working alongside John Rooney. From 2016 through 2021, Shannon did not travel with the club and only called Cardinal home games. Shannon died on April 29, 2023, after suffering a stroke. He was 83 years old.

The career **of Curt Simmons** went into a decline following the 1964 World Series. He never had another winning season. He lost 15 games while only winning nine for St. Louis in 1965. The next two seasons saw Simmons dealt to the Chicago Cubs and then to the California Angels. Although Simmons' lifetime statistics are not especially eye-catching—he had a 193–182 overall record—both Stan Musial and Hank Aaron rated Simmons as the toughest pitcher each of them ever faced because of his odd delivery. "Baseball players are trained to watch for the pitch up here (over his head)." Aaron once told a reporter. "Curt Simmons never did that. He'd pitch right from his leg, and I could never adjust to that."[22] Simmons spent most of his post-baseball life managing a golf course in Pennsylvania that he co-owned with former teammate Robin Roberts. He lived a long life, passing away at age 93 on December 13, 2022. Simmons had been the last living member of the 1950 Philadelphia Phillies NL pennant-winning team, and the last surviving Phillie to have played during the 1940s.

21. Whatever Happened To... 193

Knuckleball pitcher **Barney Schultz** is best remembered for serving up the walk-off home run to Mickey Mantle on the first pitch he threw in the ninth inning of Game Three of the Word Series. Only the most scholarly of baseball fans recall that Schultz got credit for a save in Game One. Such is the misfortune of being a relief pitcher: the failures are usually far more spectacular than the successes. Schultz spent his entire MLB career coming out of the bullpen. He had zero lifetime starts; his 227 appearances were all in relief. Following the 1964 World Series, Schultz pitched one more season in St. Louis. He appeared in 34 games and posted a 2–2 record with a pair of saves. Schultz's last MLB game was on September 6, 1965. By an odd coincidence, exactly 50 years later, in 2015, he passed away at the age of 89 in Willingboro, New Jersey.

Mel Stottlemyre, according to his SABR biography, was "one of the most underrated and overlooked pitchers of his generation. Stottlemyre won 149 games and averaged 272 innings per season over a nine-year stretch (1965 to 1973) that unfortunately corresponded with the nadir of Yankees history."[23] Indeed, because of the dismal era in which Stottlemyre pitched for New York, he generally does not get his just due as a terrific starter. After their 1964 World Series loss, the Yankees did not even seriously compete for a division title until 1974. As fate would have it, Stottlemyre was relegated to the sidelines for much of the pennant race that year. After enduring years of regular cortisone shots in his shoulder to numb the pain and make pitching possible, Stottlemyre was diagnosed with a torn rotator cuff after 15 starts in 1974, effectively ending his MLB career just before his 33rd birthday. He was unceremoniously handed his release during spring training in 1975. Stottlemyre told the media he was not surprised by the move but he was disappointed by its abruptness. He chose to distance himself from his Yankee past for many years afterward. Stottlemyre returned to Washington state and operated a sporting goods store for a time. He then joined the expansion Seattle Mariners as a pitching coach. (He resigned that post, however, when his youngest son, Jason, became terminally ill with leukemia.) In 1984 he returned to MLB to coach the New York Mets, where he stayed through 1990. After holding a similar job in Houston, Stottlemyre eventually made amends with George Steinbrenner and joined the Yankees' staff. He coached his former team from 1996 to 2005. He died at age 77 on January 13, 2019. His oldest son, Todd, born seven months after the 1964 World Series ended, was a very capable pitcher himself. He won 138 MLB games, most of them coming as a member of the Toronto Blue Jays. Unlike his father, Todd Stottlemyre played on two World Series winners.

Tom Tresh had his best year in MLB in 1965, finishing ninth in the voting for AL MVP. Not only did he bat .297 and drive in 74 runs, the 1962

AL Rookie of the Year also clouted 26 home runs. On defense, he won a Gold Glove. In 1966, Tresh upped his seasonal home run total to 27, but his batting average dropped to just .233. It was a sign of things to come. Tresh's offensive numbers dwindled steadily over the rest of his career. Partway through the 1969 season, Tresh was traded by the Yankees to Detroit. He was released by the Tigers prior to the 1970 season and retired from professional baseball. Following his playing career, Tresh returned to Central Michigan University, his alma mater. There he was employed as an assistant placement director for many years. He helped to invent the Slide-Rite, a training tool designed to teach correct sliding and diving techniques for baseball and softball players, as well as football and soccer players. At the age of 70, Tresh suffered a fatal heart attack at his Venice, Florida, home on October 15, 2008.

Carl Warwick, a journeyman player, certainly made the most of his lone World Series experience, starring as St. Louis' best pinch hitter over the seven games. Warwick was called upon to pinch hit five times—and he reached base four times in his first four appearances. His sixth-inning single in Game One off Al Downing drove in the go-ahead run in the Cardinals' 9–5 triumph. Warwick also singled and scored a run in Game Two against Mel Stottlemyre, he drew a walk off Jim Bouton in Game Three, and singled again off Downing in Game Four. That hit sparked a rally that culminated in Ken Boyer's dramatic grand slam homer. Proving he was not perfect, Warwick fouled out to Elston Howard off Bouton in Game Six. Warwick thus batted .750 in the 1964 World Series and posted an on-base percentage of .800. He scored two runs himself and had an RBI. Shuffled around to several teams beginning in 1965, Warwick retired from baseball prior to the 1967 season. He subsequently operated real estate and travel agencies in the Houston area. Warwick celebrated his 87th birthday on February 27, 2024.

Bill White continued to play excellent baseball for St. Louis until he was traded to Philadelphia before the 1966 season. He returned to Missouri to finish his MLB career with the Cardinals in 1969. An excellent defensive player, White won seven consecutive Gold Gloves as a first baseman from 1960 through 1966. His offensive numbers declined steadily after 1965, however. Following White's retirement, he moved easily into sports broadcasting. In 1971, White began calling New York Yankee games. He held the job until 1988, most often teamed with Phil Rizzuto and Frank Messer in the broadcast booth. (White did the team's broadcasts on both radio and television during most of that period.) White was a pioneer of sorts as he was the first regular black play-by-play announcer for a major-league sports team. Proving his versatility, White also called games for the NHL's Philadelphia Flyers for a time. He also worked the Winter Olympics for

21. Whatever Happened To…

ABC in both 1980 and 1984. In 1989, White was elected to replace Bart Giamatti as National League president in a unanimous vote, becoming the first black executive to hold such a high position in any major team sport in North America. He served capably through 1994. In his autobiography, White expressed concerns about having been basically a figurehead in that position, but he also said that he had accomplished some goals that he originally had set out to achieve when he accepted the job. As of February 2024, the nonagenarian White, who was born on January 28, 1934, was one of the rapidly dwindling number of participants of the 1964 World Series who was still alive.

1964 World Series Statistics

St. Louis Cardinals: Batting

Player	POS	GP	AB	H	R	AV	RBI
Ken Boyer	3B	7	27	6	5	.222	6
Lou Brock	OF	7	30	9	2	.300	5
Jerry Buchek	2B	4	1	1	1	1.000	0
Roger Craig	P	2	1	0	0	.000	0
Curt Flood	OF	7	30	6	5	.200	3
Bob Gibson	P	3	9	2	1	.222	0
Dick Groat	SS	7	26	5	3	.192	1
Bob Humphreys	P	1	0	0	0	.000	0
Charlie James	PH	3	3	0	0	.000	0
Julián Javier	2B	1	0	0	1	.000	0
Dal Maxvill	2B	7	20	4	0	.200	1
Tim McCarver	C	7	23	11	4	.478	5
Gordie Richardson	P	2	0	0	0	.000	0
Ray Sadecki	P	2	2	1	0	.500	1
Barney Schultz	P	4	1	0	0	.000	0
Mike Shannon	OF	7	28	6	6	.214	2
Curt Simmons	p	2	4	2	0	.500	1
Bob Skinner	PH	4	3	2	0	.667	1
Ron Taylor	P	2	1	0	0	.000	0
Carl Warwick	PH	5	4	3	2	.750	1
Bill White	1B	7	27	3	2	.111	2
Totals			240	61	32	.254	29

Doubles: Boyer, Brock (2), Groat, Maxvill, McCarver, Skinner, White
Triples: Flood, Groat, McCarver
Home Runs: Boyer (2), Brock, McCarver, Shannon
Sacrifice Flies: Boyer, McCarver

Sacrifice Bunts: Maxvill, Shannon, Simmons
Stolen Bases: McCarver, Shannon, White
The following players were on the 25-man World Series roster for St. Louis but did not play in any games: Mike Cuellar, Ed Spiezio, Bob Uecker and Ray Washburn

St. Louis Cardinals: Pitching

Pitcher	GP	W	L	GS	CG	IP	H	K	BB	ERA
Roger Craig	2	1	0	0	0	5.0	2	9	3	0.00
Bob Gibson	3	2	1	3	2	27.0	23	31	8	3.00
Bob Humphreys	1	0	0	0	0	1.0	0	1	0	0.00
Gordie Richardson	2	0	0	0	0	0.2	3	0	2	40.50
Ray Sadecki	2	1	0	2	0	6.1	12	2	5	8.53
Barney Schultz	4	0	1	0	0	4.0	9	1	3	18.00
Curt Simmons	2	0	1	2	0	14.1	11	8	3	2.51
Ron Taylor	2	0	0	0	0	4.2	0	2	1	0.00
Totals		4	3	7	2	63.0	60	54	25	4.29

New York Yankees: Batting

Player	POS	GP	AB	H	R	AV	RBI
Johnny Blanchard	PH	4	4	1	0	.250	0
Jim Bouton	P	2	7	1	0	.143	1
Clete Boyer	3B	7	24	5	2	.208	3
Al Downing	P	3	2	0	0	.000	0
Whitey Ford	P	1	1	1	0	1.000	1
Pedro Gonzalez	3B	1	1	0	0	.000	0
Steve Hamilton	P	2	0	0	0	.000	0
Mike Hegan	PH	3	1	0	1	.000	0
Elston Howard	C	7	24	7	5	.292	2
Phil Linz	SS	7	31	7	5	.226	2
Hector Lopez	OF/1B	3	2	0	0	.000	0
Mickey Mantle	OF	7	24	8	8	.333	8
Roger Maris	OF	7	30	6	4	.200	1
Pete Mikkelsen	P	4	0	0	0	.500	0
Joe Pepitone	1B	7	26	4	1	.154	5
Hal Reniff	P	1	0	0	0	.000	0
Bobby Richardson	2B	7	32	13	3	.406	3
Rollie Sheldon	P	2	0	0	0	.000	0
Mel Stottlemyre	P	3	8	1	0	.125	0

1964 World Series Statistics

Player	POS	GP	AB	H	R	AV	RBI
Ralph Terry	P	1	0	0	0	.000	0
Tom Tresh	OF	7	22	6	4	.273	7
Totals			239	60	33	.251	33

Doubles: Blanchard, Boyer, Howard, Linz, Mantle (2), Pepitone, Richardson (2), Tresh (2)
Home Runs: Boyer, Linz (2), Mantle (3), Maris, Pepitone, Tresh (2)
Sacrifice Bunt: Richardson
The following players were on the 25-man World Series roster for New York but did not play in any games: Archie Moore, Bill Stafford, Chet Trail and Stan Williams

New York Yankees: Pitching

Pitcher	GP	W	L	GS	CG	IP	H	K	BB	ERA
Jim Bouton	2	2	0	2	1	17.1	15	7	5	1.56
Al Downing	3	0	1	1	0	7.2	9	5	2	8.22
Whitey Ford	1	0	1	1	0	5.1	8	4	1	8.44
Steve Hamilton	2	0	0	0	0	2.0	3	2	0	4.50
Pete Mikkelsen	4	0	1	0	0	4.2	4	4	2	5.79
Hal Reniff	1	0	0	0	0	0.1	2	0	0	0.00
Rollie Sheldon	2	0	0	0	0	2.2	0	2	2	0.00
Mel Stottlemyre	3	1	1	3	1	20.0	18	12	6	3.15
Ralph Terry	1	0	0	0	0	2.0	2	3	0	0.00
Totals		3	4	7	2	62.0	61	39	18	3.77

Chapter Notes

Introduction

1. Lyndon Johnson, Azquotes.com.
2. Nate Haseltine, "Smoking Menaces Health," *Boston Globe*, January 12, 1964, 1.
3. Jeremiah V. Muphy, "In Boston: Cut Down—Not Quit," *Boston Globe*, January 12, 1964, 1.
4. Ken Burns (director), *Baseball (7th Inning)*, PBS (documentary), 1994.

Chapter 1

1. Mel Marmer, *The Year of the Blue Snow* (Phoenix: Society for American Baseball Research, 2013), 1.
2. Steve Wulf, "The Year of the Blue Snow," *Sports Illustrated*, September 24, 1989 (online version).
3. Harold Kaese, "Yankees Bury Three Jinxes," *Boston Globe*, October 5, 1964, 19.
4. "Phillies Up Lead on Bunning Job," *Schenectady Gazette*, September 21, 1964, 22.
5. Steve Wulf, "The Year of the Blue Snow," *Sports Illustrated*, September 24, 1989 (online version).
6. "Mauch Still Feels Phillies Can Win Flag," *Schenectady Gazette*, September 28, 1964, 19.
7. Ibid.
8. Steve Wulf, "The Year of the Blue Snow," *Sports Illustrated*, September 24, 1989 (online version).
9. Ibid.
10. Allen Lewis, "Mauch Finds Hunk of Gold Among Phillies' Rubble," *The Sporting News*, October 17, 1964, 10.
11. Steve Wulf, "The Year of the Blue Snow," *Sports Illustrated*, September 24, 1989 (online version).
12. Allen Lewis, "Mauch Finds Hunk of Gold Among Phillies' Rubble," *The Sporting News*, October 17, 1964, 10.
13. Steve Wulf, "The Year of the Blue Snow," *Sports Illustrated*, September 24, 1989 (online version).
14. Ibid.

Chapter 2

1. Milton Gross, "Brock Biggest Reason Cards Did It," *Boston Globe*, October 6, 1964, 51.
2. David Halberstam, *October 1964* (New York: Villard Books, 1994), xii.
3. Milton Gross, "Brock Biggest Reason Cards Did It," *Boston Globe*, October 6, 1964, 51.
4. Ibid.
5. Ibid.
6. Ibid.
7. Ibid.
8. John Stahl, "Johnny Keane," SABR Biography Project (online).
9. Milton Gross, "Brock Biggest Reason Cards Did It," *Boston Globe*, October 6, 1964, 51.
10. Ibid.
11. Harold Kaese, "Cardinals Much Like 1960 Bucs," *Boston Globe*, October 6, 1964, 23.
12. "Bob Gibson Quotes," baseball-almanac.com.
13. William Leggett, "Miracle in St. Louis," *Sports Illustrated*, October 12, 1964, 25.
14. Tim McCarver, "Former Cardinal

Tim McCarver," YouTube clip, May 26, 2014.

Chapter 3

1. David Halberstam, *October 1964* (New York: Villard Books, 1994), 316.
2. *Ibid.*, 16.
3. Til Ferdenzi, "A Year I'll Never Forget," *The Sporting News*, October 17, 1964, 1.
4. Ned Garver, Bill Bozman, and Ronnie Joyner, *Touching All the Bases* (Pepperpot Productions, 2003), 101.
5. Jan Finkel, "Johnny Sain," SABR Biography Project (online).
6. Bob Holbrook, "Yanks' Slump Follows Sale," *Boston Globe*, August 22, 1964, 15.
7. Til Ferdenzi, "A Year I'll Never Forget," *The Sporting News*, October 17, 1964, 10.
8. Harold Kaese, "Yankees Bury Three Jinxes," *Boston Globe*, October 5, 1964, 19.
9. Al Featherston, "The Demise of the New York Yankees, 1964–1966," DiamondsintheDusk.com, undated.

Chapter 4

1. Curt Smith, "More from Curt Smith on Baseball: Disappointing News Why Mel Allen Was Fired; His Rehabilitation," *Sports Broadcast Journal* (online), January 4, 2023.
2. Curt Smith, "Why Was Mel Allen Fired?" *MLB Blogs*, June 10, 2007.
3. Richard Sandomir, "Mel Allen is Dead at 83; Golden Voice of the Yankees," *New York Times* (online archives), June 17, 1986.
4. Curt Smith, "Why Was Mel Allen Fired?" *MLB Blogs*, June 10, 2007.
5. *Ibid.*
6. *Ibid.*
7. *Ibid.*
8. *Ibid.*
9. *Ibid.*
10. Curt Smith, "More from Curt Smith on Baseball: Disappointing News Why Mel Allen Was Fired; His Rehabilitation," *Sports Broadcast Journal* (online), January 4, 2023.
11. Curt Smith, "Historian Curt Smith Answers Mystery Question: Why Mel Allen Was Fired by GM Ralph Houk in '64," *Sports Broadcast Journal* (online), July 25, 2018.
12. "How About That! Yankees Fired Mel Allen in '64," *Washington Times*, December 18, 2006.

Chapter 5

1. Joe Reichler, "Ford, Sadecki Starting Pitchers for Series Opener," *Schenectady Gazette*, October 6, 1964, 18.
2. "Series Betting to Hit Record $600 Million," *Boston Globe*, October 7, 1964, 27.
3. Joe Reichler, "Ford, Sadecki Starting Pitchers for Series Opener," *Schenectady Gazette*, October 6, 1964, 18.
4. Red Smith, "Prophet Smith Favors Cards," *Boston Globe*, October 6, 1964, 23.
5. *Ibid.*
6. Harold Kaese, "Cardinals Much Like 1960 Bucks," *Boston Globe*, October 6, 1964, 23.
7. Harold Kaese, "Rocky Infield Bothers Yanks," *Boston Globe*, October 7, 1964, 25.
8. *Ibid.*
9. Joseph Wancho, "Tony Kubek," SABR Biography Project, undated.
10. Peter C. Bjarkman, "Pedro Ramos," SABR Biography Project, August 31, 2011.
11. "'I Feel Great,' Says Mantle," *Boston Globe*, October 7, 1964, 25.
12. *Ibid.*
13. Harold Kaese, "Yanks Bury Three Jinxes," *Boston Globe*, October 5, 1964, 19.

Chapter 6

1. Red Smith, "Yankees 9-5 Favorites Over Cards," *Montreal Gazette*, October 7, 1964, 31.
2. Joe Garagiola, NBC radio broadcast of Game #1 of the 1964 World Series, October 7, 1964.
3. *Ibid.*
4. Phil Rizzuto, NBC radio broadcast of Game #1 of the 1964 World Series, October 7, 1964.
5. David Halberstam, *October 1964* (New York: Villard Books, 1994), 319.
6. Joe Garagiola, NBC radio broadcast of Game #1 of the 1964 World Series, October 7, 1964.

7. *Ibid.*
8. *Ibid.*
9. *Ibid.*
10. *Ibid.*
11. *Ibid.*
12. *Ibid.*
13. Roger Birtwell, "Ford Routed; Cards Win ,9–5," *Boston Globe*, October 8, 1964, 49.
14. "Cards Knock Out Ford, Beat Yanks 9–5," *Montreal Gazette*, October 8, 1964, 29.
15. Jack Hand, "Mike Shannon Sparks Cards to Opening Victory," *Schenectady Gazette*, October 8, 1964, 44.
16. Bob Addie, "They Got the Hits—Yogi," *Boston Globe*, October 8, 1964, 49.
17. "Cards Knock Out Ford, Beat Yanks 9–5," *Montreal Gazette*, October 8, 1964, 29.
18. *Ibid.*
19. *Ibid.*
20. Jack Hand, "Cardinals Batter Yanks in Opener, 9–5," *Schenectady Gazette*, October 8, 1964, 1.
21. Jack Hand, "Mike Shannon Sparks Cards to Opening Victory," *Schenectady Gazette*, October 8, 1964, 44.
22. *Ibid.*
23. David Halberstam, *October 1964* (New York: Villard Books, 1994), 320.
24. "An Even Series—With Some Fresh Faces," *Sports Illustrated*, October 19, 1964, 24.

Chapter 7

1. David Halberstam, *October 1964* (New York: Villard Books, 1994), 322.
2. Joe Garagiola, NBC radio broadcast of Game #2 of the 1964 World Series, October 8, 1964.
3. *Ibid.*
4. *Ibid.*
5. Phil Rizzuto, NBC radio broadcast of Game #2 of the 1964 World Series, October 8, 1964.
6. Maury Allen, "Pepitone's 'Hit Me' Blackjacked Cards," *New York Post*, October 9, 1964, 112.
7. "Which Leg Was Hit?" *Boston Globe*, October 9, 1964, 33.
8. "Yanks Win, Tie Series," *Boston Globe*, October 9, 1964, 1.
9. Joe Garagiola, NBC radio broadcast of Game #2 of the 1964 World Series, October 8, 1964.
10. *Ibid.*
11. "Sinker Ball Makes Mel Toast of Yankees," *Schenectady Gazette*, October 9, 1964, 25.
12. "Yanks Blast Cards, 8-3, Knot Series," *Schenectady Gazette*, October 9, 1964, 1.
13. Maury Allen, "Pepitone's 'Hit Me' Blackjacked Cards," *New York Post*, October 9, 1964, 112.
14. Mike Rathet, "Pepitone Boasts 'Battle Scar' from Controversial HBP Play," *Schenectady Gazette*, October 9, 1964, 24.
15. "Sinker Ball Makes Mel Toast of Yankees," *Schenectady Gazette*, October 9, 1964, 25.
16. *Ibid.*
17. *Ibid.*
18. *Ibid.*
19. Jack Hernon, "Yanks Top Cards, 8-3, Even Series," *Pittsburgh Post-Gazette*, October 9, 1964, 1.
20. "An Even Series with Some Fresh Faces," *Sports Illustrated*, October 19, 1964, 24–27.
21. David Halberstam, *October 1964* (New York: Villard Books, 1994), 323.
22. "Sinker Ball Makes Mel Toast of Yankees," *Schenectady Gazette*, October 9, 1964, 25.
23. Sy Berwick, "Stottlemyre Had No Choice, Only the Yanks Offered a Contract," *Dayton Daily News*, October 9, 1964, 9.
24. "Yanks Win, Tie Series," *Boston Globe*, October 9, 1964, 1.
25. Jack Hand, "Mel Stottlemyre Squares Series for New York," *Schenectady Gazette*, October 9, 1964, 24.

Chapter 8

1. David Halberstam, *October 1964* (New York: Villard Books, 1994), 328.
2. Curt Gowdy, NBC radio broadcast of Game #3 of the 1964 World Series, October 10, 1964.
3. Harry Caray, NBC radio broadcast of Game #3 of the 1964 World Series, October 10, 1964.
4. *Ibid.*
5. *Ibid.*
6. Curt Gowdy. NBC radio broadcast

of Game #3 of the 1964 World Series, October 10, 1964.
7. *Ibid.*
8. Roger Birtwell, "The Series: Mantle Beats Babe Ruth, Cards," *Boston Globe*, October 11, 1964, 1.
9. *Ibid.*
10. *Ibid.*
11. *Ibid.*
12. "An Even Series—With Some Fresh Faces," *Sports Illustrated*, October 19, 1964, 27.
13. Roger Birtwell, "The Series: Mantle Beats Babe Ruth, Cards," *Boston Globe*, October 11, 1964, 1.
14. "Mantle Looking for Knuckler—Got It," *Boston Globe*, October 11, 1964, 50.
15. *Ibid.*
16. *Ibid.*
17. *Ibid.*
18. "An Even Series—With Some Fresh Faces," *Sports Illustrated*, October 19, 1964, 27.

Chapter 9

1. Al Abrams, "Sidelights on Sports," *Pittsburgh-Post Gazette*, October 12, 1964, 31.
2. Harry Caray, NBC radio broadcast of Game #4 of the 1964 World Series, October 11, 1964.
3. Curt Gowdy, NBC radio broadcast of Game #4 of the 1964 World Series, October 11, 1964.
4. Harry Caray, NBC radio broadcast of Game #4 of the 1964 World Series, October 11, 1964.
5. *Ibid.*
6. *Ibid.*
7. "Cards Capitalize on Richardson's Error to Win, 4-3," *Montreal Gazette*, October 12, 1964, 17.
8. Al Abrams, "Sidelight on Sports," *Pittsburgh Post-Gazette*, October 12, 1964, 31.
9. "An Even Series—With Some Fresh Faces," *Sports Illustrated*, October 19, 1964, 27.
10. Harry Caray, NBC radio broadcast of Game #4 of the 1964 World Series, October 11, 1964.
11. Rich Shook, "Roger Craig," SABR Biography Project (online), 2023.
12. Harold Kaese, "Richardson Takes Blame for Snafu at 2d," *Boston Globe*, October 12, 1964, 1.
13. *Ibid.*
14. *Ibid.*
15. *Ibid.*
16. "Cards Top Yanks on Four-Run Homer by Boyer," *New York Times*, October 12, 1964, 1.
17. "Cards Capitalize on Richardson's Error to Win, 4-3," *Montreal Gazette*, October 12, 1964, 17.
18. Harold Kaese, "Richardson Takes Blame for Snafu at 2d," *Boston Globe*, October 12, 1964, 77.
19. *Ibid.*
20. *Ibid.*
21. *Ibid.*
22. "An Even Series—With Some Fresh Faces," *Sports Illustrated*, October 19, 1964, 27.
23. Al Abrams, "Spotlight on Sports," *Pittsburgh Post-Gazette*, October 16, 1964, 19.

Chapter 11

1. David Halberstam, *October 1964* (New York: Villard Books, 1994), 337.
2. Curt Gowdy, NBC radio broadcast of Game #5 of the 1964 World Series, October 12, 1964.
3. Harry Caray, NBC radio broadcast of Game #5 of the 1964 World Series, October 12, 1964.
4. *Ibid.*
5. *Ibid.*
6. *Ibid.*
7. Curt Gowdy, NBC radio broadcast of Game #5 of the 1964 World Series, October 12, 1964.
8. *Ibid.*
9. *Ibid.*
10. Roger Birtwell, "Cards Win Battle of Dramatics in 10th," *Boston Globe*, October 13, 1964, 1.
11. *Ibid.*
12. *Ibid.*
13. Harry Caray, NBC radio broadcast of Game #5 of the 1964 World Series, October 12, 1964.
14. *Ibid.*
15. *Ibid.*
16. *Ibid.*
17. "'My Biggest Hit, Sir. Yes, Sir,'" *Boston Globe*, October 13, 1964, 20.
18. *Ibid.*

19. Tom Pendergast, "McCarver's Drive Makes Bob Gibson Happiest Man," *Springfield* (MO) *Leader and Press*, October 13, 1964, 15.
20. Harold Kaese,"10 Card Runs Due to Yank Slips," *Boston Globe*, October 13, 1964, 19.
21. "McCarver Pushes Cards Ahead," *Montreal Gazette*, October 13, 1964, 25.
22. "Careless—Mikkelsen," *Boston Globe*, October 13, 1964, 19.
23. *Ibid.*
24. Harold Kaese,"10 Card Runs Due to Yank Slips," *Boston Globe*, October 13, 1964, 19.
25. *Ibid.*
26. *Ibid.*
27. "An Even Series—With Some Fresh Faces," *Sports Illustrated*, October 19, 1964, 28.

Chapter 12

1. Jack Hand, "Simmons, Bouton Pitch Sixth Game," *Montreal Gazette*, October 14, 1964, 29.
2. *Ibid.*
3. *Ibid.*
4. *Ibid.*
5. Harold Kaese, "Bad Luck Fails to Upset White," *Boston Globe*, October 14, 1964, 39.
6. David Halberstam, *October 1964* (New York: Villard Books, 1994), 344.
7. Joe Garagiola, NBC radio broadcast of Game #6 of the 1964 World Series, October 14, 1964.
8. *Ibid.*
9. *Ibid.*
10. Phil Rizzuto, NBC radio broadcast of Game #6 of the 1964 World Series, October 14, 1964.
11. Joe Garagiola, NBC radio broadcast of Game #6 of the 1964 World Series, October 14, 1964.
12. *Ibid.*
13. "Yanks Hit Three Homers, Topple Cards 8–3," *Montreal Gazette*, October 15, 1964, 17.
14. *Ibid.*
15. Harold Kaese, "Bouton Sharpest When Cap Falls Off," *Boston Globe*, October 15, 1964, 43.
16. "Bouton Needed Pepitone Hit," *Saskatoon Star-Phoenix*, October 15, 1964, 17.
17. "Moses, Tresh 'Aided' Pepitone Grand Slam," *Boston Globe*, October 15, 1964, 43.
18. Harold Kaese, "Bouton Sharpest When Cap Falls Off," *Boston Globe*, October 15, 1964, 43.
19. Al Abrams, "Sidelights on Sports," *Pittsburgh Post-Gazette*, October 15, 1964, 33.

Chapter 13

1. Don Larsen, Quotestats.com.
2. Joe Garagiola, NBC radio broadcast of Game #7 of the 1964 World Series, October 15, 1964.
3. Phil Rizzuto, NBC radio broadcast of Game #7 of the 1964 World Series, October 15, 1964.
4. *Ibid.*
5. *Ibid.*
6. *Ibid.*
7. *Ibid.*
8. *Ibid.*
9. Joe Garagiola, NBC radio broadcast of Game #7 of the 1964 World Series, October 15, 1964.
10. *Ibid.*
11. *Ibid.*
12. *Ibid.*
13. "Gibson Pitches Cards to Series Win Over Yanks," *Montreal Gazette*, October 16, 1964, 25.
14. *Ibid.*
15. Roger Birtwell, "Gibson Gives Cards Title, Sets Record," *Boston Globe*, October 16, 1964, 19.
16. Harry Caray, *The World Series of 1964* (documentary film), MLB Productions, 1964.
17. "Long Wait for Keane," *Calgary Herald*, October 16, 1964, 53.
18. *Ibid.*
19. *Ibid.*
20. *Ibid.*
21. "Gibson Award Winner as Top Series Player," *Calgary Herald*, October 16, 1964, 53.
22. *Ibid.*
23. *Ibid.*
24. *Ibid.*
25. "Yankees Review Errors," *Calgary Herald*, October 16, 1964, 53.
26. *Ibid.*
27. *Ibid.*
28. Rob Rains, *Cardinals, Where Have*

You Gone? (Champaign, IL: Sports Publishing, 2005), 64–65.
29. William Leggett, "Speed Won the World Series," *Sports Illustrated*, October 26, 1964, 36.

Chapter 14

1. "CBS Buys 80% of Stock in Baseball Team," *New York Times*, August 14, 1964, 1.
2. Milton Gross, "Yanks to Undergo Major Shakeup Through Trades," *Boston Globe*, October 16, 1964, 20.
3. *Ibid.*
4. *Ibid.*
5. *Ibid.*
6. *Ibid.*
7. *Ibid.*
8. *Ibid.*
9. "CBS Buys 80% of Stock in Baseball Team," *New York Times*, August 14, 1964, 1.

Chapter 15

1. Sparky Anderson, Azquotes.com.
2. "Ex-Card, Yankee Manager Johnny Keane Dies at 55," *Lodi News-Sentinel*, January 7, 1967, 9.
3. Bob Burnes, "Matthews-Busch Marriage Recalls Card '64 Hassle," *St. Louis Globe Democrat (online archives)*, February 26, 1977.
4. Gary Livacari, "1964: Baseball's Version of Musical Chairs! Johnny Keane Gets Yogi's Job," Baseballhistorycomesalive.com, April 23, 2022.
5. "Why Cardinals Manager Johnny Keane Quit One Day After Winning the World Series," Stlredbirds.com, September 11, 2023.
6. "Yogi Goes Golfing After Losing Job," *Boston Globe*, October 17, 1964, 17.
7. Eric Aron, "Alvin Dark," SABR Biography Project (online), 2014.
8. Alvin Dark and John Underwood, *When in Doubt, Fire the Manager* (New York: E.P. Dutton, 1980), 98.
9. Andy Sturgill, "Danny Murtaugh," SABR Biography Project (online), 2013.
10. Craig Calcaterra, "Today in Baseball History: Johnny Keane's Firing Ends Years of Yankees Chaos," NBCSports.com, May 7, 2020.

Chapter 16

1. "Ex-Card, Yankee Manager Johnny Keane Dies at 55," *Lodi News-Sentinel*, January 7, 1967, 9.
2. Harold Friend, "Johnny Keane Was Not to Blame," BleacherReport.com, March 5, 2010.
3. William Leggett, "A Dying Team Screams for Help," *Sports Illustrated* (online archives), May 16, 1966.
4. "Johnny Keane: A Man of Quiet Dignity," Retrosimba.com, January 21, 2017.
5. Gary Livacari, "1964: Baseball's Version of Musical Chairs! Johnny Keane Gets Yogi's Job," Baseballhistorycomesalive.com, April 23, 2022.
6. John Stahl, "Johnny Keane," SABR Biography Project (online).
7. "Johnny Keane: A Man of Quiet Dignity," Retrosimba.com, January 21, 2017.
8. John Stahl, "Johnny Keane," SABR Biography Project (online).
9. *Ibid.*
10. "Ex-Card, Yankee Manager Johnny Keane Dies at 55," *Lodi News-Sentinel*, January 7, 1967, 9.

Chapter 17

1. Craig Calcaterra, "Today in Baseball History: Johnny Keane's Firing Ends Years of Yankees Chaos," NBCSports.com, May 7, 2020.
2. William Leggett, "A Dying Team Screams for Help," *Sports Illustrated* (online version), May 16, 1966.
3. Joe LaPointe, "In His Book, Fritz Peterson Discusses Pranks, Teammates and Swapping Wives," *New York Times (online archive)*, September 17, 2009.
4. Harold Friend, "Johnny Keane Was Not to Blame," BleacherReport.com, March 5, 2010.
5. David J. Halberstam, "An Empty Stadium and Red Barber's Firing," AwfulAnnouncing.com, September 22, 2016.
6. Kunj Shah, "The Story Behind the Yankees Leaving Mickey Mantle Unprotected in the 1968 Expansion Draft," Pinstripealley.com, April 7, 2016.
7. David Seidemen, "Yankee Stadium Sign, Ripped Off Right Field Wall by Fan in 1973, Soars from $200 to $46K," Forbes.com, June 6, 2018.

Chapter 18

1. Neil Russo, "Card Hurlers Were Patsies for Home Run Bats," *The Sporting News*, October 9, 1965, 30.
2. *Ibid.*
3. Terry Sloope, "Bob Gibson," SABR Biography Project (online).
4. Al Abrams, "Sidelights on Sports," *Pittsburgh Post-Gazette*, October 4, 1967, 23.
5. *Ibid.*
6. Joe Gergen, "Cardinals Scuttle Red Sox Fairytale Dream," *Montreal Gazette*, October 13, 1967, 25.
7. Lowell Reidenbaugh, "Gibson, Redbirds—Second to None!" *The Sporting News*, October 28, 1967, 5.
8. Bob Gibson, "Bob Gibson on Losing Nine Games in 1968," YouTube video, May 20, 2018.
9. Geoff Mott, "10 Questions with Jim Northrup," *Saginaw News*, October 14, 2006.
10. Neil Russo, "Red Announces Plea to New Pact: 'Get Me Some Runs,'" *The Sporting News*, October 11, 1969, 10.
11. *Ibid.*

Chapter 19

1. Danielle, "St. Louis Cardinals Celebrate the 1964 World Series Champions," Redbirdrants.com, May 26, 2014.
2. "Cardinals Celebrate 50th Anniversary of 1964 Championship," FoxSports.com, May 26, 2014.
3. *Ibid.*
4. *Ibid.*

Chapter 20. Where Have You Gone, Chet Trail?

1. Chike Erokwu, "Meet Your Neighbor: Chester Trail Dared to Dram Big," Coloradoan.com, March 2, 2014.
2. *Ibid.*
3. *Ibid.*

Chapter 21

1. Mark Feinsand, "Skowron, Richardson, Kubek & Torre Laud Teammate," *New York Daily News* (online archives), June 5, 2007.
2. Harry Caray, *Late Night with David Letterman*, July 31, 1986.
3. *Ibid.*
4. Rich Shook, "Roger Craig," SABR biography (online), June 4, 2023.
5. *Ibid.*
6. Terry Sloope, "Curt Flood," SABR Biography Project (online), 2013.
7. George Will, "Dred Scott in Spikes," syndicated article, November 21, 1993.
8. Sean Mullin (director), *It Ain't Over* (documentary film), Five by Eight Productions, 2022.
9. "Sportscaster Garagiola Quits NBC," *Lewiston Morning Tribune*, November 9, 1988, B1.
10. Matt Bohn, "Curt Gowdy," SABR Biography Project (online), 2007.
11. *Ibid.*
12. *Ibid.*
13. Red Smith, "On Howard, A Class Guy," *New York Times* (online archives), December 15, 1980.
14. Bob Nightengale, "Berra Confronts Infamous Harmonic One More Time," *USA Today* (online archives), January 21, 2013.
15. Richard Goldstein, "Phil Linz, Unlikely Baseball Celebrity, Is Dead at 81," *New York Times* (online archives), December 14, 2020.
16. Bob Costas, "Bob Costas Gives Eulogy for Mickey Mantle," YouTube video, MLB, November 12, 2015.
17. Bill Pruden, "Roger Maris," SABR Biography Project (online), 2010.
18. Dave Williams, "Tim McCarver," SABR Biography Project (online), February 16, 2023.
19. "Tim McCarver, MLB Catcher and Broadcaster, Dies at 81," Sportsnet.ca, February 16, 2023.
20. *Ibid.*
21. Len Pasculli, "Bobby Richardson," SABR Biography Project (online), October 31, 2020.
22. Andrew L. John, "Hank Aaron, Bud Selig Speak at Indian Wells Fundraiser," *The Desert Sun* (online version), May 22, 2017.
23. Gregory H. Wolf, "Mel Stottlemyre," SABR Biography Project (online), January 13, 2019.

Bibliography

Books

Craig, Roger, and Vern Plagenhoef. *Inside Pitch: Roger Craig's '84 Tiger Journal*. Grand Rapids: Eerdmans, 1984.
Dark, Alvin, and John Underwood. *When in Doubt, Fire the Manager*. New York: E.P. Dutton, 1980.
Garver, Ned, Bill Bozman, and Ronnie Joyner. *Touching All the Bases*. Pepperpot Productions, 2003.
Gibson, Bob, *From Ghetto to Glory*, New York: Penguin, 1968.
Gibson, Bob, with Lonnie Wheeler. *Stranger to The Game: The Autobiography of Bob Gibson*. New York: Penguin, 1994.
Golenbock, Peter. *Dynasty: The New York Yankees 1949–1964*. New York: Prentice Hall, 1975.
Halberstam, David. *October 1964*. New York: Villard Books, 1994.
Pappu, Sridhar. *The Year of the Pitcher*. Boston: Mariner Books, 2017.
Peary, Danny, ed. *We Played the Game: 65 Players Remember Baseball's Greatest Era, 1947–1964*. New York: Hyperion, 1994.
Pepitone, Joe, with Berry Stainback. *Joe, You Coulda Made Us Proud*. Chicago: Playboy Press, 1975.
Rains, Rob. *Cardinals, Where Have You Gone?* Champaign, IL: Sports Publishing, 2005.
Smith, Curt. *Voices of the Game*. South Bend, IN: Diamond Communications, 1987.
Stahl, John Harry, ed., and Bill Nowlin. *Drama and Pride in the Gateway City: The 1964 St. Louis Cardinals*. Lincoln: University of Nebraska Press, 2013.
Zoss, Joel, and John S. Bowman. *The American League*. New York: Bison, 1986.
Zoss, Joel, and John S. Bowman. *The National League*. New York: Bison, 1986.

Newspapers and Periodicals

Boston Globe
Calgary Herald
Chicago Daily News
Dayton Daily News
The Desert Sun
Lewiston Morning Tribune
Lodi News-Sentinel
Long Island Newsday
Montreal Gazette
New York Daily News
New York Post
New York Times
Oneonta Star
Pittsburgh Post-Gazette
Saginaw News
St. Louis Globe-Democrat
Saskatoon Star-Phoenix
Schenectady Gazette
The Sporting News
Sports Illustrated
Springfield Leader and Press
USA Today
Washington Times

Audio Recording

Caray, Harry, and Jack Buck. *1964 St. Louis Cardinals* (record album of season's audio highlights), 1964.

Documentaries

Burns, Ken (director). *Baseball*. PBS, 1994.
Caray, Harry (narrator). *1964 World Series*. MLB Productions, 1964.
Mullin, Sean (director). *It Ain't Over*. Five by Eight Productions, 2022.

Websites

AwfulAnnouncing.com
Baseball-Almanac.com
BaseballReference.com
BleacherReport.com
Coloradoan.com
DiamondsintheDusk.com
ESPN.com
Forbes.com
FoxSports.com
MLB.com
Mosportshalloffame.com
NBCSports.com
Pinstripealley.com
Quotestats.com
Redbirdrants.com
Retrosimba.com
Sportskeeda.com
Sportsnet.ca
Stlredbirds.com
USAtoday.com

Index

Aaron, Henry (Hank) 25, 85, 181, 192
Adcock, Joe 22
Ali, Muhammad 2
Allen, Dick (Richie) 8, 11
Allen, Maury 43, 81
Allen, Mel 40–47, 191
Altman, George 104
Amaro, Ruben 185
The American Sportsman (television show) 184
Anderson, Sparky 156
Andrews, Julie 1
Arnaz, Desi 109

Ball, Lucille 109
Banks, Ernie 8
Barber, Red 42, 165–166, 184
Barnett, Larry 184
Barrett, Marty 144
The Baseball World of Joe Garagiola (television show) 183
Bennett, Dennis 13
Bjarkman, Peter C. 54
Blattner, Bud 44
Boudreau, Lou 75
Boyer, Cloyd 52
Brecheen, Harry 16
Brezhnev, Leonid 3
Briles, Nelson 169
Brock, Jackie 180
Broeg, Bob 25
Broglio, Ernie 20–21, 151
Bronson, Monty 57
Brown, Joe 159
Brown, Mordecai 171
Buck, Jack 189, 192
Bunning, Jim 8, 10, 13
Burke, Mike 165
Busch, August, III 180
Busch, Susan 180

Calcaterra, Craig 159, 163
Callison, Johnny 8, 10, 11
Cantor, Eddie 92
Carlton, Steve 169
Carpenter, Bob 13
Carr, Vikki 57
Carrigan, Bill 158
Carson, Johnny 38
Cepeda, Orlando 158, 169, 191
Cerf, Bennett 110
Chesbro, Jack 96
Clark, Petula 1
Clarke, Horace 165
Clay, Cassius 1–2
Clemente, Roberto 169, 181
Cobb, Ty 35, 179
Covington, Wes 13
Cox, Billy 12
Craft, Harry 13
Criqui, Don 184
Cronin, Joe 154
Crosetti, Frank 74, 92, 126

Dalrymple, Clay 10, 14
Daley, Bud 54
Daly, John 109–110
Dark, Alvin 13, 158–159
Davis, Sammy, Jr. 110
Dean, Dizzy 16, 68
Demery, Larry 189
Dickey, Bill 35
Diller, Phyllis 109
DiMaggio, Joe 36, 89, 151, 163
Dinneen, Bill 147
Drake, Lisa 127
Drysdale, Don 20, 54, 86, 93, 169
Durocher, Leo 23, 157, 170

The Ed Sullivan Show (television program) 1, 151
Edwards, Tryon 173

Index

Featherston, Al 39
Fierson, Chuck 161
Finkel, Jan 34
Finley, Charlie 180
Francis, Arlene 110
Franks, Herman 158
Freehan, Bill 172
Frick, Ford 57, 148, 159
Friend, Bob 11, 165
Friend, Harold 161
Fusselle, Warner 47

Gagliano, Phil 174
Garver, Ned 34
Gergen, Joe 170
Giamatti, Bart 195
Gibson, Edmund Richard (Hoot) 24
Gibson, Josh 23
Giles, Warren 121, 147
Gleeson, Jimmy 61, 118, 144
Gopnik, Adam 1
Gross, Milton 21–22, 153–154

Haines, Jesse 49
Hand, Jack 68, 69, 126
Hegan, Jim 53
Hemus, Solly 23–24
Henrich, Tommy 92
Hepburn, Audrey 1
Hernon, Jack 82, 146–147
Herzog, Whitey 179
Hodges, Gil 158, 177
Holbrook, Bob 38
Hornsby, Rogers 16, 158
Howsam, Bob 169, 170
Huggins, Miller 16, 163

Isaacs, Stan 43, 44, 159
I've Got a Secret (television program) 109

Jackson, Al 22
Jenkins, Ferguson 181
Jeter, Derek 191
Johnson, Dave 176
Johnson, Lyndon 2
Johnson, Walter 41, 184

Keane, Lela 20, 156, 157, 160, 162
Kekich, Mike 167
Kennedy, John F. 2
Kilgallen, Dorothy 110
Koufax, Sandy 20, 169, 171
Khrushchev, Nikita 3
Kuhn, Bowie 178, 182

LaRussa, Tony 168
le Carré, John 3

Leggett, William 151, 164
Letterman, David 180
Lewis, Joe 160
Livicari, Gary 157
Liston, Sonny 1
Lolich, Mickey 171
Lonborg, Jim 170

MacArthur, General Douglas 23
Maddox, Garry 189
Mahaffey, Art 9
Matilla, Felix 106
Mantle, Merlyn 190
Marion, Marty 16
Martin, Billy 182
Martin, Pepper 16
Martin, Tony 86
Mathews, Eddie 92
Mauch, Gene 7–13
Mazeroski, Bill 53, 92
Mazzarella, John 94
McCarron, Anthony 167
McGraw, John 29
McKinley, William 59
McLain, Denny 34, 171
McLaughlin, Dan 173
Menke, Denis 10
Messer, Frank 194
Meusel, Bob 52
Meusel, Emil (Irish) 52
Montville, Leigh 167
Moore, Monte 180
Morris, Jack 180
Moses, Wally 135
Mozzali, Mo 50–51
Munson, Thurman 155
Murcer, Bobby 166
Murphy, Jeremiah P. 3
Murtaugh, Danny 96, 158, 159

Nixon, Marni 1
Northrup, Jim 171

Oh, Sadaharu 179

Pelekoudas, Chris 85
Peterson, Fritz 167
Powell, Boog 37
Pruden, Bill 186–187

Ramos, Pedro 53–54, 67
Rapp, Vern 179
Reese, Pee Wee 12, 185
Reichler, Joseph 48
Reidenbaugh, Lowell 170
Rhodes, Dusty 92
Richards, Paul 179

Index

Richardson, Betsy 154, 190
Rickey, Branch 16, 22
Roberts, Robin 192
Robinson, Bill 179
Robinson, Brooks 25, 37, 40, 179
Robinson, Frank 10
Robinson, Jackie 17, 142, 158
Rojas, Cookie 11, 13
Rooney, John 192
Royko, Mike 30
Ruffing, Red 182
Ruiz, Chico 9–10
Russo, Neil 168
Ryan, Irene 2
Ryba, Mike 50–51

Sain, Johnny 33–34
Sale of the Century (television program) 183
Santo, Ron 8
Scarne, John 48–49
Schecter, Leonard 178
Schoendienst, Mary Ellen 138
Scott, Mike 180
Scully, Vin 45, 47
Seaver, Tom 181, 183
Shah, Kunj 166
Shamsky, Art 172
Sheppard, Bob 91, 112
Short, Bob 182
Short, Chris 8, 10, 13
Simmons, Ted 189
Simon, Paul 5
Sisler, Dick 9–10
Slaughter, Enos 16
Sloope, Terry 169
Smith, Bob 21
Smith, Curt 40, 42, 45, 47
Smith, Kate 40
Spahn, Warren 33

Springfield, Dusty 1
Stanky, Eddie 50
Steinbrenner, George 46, 155, 167, 178, 185, 193
Stirnweiss, George 191
Stoneham, Horace 159
Stottlemyre, Jason 193
Stottlemyre, Todd 193
Sturgill, Andy 159
Sullivan, Ed 151
Sutter, Bruce 181

Tebbets, Birdie 54
Terry, Luther L. 3
Thomas, Frank 9, 10
Thomas, Lee 106
The Today Show (television program) 183
The Tonight Show (television program) 38, 127
To Tell the Truth (television program) 109
Trail, Chet 175–176
Tranströmer, Tomas 163
Tresh, Mike 87

Updike, John 184

Virdon, Bill 53

Wakefield, Bill 104
Walker, Harry 158
Ward, Preston 12
Warhol, Andy 48
What's My Line? (television program) 52, 109–110
Will, George 182
Williams, Dave 188
Williams, Ted 182
Wulf, Steve 11

York, Rudy 51

Milton Keynes UK
Ingram Content Group UK Ltd.
UKHW041843071024
449381UK00011B/145